KEEPING NEW ZEALAND GREEN
Recent Environmental Reforms

KEEPING NEW ZEALAND GREEN
Recent Environmental Reforms

P. Ali Memon

OTAGO

Published by the University of Otago Press
P.O. Box 56, Dunedin, New Zealand

First published 1993
© P. Ali Memon 1993
ISBN 0 908569 70 X

Cover design by Jenny Cooper
Typeset by Deadline Typesetting Ltd, Christchurch
Printed by GP Print Ltd, Wellington

National Library of New Zealand
Cataloguing-in-Publication data

Memon, P. A. (Pyarali Ali), 1946–
Keeping New Zealand green : recent environmental reforms /
P. Ali Memon.
1 v.
ISBN 0-908-56970-X
1. Environmental policy – New Zealand.   2. Environmental
protection – New Zealand – Management.   3. Natural resources
– New Zealand –Management.   I. Title.

Contents

The Enactment of Legislation
Wider Implications
Concluding Comments

The Parliamentary Commissioner for the Environment
Environmental Quangos
Regional and District Councils
The Maori Concerns

Figures

Tables

Foreword

The Resource Management Act of 1991 was one of the biggest law reform projects ever undertaken in New Zealand. It was massive in scope. It involved the repeal of more basic statute law than almost any other project that I can remember. It began as a zero-based study in which nothing was assumed and everything was reasoned from first principles. It came at a time in the life of New Zealand public administration when established shibboleths were being challenged. I hope the Act will be one of the more enduring monuments to come out of that febrile period of New Zealand political life.

The reform was only possible when the Ministry of Works and Development was abolished. The transfer of the Town and Country Planning and Water and Soil functions from that ministry to the Ministry for the Environment, coupled with financial support, made the reform possible.

Remarkably, for such an important and comprehensive reform, the Resource Management Law Reform Exercise (known in government by the inevitable acronym RMLR) never really generated enormous political furore or controversy. The main reason for this was the systematic and extensive public consultations which were engaged in. In many ways the reform effort was a model in terms of the principles of open government.

By now the project has attracted considerable interest overseas and many people are beginning the pilgrimage to New Zealand to study it. A useful contribution to their studies will be made by Dr Ali Memon's new book. Dr Memon is the Director of the Regional and Resource Planning Programme at the University of Otago. The University has a proud history in the discipline of geography which this book will only enhance.

This is a painstaking work of scholarship. It is based on a thorough knowledge of the official documents, extensive interviews with individuals involved and mature reflection on the issues. Obviously, as a participant in this reform exercise I do not agree with every judgement Dr Memon makes, but it is my considered opinion that this is an important book. It deserves to be widely read and I am sure it will be.

The objective of the Resource Management Act is to enhance quality of life, both for individuals and the community as a whole, through the allocation and management of natural and physical resources. Whether the Act can live up to that expectation remains to be seen. But for people who wish to understand the evolution of New Zealand's Resource Management Act, Dr Memon's book is indispensable.

RT. HON. PROFESSOR SIR GEOFFREY PALMER
College of Law
University of Iowa, USA
3 December, 1992

Acknowledgements

This study is the product of a research project that commenced seven years ago. In attaining its completion and publication I owe a debt to many, but I hope they will understand if I do not name them individually. I am particularly grateful to the officials in central and local government agencies who, over many years, have assisted my research inquiries by facilitating access to the relevant documentary sources and through discussions.

I had the opportunity to spend part of a sabbatical leave in 1990 as a research associate in the Ministry for the Environment in Wellington. This gave me the opportunity to examine the Cabinet papers and related archival sources and interview those who took part in the reforms in environmental administration, resource management and local government. I would like to thank the staff of the Ministry for the Environment and the State Services Commission for their assistance, and those former Cabinet ministers in the fourth Labour government and their policy advisers who read and commented on draft chapters for this study.

The University of Otago has been supportive over the years by encouraging and facilitating research. At various times my current and former colleagues in Geography, Professor Alan Mark and Dr Ton Buhrs have provided stimulus through discussion and comment on parts of the manuscript. The assistance of Sue Wards who worked for me as a research assistant during 1991 and Bill Mooney who prepared the illustrations is acknowledged, as well as the help of Hugh Kidd, Pauline Fraser and Ray Jackson. The task of preparing the manuscript for publication was eased by the assistance of Dr Helen Watson White, John Bourke and Wendy Harrex.

The support of my family has made this project an enjoyable endeavour and for this I am very grateful.

ALI MEMON
Department of Geography
University of Otago

Abbreviations

CEQ	Council for Environmental Quality
CPC	Cabinet Policy Committee
DoC	Department of Conservation
ECO	Environment and Conservation Organisations
EDC	Economic Development Commission
EDS	Environmental Defence Society
EIA	Environmental Impact Assessment
EIR	Environmental Impact Report
EP&EP	Environmental Protection & Enhancement Procedures
FMC	Federation of Mountain Clubs
GATT	General Agreement on Tariffs and Trade
IUCN	International Union for Conservation of Nature and Natural Resources
MfE	Ministry for the Environment
MoW&D	Ministry of Works and Development
NBR	National Business Review
NCC	Nature Conservation Council
NFAC	Native Forests Action Council
NPNCC	National Parks and Nature Conservation Commission
NPRA	National Parks and Reserves Authority
NWASCA	National Water and Soil Conservation Authority
NZFS	New Zealand Forest Service
NZPC	New Zealand Planning Council
OECD	Organisation for Economic Cooperation and Development
OND	Organisation for National Development
PCE	Parliamentary Commissioner for the Environment
PEC	Physical Environment Committee
PSA	Public Service Association
Quangos	Quasi-autonomous non-governmental organisations
RFBPSNZ	Royal Forest and Bird Protection Society of New Zealand
RMLR	Resource management law reform
SOEs	State-owned Enterprises
SSC	State Services Commission
WCED	World Commission on Environment and Development
WPEA	Working Party on Environmental Administration

1

Introduction

Objectives

Environmental issues have become an important priority for government in many countries. There is a growing public concern about the state of the environment and its significance for socio-economic wellbeing (WCED, 1987). There is also an increasing awareness that environmental problems cannot be successfully addressed on the basis of a purely scientific or technical approach, that political, economic and social factors come into play, too. Their relative significance should not be underestimated.

As a study of how New Zealand society has sought to address environmental issues, this book focuses on policies relating to the institutional arrangements for environmental administration and planning in New Zealand. The environmental restructuring policies implemented by the fourth Labour government since 1984 have been the most prominent in this respect. The task of environmental restructuring was a very complex exercise, with many facets, and the participants have had varying perspectives on it. A central objective of this book is to document and analyse these reforms. It seeks to develop an understanding of how such policy responses have evolved and how they have been implemented, examining the many significant changes which New Zealanders have seen happening around them, but may not have been able to place in context or understand. I hope it will also provide a basis for debate and discussion about these changes.

At present, New Zealand offers a particularly interesting setting for examining issues of environmental policy. In comparison with other Western countries, the recent reforms in New Zealand have been wide-ranging in nature: a concerted attempt has been made to develop an institutional framework for a national environmental policy and to establish environmental planning as an important function of central and sub-national government. Indeed, New Zealand may be the first country to have turned sustainable management into law. A review of the factors that have motivated and shaped these initiatives provides important insights into New Zealand's response to environmental concerns. Yet, with one recent exception (Britton et. al., 1992), environmental reforms have not received much attention in the recent literature on the policy initiatives of the fourth Labour government (Boston and Holland, 1987; Holland and Boston, 1990).

Despite the recent prominence given to environmental issues by the media and politicians, and contrary to commonly held perceptions, it must be remembered that environmental problems have been around for a long time in New Zealand and have periodically been the subject of public debate. Limited attempts were made to address some of these problems, through administrative reforms and through the enactment of statutes, such as the Town and Country Planning Act and the Water and Soil legislation. Despite the fact that a number of institutional reforms were implemented during the 1970s to address environmental concerns, it has become apparent that many environmental problems in New Zealand have persisted, or have even been exacerbated, during the last two decades, partly as a consequence of governmental activities.

For that reason, this study is set within an extended time frame and based on a critical understanding of the pre-1984 policy initiatives made in response to perceived needs and problems. Such a comparative approach should provide a better appreciation of the direction and extent of the more recent changes, from the perspective of students in planning and geography and in a number of related disciplines which share an interest in the study of environmental issues. It should also be of use to environmental professionals and political participants in environmental decision-making, as well as to non-governmental organisations.

Environmental Policy as a Focus for Analysis

Environmental policy is governmental action to solve the problems of a society's relationship to its environment. Thus, one writer has described the formulation of environmental policy as a normative process, designed to define the approved parameters of what is acceptable in terms of resource exploitation and environmental quality (Park, 1986). To elaborate, environmental policy is one aspect of public policy, that is, of the actions and positions taken by the state as the overriding agent of authority in society. As with many societal issues, the solution to environmental problems must ultimately be endorsed by the government; and the emphasis on the state as a collective, public entity is important in this respect (Hill and Bramley, 1986). However, even though the definition of the term "policy" has attracted considerable interest, its interpretation has not yet been fully resolved. Recent reviews of the literature on this topic conclude that the problems posed in defining the concept of policy suggest that it is difficult to treat it as a specific and concrete phenomenon since it involves a course of action or a web of decisions rather than one decision. Thus, as suggested by O'Riordan (1982), policy may refer to a set of guide-lines or principles against which possible courses of action can be evaluated, or it may relate to a declared statement of intent to do something, backed up by the provisions of an enabling statute or budget. Furthermore, it is difficult to identify particular occasions when policy is actually made. Policy will often continue to evolve during its implementation and not only in the policy-making phase of the process (Wildavsky, 1979).

The above discussion has emphasised the process of formulating policy. From our perspective, it is equally important to clarify the substance or content of environmental policy. The term "environment" also raises difficulties of defining the subject of analysis, because the concept has different connotations in different disciplines.

Environmental problems are complex, involving a wide variety of issues and subject areas. Thus, the term "environment" needs to be defined comprehensively, to include people, the natural conditions (such as climate, terrain, flora and fauna), and human artifacts (such as building structures and service infrastructures) surrounding them, as well as the physical and cultural processes which interlink the above elements. As a generic concept, "environment" provides an integrating view of society by looking at the way in which society interacts with its surroundings. Such a perspective gives an insight into the relationships between specific bio-physical, social and economic problems, and between the parts and the whole.

In view of the wide scope of the term "environment", it is inevitable that governmental decisions regarding the environment affect many aspects of life in society. The reality of integrating environmental considerations into decision-making thus constitutes a major challenge to governments (Portney, 1990). It is imperative that environmental policies reflect the full range of diverse human needs that depend for fulfilment upon the environment; these include psychological, economic, social, aesthetic and recreational needs.

Hitherto, governments have either ignored or only partially recognised the wide spectrum of values that people seek in the environment. This does not imply that governments should necessarily direct all uses of the environment. The task of environmental management is so vast and so complex that, to be accomplished, it must be broadly shared by central and sub-national government agencies, corporations and individuals (Caldwell, 1970). Plural societies, to achieve acceptable environmental outcomes, need to agree on common goals and objectives and on the means for their implementation. A national policy for the environment is a framework which provides for these common criteria for independent but mutually consistent courses of action, while its implementation may be undertaken by sub-national levels of government.

It is in this context that the organisation of responsibility for the management of the interaction between environment and society becomes a matter of major social importance. While one should not underestimate the ability of adequate scientific and technological know-how to solve environmental problems, the major challenge is to develop appropriate institutional arrangements for environmental administration and planning, as Fernie and Pitkethly observe:

all resource problems – over-population, hunger, poverty, fuel shortages, deforestation – are fundamentally institutional problems which warrant institutional solutions. The success or failure of resource management is intrinsically

tied up with institutional structures – the pattern of agencies, laws and poli-
cies which pertain to resource issues. (Fernie and Pitkethly, 1985, p.vii).

In accord with these views, this study is concerned specifically with two closely associated facets of environmental policy: administration and planning. The focus with respect to administrative structures is on the interrelated issues of the location of administrative authority and its jurisdiction. Important questions here relate to the role of the state in addressing environmental concerns, the organisation and adequacy of administrative structures, their responsibilities and procedures, and the relationship between central and sub-national levels of government.

Planning is a process of articulating needs, assessing alternative methods of responding to them, implementing such responses, and evaluating their success. Environmental planning is directed at promoting social wellbeing and attaining community goals and objectives in the course of using, modifying or protecting the environment. As a normative activity, it encompasses addressing causes of environmental problems as well as prescribing appropriate measures to mitigate the detrimental environmental impacts of human behaviour. Environmental planning constitutes a link between knowledge and action and is predicated on community consultation and participation. It has a strong sense of place and recognises the interdependence between people and their habitats. The major issues here relate to the adequacy of the process of environmental planning and its effectiveness in achieving its objectives and reflecting the aspirations of the community.

As a context for the study, the rest of this introductory chapter will briefly discuss a number of broader themes pertinent to the recent environmental administration and planning reforms in New Zealand.

Causes of Environmental Problems

The emphasis in the critical social science literature concerned with environmental issues is on the underlying causes of the wide-ranging environmental problems facing societies in different parts of the world. These include issues such as environmental pollution, resource depletion, urban malaise, rural poverty and famines. It is important to understand the underlying causes of environmental problems, even though the policy implications of this mode of analysis are not necessarily optimistic. The search for policies appropriate to address such problems seems nearly impossible at times.

The current focus in environmental studies in geography and other social disciplines is on a political-economic approach, based on a critical conceptualisation of society's relations with nature, with all the complexity and contradictions therein contained. The importance of this literature to environmental management lies in its emphasis on the actual social, political and economic factors that give rise to environmental problems, institutions, policies and outcomes. It stands in contrast to the neutrality of the dominant neo-classical economic approach, which assumes the objective of maximizing economic welfare from resource use in free markets; and also to the behaviourist theories which stress the importance of individual perceptions, attitudes and values in motivating behaviour (Emel & Peet, 1989).

Ultimately, all environmental problems boil down to a conflict between different social, economic and political interests over who should benefit from the use of the environment and the wealth or welfare derived from it. The problem is "not just a question of reordering society to respond to the demands of the population, but of deciding which demands have priority over what timescale" (Rees, 1985, p.404). Even though a significant proportion of the population in advanced countries appears to be changing, to be less materialistic, for instance, now than in the recent past, there is a historically-based inertia deeply entrenched in our value systems, and in our socio-economic and political structures. A state has numerous other important goals such as reducing unemployment, curbing inflation, or avoiding balance of trade deficits. Hence, it is not surprising that public policies to redress environmental problems are not given top priority and end up being only marginally effective (Dryzek, 1990).

Recently, the Brundtland report has advocated the principle of sustainable development, defined as a strategy that meets the needs of the present without compromising the ability of future generations to meet their own needs (WCED, 1987). Ideally, it means a development process which is equitable, conserves resources and which can be pursued indefinitely without environmental or social ill-effects. Pursued to its logical conclusion, the implementation of a sustainable development strategy entails comprehensive shifts in power relations and institutional alignments. Instead, sustainable development has been interpreted by many as a liberal, even conservative theme (Peet, 1989). Even the Brundtland report shied away from examining these socio-political imperatives for promoting sustainability.

The radical changes to systems of production and to societal relations advocated by analysts of environmental issues are unlikely to happen while environmental problems continue to escalate. Nevertheless, small shifts over a period of time have led to some rather dramatic transformations of institutions and of decision-making processes (Emel and Peet, 1989). Every society exhibits a complex and shifting structure of values and it is important to recognise these values as the basis of the policy development process. The strength of the environmental movement is now acknowledged in many countries by the creation of institutional structures designed to ensure that material goals are not pursued to the exclusion of environmental considerations. From this perspective, the recent reforms in environmental administration and planning in New Zealand may be seen as the most recent manifestation of a long process of incremental shifts in values, which has been occurring over the last one hundred and fifty years.

Environmental Values

The dominant characteristics of the physical environment in New Zealand are its diversity and dynamism. Geologically, it is relatively young, and the location of the two islands on the edge of the Pacific plate is associated with a high level of seismic and volcanic activity. The mid-latitude temperate climate is characterised by relatively high rainfall in some areas of the country while other areas are relatively dry.

The juxtaposition of widely different physical habitats in a small country of contrasting relief, with the associated variations in climate and vegetation, have presented both opportunities and constraints to successive waves of Polynesian and European immmigrants and their descendants. Although European settlement in New Zealand has been relatively recent, compared, for instance, to South Africa, North America and Australia, the environment has demonstrated a dramatic response to human impact during the course of the last one hundred and fifty years (Glasby, 1991). To a very large degree, this change has reflected the utilitarian values shared by a majority of the population, underpinned by a strong belief in the unfettered rights of the private property owner and a virtually unquestioned faith in the ability of the government (with the assistance of scientific understanding and technical ingenuity) to manipulate the environment in order to promote growth.

With a present-day population which enjoys living standards and life-styles comparable to other western countries, New Zealand society is not as utilitarian in its attitudes as it used to be. The diversity in environmental values can be illustrated most vividly with respect to the recent conflicts over management of the indigenous forests.

Indigenous forests in New Zealand are a diminishing resource, with different groups of society placing different values on them. At one end of the spectrum are the existence (the worth of knowing that a resource exists), bequest (the worth of endowing future generations with a natural resource) and spiritual values. Recently, there has been growing concern about the detrimental impact of deforestation on the global climate. Forests have increasingly been recognised as possessing scenic, wilderness and recreational attributes as well as a soil and water conservation function. At the other end of the spectrum are the utilitarian gains derived from land clearance and timber harvesting. As in other parts of the world, indigenous forests in New Zealand have been indiscriminately exploited. This exploitation, encouraged by settlement policies and land legislation, continued until well into the second half of this century. Even today, indigenous forests are being cleared for agriculture and the chipmill industry. Much of the recent clearfelling activity for the chipmill industry has occurred on Maori land.

Some of these values are compatible; others are characterised by competition and conflict. The protection of the remaining areas of lowland indigenous forests on private land is being hampered by the continuing controversy between the "protection versus development" interests, between the "greens" at

one end of the spectrum, and the local Pakeha farmers and Maori land owners and the timber industry workers at the other. The need for the wise use
of these and other resources highlights the importance of developing environmental strategies based on an assessment of social and economic, as well
as ecological, considerations.

It is instructive to reflect on the plurality of environmental values in New
Zealand from a broader, comparative stance. Figure 1.1 is a description of the
situation in Europe today (O'Riordan, 1989). As shown in this diagram,
technocentrism is a manipulative mode of thinking, as opposed to the nurturing mode of ecocentrism. Environmentalism seeks to embrace both world
views, as a constructive tension between, on the one hand, "a *conservative*
and *nurturing* view of society-nature relationships, where nature provides a

Figure 1.1 Contemporary trends in environmentalism in Western Europe

Ecocentrism		Technocentrism	
Gaianism	*Communalism*	*Accommodation*	*Intervention*
Faith in the rights of nature and of the essential need for co-evolution of human and natural ethics	Faith in the co-operative capabilities of societies to establish self-reliant communities based on renewable resource use and appropriate technologies	Faith in the adaptability of institutions and approaches to assessment and evaluation to accommodate to environmental demands	Faith in the application of science, market forces, and managerial ingenuity
'Green' supporters; radical philosophers	Radical socialists; committed youth; radical-liberal politicians; intellectual environmentalists	Middle-ranking executives; environmental scientists; white-collar trade unions; liberal-socialist politicians	Business and finance managers; skilled workers; self-employed; right-wing politicians; career-focused youth
0.1-3% of various opinion surveys	5-10% of various opinion surveys	55-70% of various opinion surveys	10-35% of various opinion surveys
Demand for redistribution of power towards a decentralised, federated economy with more emphasis on informal economic and social transactions and the pursuit of participatory justice		Belief in the retention of the status quo in the existing structure of political power, but a demand for more responsiveness and accountability in political, regulatory, planning, and educational institutions	

Source: O'Riordan, 1989, p.85

metaphor for morality (how to behave) and a guide to rules of conduct (why we must behave so)," and, on the other hand, "a *radical* or *manipulative* perspective in which human ingenuity and the spirit of competition dictate the terms of morality and conduct..." (O'Riordan, 1989, p.82). The particular challenge facing the environmental movement is to decide what particular stance to adopt in advocating change. The current situation in Europe is characterised by contradictions and tensions and by a failure to agree over cause and action. A more coherent environmentalism is yet to emerge.

Even though there are manifest differences in the characteristics of the respective environmental movements in New Zealand and the European countries, the situation in New Zealand is comparable in the above-mentioned respects. Recent opinion polls indicate that environmental issues are generally accorded a lower priority by the public than economic issues (Gold and Webster, 1990). Moreover, it is a mistake to consider the environmental lobby as a homogeneous interest group. The ideological differences amongst the groups have became increasingly apparent recently, as the "greens" have entered the political arena. Environmental groups in New Zealand have encountered some success in mainstream party politics relating to the recent environmental administration and planning reforms; but their agenda has been limited primarily to nature protection issues, such as the protection of indigenous forests, and they have failed to forge wider links, particularly with those whose concerns are more socially oriented. The links with the Maori have been nascent only, and based mainly on particular issues. As a reflection of this situation, the recent environmental reforms have in fact been driven primarily by economic rather than environmental considerations.

Economic Restructuring

The process of settlement and economic expansion in New Zealand since the 1850s was aided by the development of a political and administrative bureaucracy within the confines of a nation-state. Almost all facets of life in New Zealand progressively came to be affected by a high degree of state intervention through economic management policies, and through the provision of physical infrastructures and social welfare services. As in many other parts of the world, the state has also sought to exercise a role in managing the impact of environmental change in New Zealand.

During the mid-1980s, a series of unprecedented changes took place in the course of the country's development, changes which have left the once highly protected economy open to deregulated market forces and external competition (Franklin, 1991). Under the aegis of the fourth Labour government, these changes were conceived and executed by a small, élite group of politicians, government officials and businessmen, whose primary motivation was to increase the competitiveness of the economy in the global economic order. Besides deregulating the production and financial sectors of the economy, the reforms have been comprehensive in scope – including central and local government administration, resource management, education and the provision of social services. The dominance of the ideology of the market-place, a search for efficiency in the use of resources and the influence of Treasury have been the common hallmarks of these fundamental changes in policy direction (Holland and Boston, 1990).

With particular reference to the environmental administration and planning reforms, perhaps what is surprising is the extent to which the institutional changes advocated by environmental groups have been achieved as part of this restructuring exercise. Yet in hindsight, their collective influence in negotiating the course of recent environmental reforms may be more apparent than real.

The formulation and implementation of the environmental reforms has been dominated by a conflicting agenda. There is little doubt that the concerns of environmental groups found considerable sympathy with some politicians in the fourth Labour government. Nevertheless, the more significant consideration in directing the course of recent environmental reforms in New Zealand has been the adoption of New Right policies by the Labour administration, and by the National administration which succeeded it in 1990. The decision to abandon the historically important role of the state as a developer and to curtail public sector expenditure appears to have been the crucial one in this respect.

During the first term of the fourth Labour government, central government administration was subject to drastic reforms on the basis of principles such as transparency, the separation of policy and regulatory functions and other concepts related to public choice theory. As one of the first sectors to which these policies were applied, the central government environmental bureaucracy was restructured as part of this wider process. Subsequently, the reforms of local government, of resource management statutes and of the environmental quangos followed during the second term of the fourth Labour government, and were completed by the National government, driven by similar considerations.

A Maori Perspective

The implications of the recent environmental administration and planning reforms from a Maori perpective also emerge as a significant theme in this study. As in other New World societies, racial disputes in New Zealand over the ownership and management of land and of other environmental resources have been a source of many long-standing grievances. These grievances have centred on the failure of successive governments to honour the Treaty of Waitangi negotiated in 1840 between the Crown and the heads of Maori tribes. Under the Treaty, the Crown guaranteed to Maori the full, exclusive and undisturbed possession of their lands, estates, forests, fisheries and other properties.

The pre-colonial Maori tribes shared, to varying degrees, a combined land-

and water-based culture. Despite their relatively small numbers, they had a considerable inadvertent impact on the environment, and large areas of the indigenous forest cover had been cleared and destroyed for purposes of hunting and cultivation before organised European settlement began in 1840. But progressively, these descendants of the Polynesian immigrants to New Zealand had learnt, over the course of a thousand years, to develop successful niches within a changing physical and cultural environment. Any propensity for over-using environmental resources was mitigated by taboos (literally, tapu, prohibitive restrictions) regarding certain seasons, times or areas of harvest and by social norms based on sharing and reciprocity. Thus, on the eve of European settlement in New Zealand, the early explorers and missionaries recorded, in a number of regions, several relatively large, flourishing coastal communities. However, within a few decades, European settlement led to the disintegration of the traditional Maori economy, and to the growth of an export-oriented economy within the global mercantile framework.

In many societies affected by European colonisation, particularly in Africa and Asia, the agricultural and mineral export enclaves which developed were juxtaposed with the traditional subsistence economies of the indigenous people. Over time, a significant degree of dependence emerged between the two sectors, but often to the greater advantage of the former. By comparison, Maori traditional economic systems were not able to survive to any significant degree in New Zealand. While it may have been assumed that Maori would eventually become assimilated into the modern mainstream economy, it can be argued that they were marginalised to a far greater degree than were a number of other societies colonised by the Europeans during the nineteenth century. Explanations for this marginalisation include the imposition of a system of individual property rights on all resources and the rapid outnumbering of the Maori population by the colonists. While the Maori population in 1840 exceeded the European population by perhaps 70 to 1, numbers were equal within twenty years. By 1921, the Maori population had fallen to 4.5 percent of the total population (Memon and Cullen, 1991).

At present, Maori people constitute approximately nine percent of the total New Zealand population and in terms of their current socio-economic status, generally occupy a lowly position within New Zealand society. The development of New Zealand society has, to a very large extent, been dominated by European values. Maori values, economic systems and forms of government, including traditional institutions for resource management, became marginalised. The guarantees and privileges accorded to Maori by the Crown, including their rights of access to land and water resources, and their participation in management decisions, were overlooked or deliberately ignored in the growing apparatus of state-sponsored legislation and related instruments for resource allocation and management.

Only very recently have the concerns of the Maori people been accorded some degree of political recognition (Douglas, 1991). However, one of the main unresolved issues in the environmental restructuring process is the implications of Maori ownership and management of resources.

Synopsis   A CHRONOLOGICAL LOOK AT GOVN'T CHANGE

Chapter 2 reviews the contextual background and history of environmental administration and planning in New Zealand from the 1870s to the 1980s. As the largest developer in the country, central government reflected utilitarian and exploitative attitudes towards the environment. Its activities were based on the values of a materialistic society and conservative political institutions. In the 1970s there was an unprecedented expression of public concern about declining environmental quality. As in a number of other western countries, the roots of recent environmental initiatives can be traced to the 1970s, when changing public attitudes, accompanied by wider socio-economic influences, provided a catalyst for the incremental reforms in the administrative structures and processes for environmental decision-making. The fourth Labour government in New Zealand, in office from 1984 to 1990, implemented policies that have led to fundamental changes in institutional arrangements for environmental administration and planning. Collectively, these reforms have precipitated the most radical changes in living memory to the public sector.

Subsequent chapters examine the major facets of the fourth Labour government's environmental initiatives: central government environmental bureaucracy (chapter 3); local and regional government restructuring (chapter 4); environmental planning functions of central, regional and local governments (chapter 5) and the role of environmental quangos (chapter 6).

The speed with which the above policy initiatives have been developed and implemented is striking. The major policy decisions pertaining to central government's environmental bureaucracy were made and implemented primarily during the first term of the fourth Labour government, between 1984 and 1987. The reform of environmental quangos and the local and regional government restructuring exercise were accomplished during the second term of office from 1987 to 1990. The parallel resource management law reform proposals came to completion in July 1991 under a National government administration.

The implications of these reforms are more fully understood if the different components are viewed in relation to the broader context discussed in chapters 1 and 2. This is the objective of the concluding chapter 7.

2

An Historical Perspective

Introduction

Environmental problems demand effective action by government. However, central as well as local government agencies confront deep-seated obstacles to effective environmental management, as has long been recognised by those seeking to promote decentralisation and participation in decision-making (Walker, 1989; Paehlke and Torgerson, 1990; Pickvance, 1990; Bartlett, 1990). These constraints stem primarily from the fact that the state has priorities which have little to do with environmental concerns, so that environmental concerns may be overridden when they come into conflict with other priorities such as economic growth. While environmental regulation during periods of rapid urban growth of industrial cities may have brought improvements in environmental quality, the question of whether further policy efforts would produce sufficient benefits to justify their costs has become increasingly controversial (Dryzek, 1990). Moreover, public intervention has been associated with the growth of large bureaucracies that lack public accountabililty. Any intervention to achieve environmental objectives has tended to be poorly targeted, fragmented and ad hoc, and based on inadequate information.

The objective of this chapter is to review the state's role in environmental administration and planning in New Zealand. It provides a broad historical perspective on the evolution of the institutional arrangements for environmental administration and planning up to the 1980s, within the wider framework of the country's political economy and the public policy process. Such a wide-ranging review is useful for two reasons. First, it demonstrates the obstacles to effective environmental management in New Zealand during the period prior to 1984. Second, from a comparative perspective, it helps to appreciate the extent of restructuring in the fields of environment administration and planning during the post-1984 period which will be examined in the subsequent chapters.

The Wider Context

With the establishment of a European-dominated society during the mid-nineteenth century, the pace of environmental change in New Zealand rapidly accelerated. The Polynesian inhabitants also had a significant impact on the New Zealand environment before European colonisation, particularly in the

South Island. Elsewhere, any change tended to be localised and large areas were still intact under a luxuriant forest cover. The Europeans perceived forests as an impediment to settlement and to other uses of land. By 1880, forest covered only a third of the country, compared with a little less than half in 1840. Agricultural and pastoral settlement, the growth of towns and the demands of the gold and timber industries decimated the forest cover and drastically changed the face of the land (Wynn, 1979). Since then, during the comparatively short history of modern New Zealand society, the face of the country's landscape has altered almost beyond recognition in response to the ways it has been perceived, utilised and managed by New Zealanders.

The root causes of such environmental changes have been universal. Since the industrial revolution, humans have gained an increasing technological power to subdue and exploit nature (Thomas, 1956). With the development of a global economic system based on the principles of international division of labour, specialisation and exchange, the combined power of the technological and political forces has produced the period of greatest change in the environment so far. The momentum of such expansionist attitudes has continued as an accelerating, cumulative process throughout this century, often in response to considerable economic and bio-physical adversity. Thus, as observed by Cumberland (1961), humans did more to alter the landscape in the previous hundred years than nature and humans together accomplished in the previous five thousand.

The nature and impact of these changes have been subject to wide-ranging studies in several disciplines (for example Anderson, 1980; Molloy, 1980; Williams, 1973). The significance of earlier environmental changes and their impacts were initially most visible in the countryside, and were associated with the expropriation, settlement and exploitation of land, forest and mineral resources as the foundations for a modern economic system. But even as the New Zealand countryside was being subjugated, equally pervasive changes, linked with urbanisation and the development of manufacturing and tertiary economic activities, were beginning to have an impact. By the 1920s, New Zealand was well on the way to becoming an urban society, and by 1961, more than sixty percent of the country's population lived in centres with more than one thousand inhabitants.

The economic strategy found its vindication through the successful development of a predominantly grassland economy based on the export of primary produce, which was subsequently followed by a limited degree of product diversification. Prosperity from this growth flowed from the country's farms and processing industries to urban industries and services (Hawke, 1985). By these means New Zealand was able to carve out and occupy a comfortable niche within the global capitalist economy, even though that niche was a fragile one and the source of continual insecurity to its citizens (Franklin, 1978).

For nearly a century and a half, the state played a pivotal role by, on the one hand, promoting and facilitating these changes, and on the other, seeking to regulate and manage their impact. It is appropriate, therefore, that the development of institutional arrangements for environmental administration in New Zealand should be seen within the context of the wider public policy process. Three aspects of this process are particularly relevant.

First, the dominant focus of public policy debate in New Zealand has inevitably been on the issue of economic growth. This is a reflection of the country's dependent position within the international mercantile economy. This objective engendered government intervention in the form of wide-ranging policies and programmes to foster the utilisation of land, energy, mining, fisheries, forestry and tourism resources. Alongside such wealth-generating initiatives, central government also came to play an important role in the delivery of services, such as the provision of housing, hospitals, roads, railways and schools.

Pragmatism, based on responding to perceived issues in a politically acceptable fashion rather than on a particular ideological platform, has been identified as the instrumental force in guiding the development of the government's role in this field (Hawke, 1982; Mascarenhas, 1982; Jackson, 1988). But what is even more significant is the overriding importance attached by successive governments, in spite of their political differences, to the role of the state itself as a large scale developer. Its many-sided involvement has stretched beyond merely encouraging and assisting the corporate sector and private individuals to undertake the task of development through resource exploitation. The state was itself directly involved in this process as an entrepreneur. Such involvement should not be viewed as merely having been inherited from the pioneer economy of the nineteenth century. In fact, it persisted and significantly increased under successive governments through various programme initiatives, in response to the expansion of the New Zealand economy and population after 1946. Not only was the state the country's largest land owner,[1] it was also a major business entrepreneur, being the owner and manager of coal mines, forestry estates, farms, irrigation schemes, power stations and hotels.[2]

Second, since the 1870s, a strong centralist stance has pervaded the formulation and implementation of public policies and programmes for resource utilisation and for the provision of infrastructure in New Zealand. Within the framework of the unitary state, the objectives of promoting economic growth and infrastructure provision have tended to be regarded as a national rather than sub-national matter and hence the primary responsibility of central government. From the state's perspective, functional economic considerations, although underlined by an implicitly egalitarian ethos, have been perceived as its primary policy goals, and as being far more important than community well-being in the local and regional context. Because the formulation and implementation of public policies have been imbued with a strongly centralist perspective, it has been difficult for decision makers to appreciate the implications of territorial diversity and the desire to permit local and regional flexibility in the choice of policy options. Policy solutions formulated at the national level were assumed to be universally appropriate to all localities and groups, because New Zealand was perceived as a relatively homogeneous, egalitarian society.[3]

Third, despite direct public involvement in the New Zealand economy, and irrespective of the ideological leanings of the party in power, New Zealand politicians have been extremely solicitous of the freedom of private property owners. Rural and urban land owners have always successfully and jealously guarded their assumed right to make land utilisation decisions unencumbered by what they perceived as excessive regulations. Indeed, state involvement in resource utilisation projects and the provision of infrastructure services such as electricity and transportation was perceived as necessary in order to encourage private sector development. These roles were seen to complement rather than contradict each other.

When one considers this wider public policy framework, it is evident that while the cumulative growth during the last five to six decades of environmental legislation administered by central and local government may have served an important symbolic role, it failed to be particularly effective in satisfactorily resolving conflicts over resource utilisation and in addressing important environmental issues. Because of the ideological premises on which legislation and decision-making were based, and given the deeply entrenched interests of the state as a major developer, there were inherent constraints on the ability of central government to promote appropriate policies derived from informed judgements about alternative options for resource utilisation and service delivery. The justification for environmental planning was seen in utilitarian terms: for example, in the light of the benefits of increased production from land conservation measures, or in terms of functional efficiency in urban land use. Intervention in the right of the developers to make land utilisation decisions has been sanctioned only in the last few decades but has been limited to taking care of undesirable "externalities"; in other words, to minimise the unwanted consequences arising from individual and corporate decision-making.

At the same time, the state was able to continue its long-standing preoccupation with economic growth. Public concern about the potential impact of environment planning initiatives at the central government level was, to a considerable extent, marginalised, because such initiatives were institutionally co-opted within the mainstream development-oriented bureaucracy. Environmental conflicts were effectively suppressed and therefore prevented by bureaucrats and politicians from entering the political arena unless forced to by public pressure. Likewise, the role of local government was also marginalised. Even though a number of environment planning functions, such as town and country planning and water and soil management, were delegated to local government, central government was careful to protect its overriding political and bureaucratic supremacy.

The Formative Years

In discussing the growth of government agencies during the period 1840 to 1876, Polaschek (1958) remarked on the inevitable preoccupation of the early colonial officials with the wars with indigenous peoples over land. It was only after 1870, once British supremacy had been confirmed, that the government was able to turn its attention to economic issues.

The early colonial administration was modelled on the typical Crown Colony pattern, and the rudimentary departmental structure was derived from existing English institutions. More significantly, the early form of administration was centralised. The trend towards increasing centralisation and dominance by central government, which became even more clearly apparent in later years, was briefly reversed for a short duration of some twenty years when provincial governments were more important than central government, even though they did not enjoy the sovereignty of states in a federal system.

The creation of the provinces in 1852-53 provided for a representative and responsible form of government for New Zealand. The provinces were seen then to be better suited to the needs of New Zealand as a newly developing country with a scattered population and a rugged terrain. The six provinces (subsequently increased to nine) stood to play a potentially significant role in resource planning and management, had this form of government been able to survive. Central government delegated to the provinces a number of functions including land administration, the running of hospitals, public works, and the administration of harbours and gold mining. Unfortunately, the continuing conflict over the division of the responsibilities and financial resources of central and provincial government culminated in the abolition of the provinces in 1876. The situation in some of the provinces had also become exacerbated by increasing financial difficulties, caused in part by the land wars of the 1860s. From the central government's perspective, the provinces had become an impediment to its own borrowing and investment plans to further the development of the country (Hawke, 1985).

Central government thus resumed control over a number of important functions, such as public works and immigration, which had previously been almost exclusively the functions of the provincial government, and an attempt was made to create active departments within the framework of a more unified structure. This move was also made partly in response to the increasing pace of population expansion and economic growth which had been prompted by the vigorous public works and immigration programmes initiated by the Vogel administration. That administration established the Public Works Department, the forerunner to the Ministry of Works and Development, linking it initially with immigration. Loans obtained on the London money market were used to build railways, telegraph lines, roads and bridges, and to subsidise large scale immigration.

The increasing importance of central government in promoting growth was reflected over the years in an expansion of the public bureaucracy. The fundamental ideology prevailing in government and underlying its activities during the nineteenth and early twentieth centuries was a laissez-faire exploitation of the country's wealth. The legislature played an instrumental role in creating the institutional basis for the rapid private appropriation and exploitation of resources, a process equated with economic growth, individual advancement and community betterment (Hearn, 1982).

Given this situation, it is not altogether unexpected that central government demonstrated a partisan attitude when conflicts emerged over the utilisation of resources. A number of studies of such conflicts underline the significant role of small environmental interest groups in promoting an awareness of the undesireable implications of prevalent laissez-faire attitudes, and the lack of an appropriate political response to effectively address such issues (Wynn, 1977 and 1979; Mather, 1982; Hearn, 1982 and 1983; Roche, 1984a and 1987). Given the relative cultural homogeneity of European society in New Zealand, it is perhaps surprising that such conflicts did arise. Material values were subscribed to by a majority of Pakeha New Zealanders, and government policies mirrored these. Groups who questioned such policies, including the Maori, were in the minority and lacked the political clout to influence decision-making. They may be regarded as the pioneers of the environment lobby, whose significance in questioning government policies has become much more apparent only relatively recently.

Nevertheless, the achievements during the nineteenth and early twentieth centuries must not be underestimated. Foremost amongst these was the establishment of a system of national parks and other protected areas, beginning with the creation of the Tongariro National Park in 1894 and Egmont in 1900. These developments reflected, to some extent, the influence of American initiatives. The Land Act 1892 made provision for a range of protected areas: scenic reserves, flora and fauna reserves and timber growth and preservation reserves. The Scenery Preservation Commission of 1904-6 went further and endeavoured to repurchase freehold lands of scenic interest for return to "public" ownership. The range of protected areas, including national parks, has been augmented since then, often at the urging of various interest groups (Roche, 1984a and 1984b).

While the government initially managed largely to distance itself from issues of environmental management and regulation, the increasing visibility from the 1920s and 1930s of the detrimental impact of human activities associated with population growth and settlement, led to remedial government action, which sought incrementally to mitigate this impact. For example, the cumulative impact of farming and of associated land management practices, such as periodic burning of forests and tussock mountain lands, led to problems of declining soil fertility, erosion and flooding in a geologically young country, highly susceptible to environmental hazards (Gibbs, 1974).

The results of field studies by scientists, together with the experience of other nations, provided a better insight into such relationships and their implications for sustained yield management. Parliament responded to this by enacting the Soil Conservation and Rivers Control Act 1941. Catchment authorities were created and funded by central government to undertake resource planning on a watershed basis. The task of co-ordinating the conflicting demands for increasingly scarce water resources under the Water and Soil Conservation Act 1967 was subsequently delegated to these agencies. The undesirable impacts of unregulated land subdivision and urban expansion on the quality of the urban environment had been evident from the early days of settlement. The increasing pace of urban growth, accompanied by new concerns such as co-ordinating the pace and incidence of growth in metropolitan regions and the loss of valuable agricultural land on the urban periphery, led to the Townplanning Act 1926, its amendment to make provision for regional planning in 1929, and the revised Town and Country Planning Act in 1953. Significantly, the task of administering the town and country planning functions was also delegated to local government.

Over the years, a large body of related environmental statutes has been enacted, and policies adopted relating to issues such as environmental pollution control, urban renewal, agricultural chemicals, native forests, national parks, heritage preservation, mining and waste disposal.[4] Such legislative responses invariably tended to be reactive rather than proactive, and even then were very slow to eventuate, despite claims made during the parliamentary enactment debates regarding their potential effectiveness. While it was generally deemed more appropriate to delegate a number of these functions to agencies of sub-national government, central government nevertheless jealously guarded its vested interests. In order to ensure that the construction of public works and related projects was unfettered by having to obtain local consent, and because of a general lack of trust in the capability of local government, the institutional arrangements for delegating functions ensured that the Crown was not bound by such legislation. In addition to this, in view of the control by the central government of the purse strings for funding local government activities such as soil erosion, flood control, infrastructure services and urban renewal schemes, the priorities of local authorities were effectively centrally rather than locally determined.

The Development Bureaucracy

As I have already remarked, a characteristic feature of central government in New Zealand until 1984 was the existence of large state bureaucracies, whose primary commitment was to promote the utilisation of natural resources such as land, forests and minerals in order to engender growth. Furthermore, the bureaucracy considered itself responsible for providing infrastructure such as housing, hospitals, electricity and roads, even to the extent of building and operating hotels in National Parks. Such multifarious involvement was reflected in the emergence of a series of big and relatively powerful state departments: Agriculture and Fisheries; Energy; Forest; Lands and Survey; Mining; Housing; Health; Tourism; and Works and Development.

Their underlying philosophies were strongly production oriented and the main thrust of their policies was towards expansion. They operated within a tightly defined compartmentalised bureaucratic framework. This compartmentalisation was partly a consequence of the fragmented legislative mandate, and partly characteristic of a central government bureaucracy with departments organised on a functional basis. Over the years, special legislation had been enacted specifically geared to individual agencies and their particular responsibilities. There was a noticeable absence of an agency with a general legislative mandate for environmental administration and co-ordination at the central level.

Internally, these agencies were characterised by hierarchical power relations. Authority was clearly concentrated in Wellington with established organisational lines for decision-making. The formalised style of decision-making was "from the top down". Head offices set targets based on resource inventories and national harvest or demand projections. Public involvement in decision-making was limited or non-existent. These agencies consequently lacked the ability to adapt creatively to controversial situations. They were unable to mediate, for instance, in cases of conflict between competing groups, or to recognise the need for local and regional flexibility in the delivery of services.

Public concern began to focus on such issues during the 1970s. Individuals and groups began to fear the potentially dire consequences of growth: irreversible damage to scenic landscapes and ecosystems, together with the detrimental impact on local and regional economies through the loss of valuable farm land and irrigation opportunities. They also criticized the bureaucracy for its cultural insensitivity towards the values of the local Maori communities and inner city neighbourhoods, and were instrumental in exposing more deepseated political and administrative biases in the manner in which policy decisions were made by central government.

One such issue, with complex environmental implications, arose in the energy sector. The first major public exposure of the extent to which the state was willing to compromise its constitutional mandate to achieve limited economic objectives was in 1960, when it ignored a political commitment and signed an agreement with an overseas consortium, the Commonwealth Aluminium Company (Comalco). The agreement permitted the company to exploit the combined water resources of Lakes Te Anau and Manapouri, the two largest glacial lakes in the Fiordland National Park, for the purpose of generating electricity to smelt bauxite imported from Australia. The contract permitted the company to raise the levels of both lakes and to drown forests along 320 miles of shoreline, a proposal which constituted a gross abuse of the National Parks Act passed little more than a decade earlier. By passing legislation which overrode this legislation, the government also ignored a petition of close to 25,000 signatures.

Comalco secretly renegotiated the agreement with the government in 1963 on account of financial difficulties, thereby exchanging its water rights for a commitment from the government to assume the responsibility for constructing the power scheme and guaranteeing a power supply to the company. The government also inherited the obligation to raise the levels of both lakes, and despite growing public opposition during the decade, based on economic, ecological and engineering evidence as to the questionable merits of the scheme, felt compelled to respect that obligation. Nationwide protests turned this into a major political issue in the 1969 general election (Cleveland, 1972b). The government response to this disquiet was to set up a Cabinet Committee on Manapouri, followed by a Commission of Inquiry and, finally, a Parliamentary Select Committee which was convened to consider a second petition endorsed by 264,908 signatures. The Select Committee recommended "favourable" consideration of the petition and supported the view that Lake Manapouri should not be raised at this time. The government was compelled to announce in September 1971 the revised terms of the Comalco concession which provided protection for the natural shoreline environment of Lake Manapouri.

Unwittingly or otherwise, the state displayed a staggering inability to learn from this experience. During the 1970s and the early 1980s similar conflicts emerged over comparable large-scale resource development projects.

The Electricity Division of the Ministry of Energy, the advisory agency to the Cabinet on how best to satisfy the country's power needs, together with the Ministry of Works and Development as the national construction agency, had acquired a strong vested interest in the construction of new power projects. However, exponential increases in power requirements predicted by the energy advisers appeared questionable, especially when the two departments concerned were not prepared to demonstrate how these estimates were arrived at.

Unfortunately during the late 1970s and early 1980s, these professional advisers to the government found allies amongst the politicians. The National government at that time was keen to promote large-scale energy projects as the basis of a "Think Big" political platform deemed essential for New Zealand's economic revival. It has been argued that an understanding of such alliance-making behaviour requires an appreciation of the close relationship between government and business interest groups, a relationship which was rooted long ago in the colonial origins of the country and the style of New Zealand politics (Cleveland, 1972a; Kellow, 1986). As a consequence of this alliance, the construction of a number of energy and related downstream projects was politically sanctioned, even though their respective economic merits appeared marginal in the context of a worsening national debt crisis.

It is not surprising, therefore, that from the viewpoint of some sectors of New Zealand society, the record of these government agencies in managing resources began to arouse increasing dissatisfaction. The New Zealand Forest Service, for instance, had for many years been involved in a running controversy over the logging of native forests. With the adoption by the government of an indigenous forest policy in 1975, the public was assured that the previously wasteful and destructive practices of forest management would be phased out. In practice, however, the clear felling and conversion of native forests continued. The Forest Service, having exclusive control of state forests, was in a powerful position and could violate the indigenous forest policy which was intended to control its management practices.

Because they were under the control of a production-oriented agency with an overwhelming emphasis on active forest manipulation and wood production, unique forest habitats and forest areas set aside as reserves were considered by the Service to be available for multiple-use management. Management advice and reserve proposals from other government departments and from conservation organisations were rarely accepted, with the Service preferring to listen to its own advice on these matters (Lees, undated). Again, unfortunately, the mainstream political parties did not provide an adequate channel for the articulation of public concerns. This was because many issues of public policy were largely determined by government in its interactions with experts, the administrative officials and established pressure groups (Cleveland, 1972a).

Concerns expressed by environmental groups were mirrored, and sometimes overshadowed, by the growing articulation of Maori discontent (Horsley, 1989). The fundamental basis of concern on the part of the Maori related to the lack of government commitment to the Treaty of Waitangi which guaranteed Maori control over resources. From the earliest contact with the Europeans, Maori groups had been fighting to retain their economic base and to ensure the survival of their spiritual and cultural beliefs. Their sense of powerlessness was compounded by the fact that there was negligible legislative provision for Maori concerns to be considered when developmental decisions were made. The "Think Big" policies associated with the Taranaki energy projects, Waikato power generation and coal mining, and the expansion of the New Zealand Steel complex at Glenbrook on the Manukau Harbour, raised major environmental concerns for the Maori in these regions. Yet, as observed recently by members of the Tainui tribe,

Traditionally Maaori groups have not been directly involved in project initiation and planning. This has been the prerogative of the large public development agencies such as Ministry of Works and Development, or Ministry of Energy. Attempts to input a Maaori perspective, or to gain access to resources necessary to expedite input into the process, have operated under severe constraints. This is largely because agency decision makers, who are almost exclusively Paakeha, control the process and the resources necessary to project planning. These people ... control concerns such as the project time frame, finance, expertise, information and ... capital flows associated with large scale projects. ... A further constraint on Maaori participation in the planning process is the Paakeha power structure. As it currently exists the power structure would rather deal with Paakeha organisations and penalises Maaori people who seek to have an input into the planning process. (Mahuta et. al., 1985, p.12).

The Waitangi Tribunal was established by the Treaty of Waitangi Act in 1975 to address the question of Maori rights under the Treaty of Waitangi; but the powers of the Tribunal were limited then to Crown actions after 1975 and did not significantly allay Maori concerns. It was not until 1985 that the Waitangi Amendment Act was passed permitting the Tribunal to make recommendations on claims dating back to 1840.

The Search for an Effective Environmental Administration

It is not as if an official awareness did not exist, prior to 1984, as to the wider environmental implications associated with the activities of the state development agencies. In fact, as discussed earlier, comparable concerns regarding deforestation had been debated in Parliament as early as the 1880s (Wynn, 1977). More recently, similar concerns, focused on the formulation and implementation of central government development policies, were occasionally canvassed within official circles (for example the Interdepartmental Committee on the Pollution of Waters, 1952). But the fact that the same issues continued to reappear periodically on the public policy agenda attests to the inability or unwillingness on the part of the state to address them effectively.

Since the 1960s, a number of potentially significant initiatives have been made to develop appropriate institutional arrangements for effective environmental administration. Although these initiatives were sequential, they represented parallel and, to some extent, competitive bureaucratic approaches. Their common objectives were to enable better consideration of the wider socio-economic and bio-physical implications of government policies and to resolve conflicts in the utilisation of resources by adopting a common national stance based on good advice. The reforms sought to achieve this objective through a more balanced perspective on conservation and development priorities within the process of public policy formulation and implementation. They constituted, in a sense, a search for an effective model that was compatible with the role of central government in New Zealand as a major developer, and with the notion of a unitary public interest represented by central government. Finally, such initiatives were based on monocultural norms, with little or no consideration being accorded to Maori values.

The Ministry of Works and Development as a National Land and Water
Resources Policy Agency

The primary function of the Ministry of Works and Development was as a national construction agency. As an appendage to this role, it also served until 1988 as a national land and water resources policy agency. The former function was undertaken through its Town and Country Planning Division and the latter function through its Water and Soil Division.[5] The respective antecedents of these two functions may be traced to the demise of the Organisation for National Development (OND) in 1945, and to the enactment of the Soil Conservation and Rivers Control Act in 1941.

Established in 1943, and attached to the Prime Minister's Department with an ambitious mandate to co-ordinate the task of post-war reconstruction, the OND, in fact, had a very short life. Through its links to local government, it was expected to co-ordinate proposals for consideration by the Cabinet Committee on Reconstruction, as well as to administer the Townplanning Act 1926. The main reasons for its premature demise in 1945 were the "pressures of a triumvirate of major departments fearful of the birth of this instrument of overall policy control whose diverse interests were getting much too close to what had always been their prerogatives" (Cox 1980). Senior officials in the Ministry of Works, as well as in the Treasury, saw it as usurping direct access to the Ministers.

Having inherited the planning functions of the OND and the Department of Housing Construction, the Ministry sought to develop a policy advisory role on the national use of land, to complement its principal function as a public works programming and construction agency. A national perspective was perceived to be necessary in view of the diversity of statutes enabling the use and development of land, without any co-ordination amongst administering government departments. Such views were influenced by contemporary developments in Britain, where a comparable national land-use planning framework had been recently established (Cullingworth, 1964).

It was proposed to adapt this approach to the New Zealand situation, with recommendations that the Minister of Works be charged with the responsibility to secure "consistency and continuity in the framing and execution of a national policy with respect to the use and development of all land in the Dominion"; that the Minister be given the power to "control, co-ordinate and plan the right use and development of land in the national interest"; and that he should have a reserve power to require that a development which is of more than local interest be referred to him for a decision (Cameron, 1947). The scope of the proposed national planning policy was all-embracing: it included policies relating to the location of population, industry and new towns, to agriculture, rural development, energy, transportation and communication.

In the event, the Ministry was denied such an explicit and wide-ranging legislative mandate, even though it sought to exercise that role implicitly through the Town and Country Planning Branch. Given the overriding mission of the Ministry as a central government construction agency, it was by no means clear that such a role was, in the first place, even appropriate for it. It would have been akin to appointing the poacher as a gamekeeper. As a matter of fact, the town and country planning function within the Ministry became essentially a handmaiden of public works. With the enactment of the Town and Country Planning Act 1953, in response to increasing pressures on the environment, the responsibility for land-use planning was delegated to territorial local authorities, and a Planning Tribunal was constituted to resolve disputes between land owners and local authorities. However, the Crown was not bound by the requirements of the Act or by the local and regional planning policies approved under the Act and openly ignored them (Commission of Inquiry Into Housing, 1971). As the central government agency responsible for administering the legislation, the Ministry chose to adopt a largely one-sided perspective of its role, limited to servicing the physical planning requirements of the state sector. Because of the extensive involvement of the state in resource utilisation and the provision of service infrastructure, planning became closely associated with promoting public works projects. Planners were forced to operate within the framework of the already well-entrenched central and district organisational structures of the Ministry, which was dominated by engineers. Planning was perceived as technically a land development process involving the construction and coordination of settlements in an "orderly" manner.

Even the success of this limited form of deterministic, physical planning was judged equivocally, as one member of parliament observed when commenting on the planned state housing suburbs that were rapidly coming to dominate the urban landscape of the larger cities:

In many cases the nature of town planning has been conditioned by the consequences of a sterile public means test housing policy. Money costs have too often [been] allowed to exclude social values. Far too often the curve of concrete has been regarded as more important than the shape of the society that was being created. Town planning has mainly been a matter of placement. A place for industry, a place for houses, a place for roads, a place for commercial activity. But if the place for houses is filled with buildings of a similar construction and design, all squeezed down in size and quality into the corset of an artificially low lending limit; if they lack good access, proper sporting, recreational, and cultural outlets for their inhabitants; if they are all jammed together, one on top of the other with privacy and open living space treated as disposable luxuries, instead of creating a well planned, bright, integrated community, with a happy social climate and an attractive environment, there will be created a high-density conglomeration of buildings which are not much more than a collection of storage spaces, in which industrial workers and their families are put away at night – a utilitarian, but unattractive social wasteland that is productive of social problems. (McMahon, 1972, p.48).

New Zealand's cities have evolved primarily as a product of established interests in land development. Central government urban development decisions had significant impacts on the quality of life in terms of location of jobs and housing and access to services. These social considerations were not addressed within the framework of the planning legislation.

Since the mid-seventies, the Town and Country Planning Division came to exercise a significant role in co-ordinating the implementation of the "Think Big" resource development strategy on behalf of the Crown. It succeeded, to some extent, in securing limited acceptance of, and providing a base for, undertaking social impact assessments of policy decisions. Periodically, it also sought to address wider issues such as pollution control, coastal planning and regional development, but in an advisory fashion only, by convening inter-departmental committees. The scope of such deliberations was typically limited to highlighting the problems, rather than formulating explicit policies to be adopted by the government.

During the 1980s, the Town and Country Planning Division came under increasing political and bureaucratic scrutiny. The circumstances which led to its demise have to be understood with reference to the wider strategic planning role that the Division sought for itself within the framework of central and regional government, following the enactment of the revised Town and County Planning Act in 1977. A significant objective of this Act was to enable communities to have a greater influence over central government's sectoral development plans. Communities were allowed to make an independent review of key sector policies, their interrelationships and possible social implications. Regional plans, prepared by the United and Regional Councils, were promoted as a "contract" between the regions and central government. With the growing realisation of the social implications of the Labour government's policies to deregulate the economy, the Directorate sought to bring to Cabinet's attention the strong concerns expressed in the provinces affected by these policy decisions. It had become apparent that such concerns had not been anticipated nor taken into consideration when those decisions were made. The advice of the Division proved to be politically unpalatable and it was strongly rebuked for going beyond its legislative mandate.

The Ministry of Works and Development also exercised a role in the management of water and soil resources through its Water and Soil Directorate. Surprisingly, in spite of their being located in a single and highly centralised agency, there were few direct parallels, or professional and organisational links, between the land-use and the water and soil resource planning functions of the Ministry. While the former function was initially adapted from the English model, the latter was influenced by American experience and practice. Successive decades of bush clearance and land development had increased the risk of flood hazard in many communities. Reluctant recognition of the relationship between flood revention and soil conservation, in spite of direct opposition from the Department of Agriculture, led to the enactment of the Soil Conservation and Rivers Control Act in 1941 (Kellow, 1983). The Act created the Soil Conservation and Rivers Control Council, which represented various interest groups and was charged with both the promotion of soil conservation, and the prevention of erosion and damage by flooding. One of the major tasks of the Council was to co-ordinate the policies and activities of government departments and local authorities in order to reduce erosion and flood damage. Regionally elected catchment boards were established as the appropriate units for resource planning; subsidies were then made available to promote both the adoption and implementation of soil conservation plans by farmers and the construction of flood protection works by the boards.

Subsequently, in 1967, water resource planning was incorporated as an additional function within this institutional framework. The accelerating pace of population increase, urbanisation and related industrial development following the Second World War led to increasing pollution of the New Zealand environment (Nielsen, 1975). Between 1923 and 1965, no fewer than 60 separate pieces of legislation were brought into force to regulate pollution. But this proliferation in legislation did not result in eliminating pollution or even preventing its spread to a wider area of the country. The situation was particularly bad with regard to water pollution, notwithstanding the fact that a Pollution Advisory Council had been created under the Water Pollution Act 1953. This Council had proved to be ineffective because its role was only advisory and it had no powers to enforce its policies on water quality. The ultimate responsibility to do this was left with local authorities and government departments, who did not have to act on the advice of the Council.

The objectives of the Water and Soil Conservation Act 1967 were to promote a national policy for water management, to make provision for water allocation, and to promote multiple water utilisation. A National Water and Soil Conservation Authority, chaired by the Minister of Works, was created with an ambitious mandate.[6] It was required to advise the Minister on the co-ordination of public policies related to water and soil, to set the broad national policy on water management and to supervise its implementation. The Authority was designed to secure a working consensus amongst those who had a vested interest in aspects of water resource utilisation. It was expected that the general consensus established by the representative character of this decision-making structure would enable it to establish priorities in water resource use.

But above all, the Authority was also a quasi-judicial body expected to resolve conflicts in the allocation of water resources. Thus, in performing its functions, it had the investigative power of a Commission of Inquiry, and for several specific tasks the requirement to act as a determining tribunal. The managerial, technical and research services to the Authority were provided by the Water and Soil Division of the Ministry of Works and Development.

The Water and Soil Conservation Act 1967 also gave catchment authorities a more important role as regional water boards, in addition to their flood protection and soil conservation functions. This was seen as establishing a partnership between the central government and the region. Supervised by the Authority, the regional water boards were empowered to deal with water right applications to use water or to discharge into water; to promote conservation and the most beneficial uses of natural water; to recommend maximum and minimum levels and flows and minimum standards of quality for waters; and to investigate and record all water resources. However, while the Act bound the Crown, it also reserved to the Crown a privileged position for obtaining water rights. Crown water right applications were decided directly by the Authority, with regional water boards only able to make recommendations to it. The reason for this was to protect the interests of the New Zealand Electricity Department (Interdepartmental Committee on Water, 1965).

In the event, the Water and Soil Division established a powerful position for itself in relation to the Authority as well as to the catchment authorities and regional water boards. The Division advised the Minister in two different and potentially conflicting capacities: directly in connection with the Authority's responsibilities on the co-ordination of public policies related to water and soil; and through the Commissioner of Works when considering matters for which the Ministry had responsibilities as a national construction agency. Likewise, the Minister was put in a position of conflicting interests: as an advocate on behalf of the Crown, and as a policy co-ordinator and adjudicator for the Authority. The Authority, which already had a significant development bias among its members, found that it could not fulfil its objectives when major conflicts arose over the allocation of water resources.[7] Furthermore, the Division also exercised a very close technical and financial control over the activities of catchment authorities and regional water boards. From a local and regional perspective, the Division came to be seen as paternalistic and inflexible. The partnership model on which the water and soil management reforms had been based did not prove to be very workable. Thus, by the mid-1980s, the scene was set for a radical review of the institutional arrangements for water and soil resource planning, arrangements which had been hailed as progressive and far reaching when they were conceived two decades earlier.

Environmental Policy Reforms During the 1970s

As in a number of other Western countries, the growing concern with environmental issues in the 1970s led to reviews of the institutional structures for making public policy. However, the structural reforms which took place as a consequence were not the result of a process of wide-ranging assessment of rational requirements for environmental policy; rather, they appear to have evolved in an ad hoc manner. While it was recognised that environmental problems were interrelated and could not be tackled in isolation by individual departments, the notion of a single agency – a ministry for the environment – at this stage proved politically too radical. Creating such an organisation was seen as tantamount to carving different-sized pieces off nineteen departments charged with various environmental responsibilities and combining them into one. This option was deemed unpractical and inefficient by the government (Norman, 1973).

Instead, the framework that developed over a decade comprised:

- a Minister for the Environment;

- a Cabinet Committee to co-ordinate environmental policy, chaired by the Minister for the Environment, and including the Deputy Prime Minister and the Ministers of Health, Works, Agriculture, Electricity and Internal Affairs;

- an Officials Committee, to provide information and advice to the Cabinet Committee and consisting of the Permanent Heads of the departments of Lands and Survey, Internal Affairs, Health, Works, Treasury, State Services Commission, Agriculture, Electricity, Forest Service, Marine, Maori and Island Affairs, Scientific and Industrial Research, and Transport;

- the Environment Council, comprising certain central government officials and selected private individuals with an interest in environmental affairs. Initially created as part of the National Development Council system, it also reported directly to the Minister for the Environment.

The Ministry of Works served as the secretariat for the above two committees and for the Council. In addition, there were:

- the Commission for the Environment, with responsibility to co-ordinate environmental policy, to advise the government and to administer environment impact assessment procedures for government-funded projects and for private-sector projects which required government consent;

- the Nature Conservation Council, comprising up to seven members appointed by the government on the recommendation of the Minister of Lands, to assess the likely impact of proposed public works on the biophysical environment and to advise the government accordingly.

The above institutional framework evolved in a piecemeal fashion. The earliest achievement, the Nature Conservation Council, was marginally successful in providing a platform for the expression of public opinion on environmental issues and as a source of relatively independent advice to the government. It was established in 1962 in the wake of the initial proposals for the Lake Manapouri power scheme, and in response to concerns expressed by groups such as the Royal Forest and Bird Protection Society. A major role envisaged for the Nature Conservation Council was to assess and help mitigate the likely impacts of public works on the natural environment (Wells, 1984). It had powers to conduct inquiries on matters of national importance and to recommend to the Minister a national policy for the conservation of nature; but it was not particularly effective in this way, partly because the Act did not bind the Crown by the recommendations of the Council. In the event, even though the Council consistently and repeatedly advised against raising the level of Lake Manapouri, its recommendations were overruled. Subsequently, a number of other major projects in the areas of communication, forestry, irrigation, wetland drainage and coastal development came under the scrutiny of the Council. But once again, the effectiveness of the Council was constrained because its findings were not binding on the government.

The experience of the Council as an advisory agency demonstrated that, in the final analysis, the protection and improvement of the environment depended on central government and local authorities being obliged to accept and observe the same requirements laid down for the private citizen. For historical reasons, public policies and projects in New Zealand have tended to produce much bigger impacts than private development initiatives.

Further attempts, with a much greater degree of promise, were made to address environmental concerns during the early 1970s, under the aegis of the National Development Conference. The National Development Conference (NDC) was established in 1968-70 to review New Zealand's resources and to agree on development strategies by setting targets and programmes. It was an exercise in indicative economic development planning, made in response to the perpetual crisis of the country's export based economy. A series of sector committees, representing major interest groups, were convened to undertake detailed investigations, and a group of advisory sector councils was then established as a form of continuing planning machinery.

The Physical Environment Committee (PEC) was convened, almost as an afterthought, by the Steering Committee of the National Development Conference, primarily at the behest of interest groups such the New Zealand Institution of Engineers and the Urban Development Association. Its terms of reference were potentially wide-ranging, to include consideration of the kind of physical environment to which New Zealand might aspire; to identify problems in attaining these desirable outcomes; and to examine the measures, organisational machinery and policies for addressing problems then perceived as significant. Some of these problems were: population distribution and internal migration; land use competition for agricultural, residential and recreational purposes; land tenure; preservation of natural, scenic and recreational endowments; and environmental problems such as water, air and noise pollution (National Development Council, 1969).

The institutional arrangements for environmental management were one of the four key topics which provided the focus for the Committee and its working parties (O'Riordan, 1971). The Committee was unfortunately not in a position to do justice to such an important subject. Its deliberations were dominated by government and professional group representatives, working within the framework of the NDC exercise. The environmental groups lacked the capability to play an active role in this consultative process, with the possible exception of the Royal Forest and Bird Protection Society.

The conservative stance of the Committee on the question of reforms for environmental administration was clear in its report to the Physical Environment Conference convened by the NDC in 1970:[8]

> *What did appear to us ... is the enormous complexity of the structure that exists already; the fact that far from being stable or out of date or locked in some conservative self contemplation of its own virtues, it is rapidly changing and there have been most important developments in environmental control in quite recent times. These must be given time to work out. Their effectiveness must be assessed and in addition to this of course, the importance of local government and its enormous contribution to the work of environmental control had to be recognised. ... the Local Government Commission is in [the] process of [conducting] a complete review of the structure of local government in New Zealand.... Until the review is completed and the investigations are in, and the possibilities for change are assessed, a somewhat amateur recommendation for striking reforms would be in fact both otiose and presumptuous. For this reason the report deals with the possibility of working towards change by collaboration rather than by an attempt to make any sort of conscription for alteration. (McMahon, 1972, p.31).*

The Committee rejected outright the notion of a single environmental ministry because this would "disrupt many long-established agencies while leaving others equally relevant to environmental policy untouched". Such a conservative stance continued to prevail within central government until 1984.[9] Thus, the most significant recommendation of the Committee was limited to establishing an Environmental Council as a sector council within the NDC structure, as an advisory body to Ministers and the NDC, despite its obvious overlap with the Nature Conservation Council. The Environmental Council was seen as "an excellent way in which the interest groups can be consulted, their points of view taken into account, and authoritative advice tendered to Government in collaboration with those who have the institutional experience necessary for effective change" (McMahon, 1972, p.31).

Shortly after the creation of the Environmental Council, a Cabinet Committee for the Environment, chaired by the Minister of Works, was set up to bring together, on a consultative basis, ministers and officials involved in major works which had environmental significance. The Cabinet Committee was assisted by an Officials Committee. Meanwhile, growing pressure from interest groups to see stronger government involvement in environmental assessment and monitoring led to the establishment in 1972 of the portfolio of the Minister for the Environment and also of a Commission for the Environment, with a small administrative and professional staff. The Commission's principal tasks were to co-ordinate departmental activities, reconcile conflicts, seek action to protect environmental values and, from 1974, audit environmental impact reports (Norman, 1973).

Even though its immediate achievements were limited, the creation of the Physical Environment Committee (PEC) has to be seen as an important initiative in the history of environmental administration. It created the momentum for subsequent environmental policy reforms. A number of other factors were also influential in this respect: the impact of the Save Manapouri campaign and the growing environmental lobby; the rise of the Values party and the recognition of the electoral significance of environmental issues by the mainstream political parties; the United Nations Conference on the Human Environment held in Stockholm in 1972; and the responses of countries such as Britain, the United States and Canada to environmental problems.

Without underestimating the significance of the above institutional reforms, I believe they did not prove as far-reaching in their impact on the central government policy process as may have been anticipated. Only passing consideration appeared to have been given during the course of the above reform exercise to a review of the many forms of resource management legislation relating to, for instance, land use, water and soil, forestry and coastal areas, or to the practices of agencies when administering these statutes. The potential power of the Environment Council was vitiated by its being made responsible to the Minister rather than directly to Parliament. The Minister was not given a wide-ranging responsibility for the environment portfolio, compared with his counterparts in other countries such as Canada and Britain. In these countries, there were a number of existing or newly created government agencies with environmental responsibilities that came directly under the command of the Ministers of the Environment. By comparison, the New Zealand Minister had very limited staff resources and an all-embracing watch-dog brief over any developments of environmental significance within the public sector. The government was able to continue making its decisions in the secrecy of the Cabinet, without having to justify them in the public.

The Cabinet Committee for the Environment remained in existence until 1975, even though it hardly ever met. Thereafter, important environmental issues were mostly dealt with by other Cabinet committees on an ad hoc basis, such as by a Cabinet Works Committee in the case of major development proposals, and sometimes by Cabinet as a whole (Buhrs, 1990). The Officials Committee for the Environment, chaired by the Assistant Commissioner of Works, also became inactive after the Commission for Environment became fully active. Hence:

Although in appearance, then, the responsibility for the co-ordination of environmental policy shifted from Cabinet as a whole to the Minister for the Environment, and from the Officials Committee for the Environment to the

Commission for the Environment on an administrative level, there was in fact little change. Environmental policy co-ordination continued to take place as before: by ad hoc deliberation between those ministers, officials and agencies most directly involved. (Buhrs, 1990, p.23)

Vested interests within the central government bureaucracy forestalled the creation of a strong, independent Ministry for the Environment, with reporting powers to Cabinet, parallel to those of Treasury. The role of the Commission was more akin to a government department rather than to a commission of inquiry (Mills, 1979). The decision to create a new environmental policy agency, rather than charge an existing government department with this responsibility, was a reflection of a lack of confidence in the ability of existing departments, such as the Ministry of Works and Development, to perform such a function satisfactorily. Yet, in hindsight, during its fourteen years of existence, the Commission found it difficult to do its job effectively on account of political and institutional constraints (Buhrs, 1991). While it had the mandate, it did not have the legislative power, executive authority, status or management responsibility to do the job. The large state agencies (the Lands and Survey Department, the Forest Service, the Ministry of Works and Development, the Ministry of Energy) found it very difficult to accept that co-ordination was necessary, except where they saw themselves doing it.

Likewise, the success of the Environment Protection and Enhancement Procedures (EP&EP) proved variable (Morgan, 1983 and 1988; Gilbert, 1986). The ineffectiveness of the Town and Country Planning Act as an environmental management measure, on account of the persistent refusal of the Crown to bind itself under the Act, was a factor in the creation of the EP&EP. But the latter lacked a statutory base to enforce compliance, in a policy-making environment dominated by inter-organisational rivalry and fragmented decision-making.[10] It would have seemed appropriate to incorporate such procedures within a planning act which was binding on all developers, including the Crown. The lack of apparent and real co-ordination between the EP&EP and the parallel decision-making processes under the Town and Country Planning Act and the Water and Soil Conservation Act came to be perceived by developers as unnecessarily expensive and bureaucratic.

Concluding Remarks

As a context for the evolution of environmental policies, public awareness of, and attitudes to, the environment have changed considerably since the mid-nineteenth century. While public interest in environmental issues has waxed and waned in response to particular concerns of the time, the environmental movement has gradually acquired a public standing comparable to other pressure groups, such as those representing farmers and manufacturers. The Maori people have also come to articulate their particular environmental concerns more forcefully.

As in many other western societies, where well over eighty percent of the population now live in urban areas, for a majority of New Zealanders the most immediate environmental problems are likely to be urban based. One would expect people to be most concerned about poor urban form and design, inadequate planning, waste disposal, proximity to hazardous toxic substances, crime, access to adequate housing and related amenities, and long journeys to work. Important issues further afield include the destruction of indigenous vegetation, inappropriate coastal development, loss of high-potential soils and wetlands, heavy metal accumulation in pastures and orchards, water pollution, environmental hazards such as droughts, species loss and unsustainable agriculture. Such concerns are not different from those recently experienced in other developed societies (for example, see Park, 1986). Material progress, with its associated scientific and technological capabilities, has allowed these societies to place more emphasis on the quality of life.

Nevertheless, compared to people in other western countries, many New Zealanders tend to perceive their cities and the countryside as relatively environmentally clean. Such a "green" image may be justified to some degree, in that New Zealand does not suffer from the worst excesses of environmental degradation, such as dilapidated inner cities and urban obsolescence, famines and poverty, acid rain and severe atmospheric and water pollution, that confront many developed and under-developed countries.

In some respects at least, such differences are only a matter of degree and time, and there may, indeed, be an element of false security here. The extent of environmental damage is particularly evident in terms of problems such as deforestation, loss of species and agricultural pollution caused by heavy metal accumulation in pastures and orchards. New Zealand has for far too long been a most wasteful nation. For instance, compared to other OECD countries, it ranks poorly in terms of the amount of energy it takes to produce a unit of gross domestic product.[11]

The increasing incidence of environmental problems that have come to face many societies, including New Zealand, has been attributed to a number of common, interrelated, causes: economic and population growth (Meadows et.al.,1972), technology (Commoner, 1972), affluence and consumerism brought about by industrial civilisation (Roberts, 1973), the Judaeo-Christian tradition (White, 1968), and capitalism (Weisberg, 1971; Sandercock, 1975 and 1977). The fact that New Zealand may be marginally better off is, in many respects, a reflection of its peripheral position in the global capitalist economy. Even though it is a highly urbanised society, it has not faced to the same degree the pressures associated with, for instance, large-scale, heavy industrialization concentrated in urban agglomerations. Furthermore, New Zealand is a society comparatively rich in natural resources. Labour and capital are the relatively more scarce and expensive factors of production. There has also been a time-lag in the diffusion throughout New Zealand society of the modern industrial technology, life-styles and values that have contributed to the environmental crisis in other advanced capitalist societies. Thus, while the pace of environmental change has gathered increasing momentum in New Zealand since the mid-nineteenth century, the above factors have served, to some extent, to mitigate the impact of this process.

A distinctive feature of the New Zealand experience has been the role of the state as a contributor to, and manager of, the process of environmental change. Compared with the experience of other developed capitalist societies, the growth of the New Zealand economy has been significantly aided by the establishment of a centralised political and administrative bureaucracy. Since the pioneer era, the state has been expected to develop resources to generate wealth and to provide a wide range of services. The role of the state may be described in terms of Marxist and corporatist theses in this respect. Its principal economic function has been to create conditions that are favourable to the accumulation of capital and in this aim it has had the support of the business and labour elites (Miliband, 1969; Middlemas, 1979). In order to achieve such objectives, public intervention by the state in the New Zealand economy was undertaken in a proactive fashion. The state acted as an entrepreneur engaged in wide-ranging activities and serviced by a massive central government bureaucracy. Such a role was subscribed to by the mainstream political parties. The attitude of the state to the environment has been dominated by ideologies of material progress and technological superiority. Environmental policies, such as land-use planning and flood protection legislation, were justified primarily in functional terms to increase output and prevent the worst excesses of free market capitalism.

The detrimental environmental impacts of state activities began only relatively recently to be perceived as unacceptable by sections of New Zealand society. The environmental and Maori groups repeatedly exposed deep-seated political and administrative biases in the manner in which public policies were formulated and implemented. The government responded to these concerns by adopting environmental policies. But the implementation of these policies was internalised within the mainstream development agencies and consequently marginalised. While attempts were made by central and local government agencies to deal with problems such as urban sprawl, coastal development, environmental pollution, urban renewal and the protection of natural areas and historical buildings, these constituted a compartmentalised environmental strategy. This also meant that administrative and legal boundaries were drawn around resources such as water, land, air, energy and forests, and between urban settlements and the countryside. Human communities and natural systems do not recognise these artificial boundaries.

Parallel attempts to create more autonomous environmental policy agencies can only be described as an incremental improvement on this situation; but they do symbolise a greater measure of political acceptance of environmental management as a legitimate role of government, alongside economic management and the protection of the health and safety of individuals. The catalysts for such initiatives can be traced to the rising global concern for the environment since the 1960s, and the mobilisation of public interest in environmental concerns. There was also some recognition amongst New Zealand policy makers and their advisers of the political significance of social change. Unfortunately, however, compared with the innovations in institutional arrangements in countries such as the United States during the 1970s (O'Riordan and Sewell, 1981), the tide of environmentalism did not bring about major changes in the styles of decision-making in New Zealand. The institutional innovations in New Zealand pale into insignificance compared to the extent to which the state was willing to use its political muscle and bureaucratic powers to promote its expansionist economic policies. This expansionist movement was reinforced by the perpetuation of a complex system of financial subsidies and guaranteed prices that encouraged production in the primary sector. Environmental issues were isolated from related social concerns, such as the recognition of Maori values in the management of natural resources. The assumptions underlying the basic ideological framework within which the role of the state in the New Zealand society had evolved went unquestioned. Ironically, such reforms had to await the restructuring policies of the 1984 Labour government, inspired by neo-liberal economic philosophies.

3

Environmental Administration Reforms in Central Government

Introduction

The role of central government in environmental administration and planning, as it had evolved since the 1870s, has been radically recast since 1984. Recent innovations in the institutional framework for environmental administration within central government have been implemented by means of two key legislative enactments: the Environment Act 1986 and the Conservation Act 1987. These innovations represent the outcome of policy developments stretching over a number of years. They are the product of a complex and changing interplay between competing and conflicting forces as they were perceived by the decision-makers in a rapidly changing policy environment.

The antecedents to these reforms may be traced back to the environmental issues of the 1960s and the 1970s, such as the Lake Manapouri proposals and the deforestation of the West Coast, as discussed in the preceding chapter. The election promises made by Labour in its 1984 manifesto to address deep-seated conflicts in the operation of the central government development agencies provided the initial momentum for environmental reform. However, it was the incorporation of the environmental reform momentum within the much wider ranging political agenda, to deregulate the economy and radically restructure the public sector bureaucracy, that was ultimately instrumental in achieving the outcomes advocated by the environmental groups. From a broader theoretical perspective which questions the ability of the state to accord priority to environmental objectives when they come into conflict with economic objectives (Emel and Peet, 1989; Paehlke and Torgerson, 1990), the recent New Zealand experience demonstrates that fundamental changes to the framework for environmental administration have eventuated primarily as an inevitable consequence of, and as a convenient adjunct to, the wider restructuring agenda of the fourth Labour government. In the absence of such an agenda based on neo-liberal economic philosophies (Boston et al, 1991), it is quite likely that the scope of the environmental reforms would have been limited to incremental changes, as had been the practice prior to 1984.

Following the implementation of the recent changes in environmental administration in New Zealand, a logical question that should now be asked is the appropriateness of the new institutional arrangements to effectively pursue environmental objectives within the public policy process. Before examining the reform process and its implications in terms of the potential effectiveness of the new environmental agencies, it may be useful to describe first the new organisational framework for environmental administration. [1]

The Agency Framework

A new public bureaucracy responsible for environmental and natural resource management came into being in 1987. Compared with the preceding bureaucratic regime, the changes that took place implied a different attitude towards the administration of New Zealand's environment. The key agencies, established in 1987, that now have a major role in environmental administration at the central government level are the Ministry for the Environment (MfE), the Department of Conservation (DoC) and the Parliamentary Commissioner for the Environment (PCE).

The administrative framework within which the above agencies operate is illustrated schematically in Figure 3.1. The agencies that formerly had the responsibility for environmental administration have either been abolished, as is the case for the Ministry of Works and Development, the Department of Lands and Survey, the New Zealand Forest Service and the Commission for the Environment, or substantially restructured as has been the case with the Ministries of Transport, Agriculture and Fisheries and Internal Affairs (Figure 3.2). In addition, the former resource production functions of the public sector, such as mining, forestry, land development and electricity generation,

---

Figure 3.1 The environmental administration framework, 1987

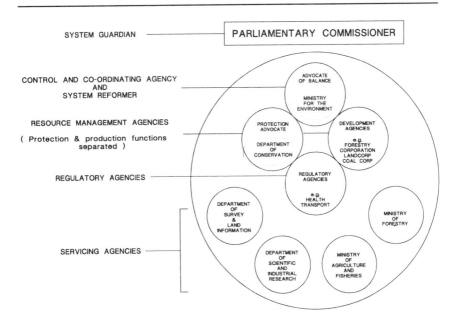

Figure 3.2 Reallocation of functions

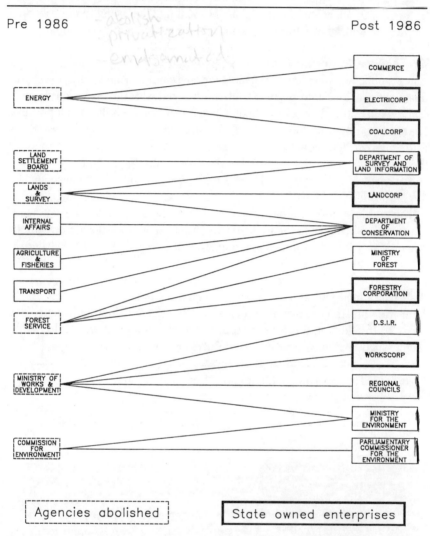

Pre 1986   *abolish privatization envisnmted*   Post 1986

have been devolved to state-owned enterprises or privatised.

The Environment Act 1986 created the MfE and the office of the PCE and these two agencies operate in the context of the objectives of the Act. Tantamount to an expression of a national New Zealand environmental policy, the objective of this statute, outlined in its long title, is to ensure that in the management of natural and physical resources, full and balanced account is taken of:

i. The intrinsic values of ecosystems; and

ii. All values which are placed by individuals and groups on the quality of the environment; and

iii. The principles of the Treaty of Waitangi; and

iv. The sustainability of natural and physical resources; and

v. The needs of future generations.

In this context, "environment" includes not only the natural elements, but also people, their communities and their cultural beliefs. In carrying out their functions, the MfE and the PCE are also required to have regard to matters set out in Section 17 of the Act.[2]

The MfE is a relatively small, primarily policy-oriented agency with approximately 110 staff based in Wellington and the regions. It is typically portrayed as "the ministry in the middle", or as a "neutral" policy agency. The Act defines the principal responsibilities to include:

To advise the Minister on all aspects of environmental administration, including – (i) Policies for influencing the management of natural and physical resources and ecosystems so as to achieve the objectives of this Act: (ii) Significant environmental impacts of public or private sector proposals, particularly those that are not adequately covered by legislative or other environmental assessment requirements currently in force: (iii) Ways of ensuring that effective provision is made for public participation in environmental planning and policy formulation processes in order to assist decision making, particularly at the regional and local level. [Environment Act, 1986, Section 31(a)]

development.

Potentially, this is an important power-base for the new Ministry, a position formerly monopolised by the Treasury and the State Services Commission.[3] The Ministry is expected to act as a counterbalance to the Treasury within the machinery of government.

The control function has two elements: first, the power to investigate and certain limited powers to obtain information; and second, the provision for mandatory reports on proposals submitted to Cabinet or its committees. Hence, there is mandatory provision for the MfE to report on any policy proposals with significant environment implications submitted to Cabinet or its committees.

While the MfE sees itself as "a neutral advocate of balance" within the government, DoC is an advocate of conservation values as well as a national heritage management agency, with specific "hands on" responsibilities for managing the Crown's conservation estate, including national parks, wildlife sanctuaries and historic reserves. DoC was established under the Conservation Act 1987, and this act's primary objective is to promote the conservation of New Zealand's natural and historical resources. The Act defines two primary functions for DoC:

1) *to manage all natural and historical resources allocated to it for conservation purposes;*

2) *to advocate and promote the conservation of natural and historical re-*

sources, and to allow and foster use of these resources for recreation and tourism, consistent with its conservation priorities.

The Conservation Act is less environmentally neutral than the Environment Act. The term conservation is defined in the Act as: "the preservation and protection of natural and historic resources for the purpose of maintaining their intrinsic values, providing for their appreciation and recreational enjoyment by the public, and safeguarding the options of future generations." (Conservation Act, 1987, Section 2(1))

Thus, the Act takes a clear preservationist and protectionist stance. This is in contrast to the Environment Act, which requires a balancing of conservation and development issues, therefore reflecting a much wider spectrum of values. As an advocate of conservation values in the public sector policy process, DoC is expected to provide a counterweight to agencies that are development oriented.

DoC is a relatively big, programme-oriented agency with considerable management responsibilities. The third of the country's total surface area which the department administers includes 13,000 km of coastline, as well as intertidal zones and the sea bed to a twelve mile limit.

While the MfE and DoC are an integral part of the executive branch of government, and are directly accountable to the Cabinet, the PCE is essentially autonomous. As an officer of Parliament, the PCE is an environmental auditor and ombudsman, with the mandate to act as a watch-dog over the environmental administrative system and to conduct inquiries on matters of particular environmental sensitivity. Hence, while there may appear to be an overlap in the functions of the MfE and the PCE, there is a fundamental constitutional difference in their accountability. The PCE places considerable emphasis on the independence of the office from any vested interests, including the executive branch of the government.

The primary role of the Commissioner is to monitor and report directly to the House of Representatives on the performance of agencies and processes that may have adverse effect on the environment. In undertaking this role, the Commissioner is expected to take into account the values set out in the Environment Act. The PCE's mandate, as defined in this Act, is wide-ranging: it includes the power to monitor the activities of all environment-related agencies and the authority to obtain information and conduct formal inquiries. The PCE has a small office with a staff of fewer than twenty.

The PCE's functions relate both to policy matters and to specific projects. Its policy function includes reviewing the agencies and processes established by government to manage the allocation, use and preservation of natural and physical resources, with the objective of maintaining and improving the quality of the environment; investigating the effectiveness of environmental planning and management by public authorities; and investigating and reporting to Parliament on matters before the House or its Committees which may have a significant effect on the environment.

The jurisdiction of the Commission in relation to particular projects includes the powers to investigate any matter in respect of which, in the Commissioner's opinion, the environment may be or has been adversely affected. It can inquire, on the direction of Parliament, into any matter that has or may have a substantial and damaging effect on the environment. The Commission can also participate in proceedings related to or arising from the obtaining of any resource consents.

Objectives Governing the Reform Process

In order to understand the rationale underlying the restructuring of environmental administration, it is important to see these changes in the broader context of the deregulation of the New Zealand economy and of the state sector reforms. The environmental administration reforms signify a radical restructuring of the historically long-standing role of the state as a development agent, that dates back to the 1870s. Such a metamorphosis was precipitated by a questioning of the traditional functions of central government in promoting settlement and in harnessing the country's resources, and by concerns relating to the structure and performance of the public sector. Past governments, irrespective of their political leanings, had been motivated to undertake such activities to promote economic expansion; but the difficulties inherent in pursuing these policies over the years made them progressively less attractive politically and led to a major challenge to the philosophy and practice of environmental administration.

The relinquishing of the national development role of government in New Zealand during the last half of the 1980s was precipitated by two main factors. On the one hand, a fiscal crisis common to a number of other western countries put significant constraints on the ability of the government to fund infrastructure and resource development projects. On the other hand, the environmental lobby, which had become more sophisticated and enjoyed increasing public support, became a significant pressure group. Its concerns regarding bureaucratic agencies with multiple and conflicting objectives could not be so easily sidestepped.

By divesting itself of the role of developer, central government has come to adopt what it sees as a neutral stance. While an incipient public policy shift in this direction may have been anticipated earlier by the New Zealand Planning Council (NZPC, 1979), it became a major objective during the first term of the Labour government. The Treasury played a major part in establishing the reform agenda for this purpose (Treasury, 1984a), backed by the Hon. R.O. Douglas, an influential Finance Minister.

The rationale underlying the recent economic reforms lies in a belief that an open and more competitive economy will propel growth and increase living standards. This was combined with with an ideological desire on the part of the government to let the market determine the allocation of resources.

The key elements of the changes include:

- *the dismantling of economic protection and excessive regulation to permit greater competition and thereby encourage better economic performance; and*
- *the removal of subsidies and other forms of incentives or intervention to ensure that industry operates efficiently and resources are channelled to the most productive areas of the economy.*

The above measures to restructure the economy were complemented by parallel reforms to improve the efficiency and accountability within government agencies (Treasury, 1984b). These reforms were initiated by the Treasury and the State Services Commission, with the rationale that commercial models of control could be applied to the public sector (Boston et. al., 1991). A number of considerations have underpinned these recent reforms: to avoid conflicting objectives of the state by separating its commercial activities from the non-commercial ones; to separate policy formulation from service delivery functions; to permit contestability of advice to Ministers to enable them better to judge the trade-offs in making policy decisions; to improve transparency of departmental operations and provide greater accountability for performance. This rationale has pervaded, to a very significant extent, the major policy decisions relating to restructuring environmental administration within central government.

Ironically, the environmental groups had been lobbying the government for several years to separate its resource production and conservation functions, but for very different reasons. They had become ardent advocates of the separation of nature conservation functions from the Departments of Lands and Survey and the Forest Service. Both of these agencies tended to be dominated by production objectives and did not appear very willing to publicly reveal the basis on which such trade-offs were often made during the decision-making process. In this way, the environmental reform policies that came to be adopted and implemented during the mid-1980s were based on an uneasy, fortuitous alliance between two significant interest groups: the economic non-interventionists and the environmentalists, but with the former having the upper hand in shaping the final outcomes.

While this was the broad context within which the major policy choices relating to environmental administration were finally made, the course of policy development and its implementation was the subject of considerable discussion and negotiation amongst several groups with vested interests in the anticipated policy outcomes.

Policy Antecedents

The environment has become an important public concern in many countries during the 1980s and this is equally the case in New Zealand. What is interesting in New Zealand is the extent to which the fourth Labour government responded to these concerns and implemented policies it deemed appropriate within a relatively short time.

A number of factors have been instrumental during the last decade in raising the stature of the environment as a domestic policy issue and, more specifically, influencing the 1984 Labour party manifesto. Significant amongst these have been influences emanating from abroad, generated by an increasing awareness of the human impact on the environment. Supported by local environmental groups, the Organisation for Economic Cooperation and Development (OECD), for instance, has since the beginning of the 1980s been a significant catalyst for change. To a lesser extent, the International Union for Conservation of Nature (IUCN) was also instrumental in focussing attention on environmental issues. International concern over population growth, environmental degradation and the depletion of living resources prompted the preparation of the World Conservation Strategy by the IUCN. It argued that conservation and development are mutually dependent and that sustainable development must be guided by ecological considerations. The IUCN report was endorsed by the New Zealand government and prompted the New Zealand Conservation Strategy.

Following reviews in Sweden and Japan, New Zealand's environmental policies were reviewed by the OECD in 1980 (OECD,1980). Initiated at the request of host governments, such reviews, undertaken by a panel of experts from member states, were designed to identify the goals and performance of environment management policies and practices. They were also used to encourage the countries reviewed to place environmental concerns higher on the policy agenda. As a baseline for assessing the evolution of recent policies, it is appropriate to examine the OECD report.

The OECD report identified major weaknesses in the public policy process from an environmental perspective. Two related considerations were singled out: a need to strengthen the primary source of advice on environmental policy within central government; and a need for a more effective co-ordination of environmental policy within central government and between different levels of government, in order to permit the early integration of environmental concerns in projects for energy, agriculture, forestry and mining development.

While effective in posing questions and directing attention to perceived constraints on policies, the OECD panel, in forming recommendations to address these concerns, in fact proved disappointing. The recommendations reflected a reluctance on the part of the visiting experts not to offend the host government.[4] An important but implicit assumption made in the report was that the state would have a continuing role as a large-scale resource developer. Moreover, the deliberations of the panel were directed by the host government's officials and this may also have been a constraint.

The panel identified three possible models of institutional reform, but favoured an alternative which was only marginally different from the status quo. This alternative was tantamount to according statutory recognition to the existing Commission for the Environment. Even then, the political as well as the bureaucratic environment did not prove receptive towards taking action to implement this particular proposal.[5] The only initiative promoted by the National government contradicted the recommendations of the OECD report. The controversial 1982 proposal to amalgamate with undue haste the Department of Lands and Survey and the New Zealand Forest Service was motivated by the perceived overlap between the two agencies and the possible financial savings from economies of scale through the rationalisation of public land management activities (Department of Lands and Survey and NZFS, 1983). This proposal was abandoned because of both bureaucratic inertia and opposition from environmental groups. These groups objected to the creation of a very large and potentially more powerful bureaucracy with both conservation and production responsibilities, but dominated by production interests.

However, the significance of overseas influences should not be overstated. While the OECD mission was certainly instrumental in highlighting the institutional constraints on effective policy, the primary impetus for establishing a political platform to eventually secure successful government action must go to the environmental groups. The recent reforms must ultimately be seen as a response that evolved within the context of the domestic political process. Compared to their image only a decade earlier, the environmental groups emerged during the 1980s as articulate and well-informed advocates. Their concerns came to acquire an increased measure of legitimacy in the eyes of the general public. The strength of their collective power-base was, by now, comparable to the more conventional advocacy groups representing farmers and manufacturers. Built on a specific issue or regional base, and zealously autonomous in pursuit of their particular objectives and concerns, they formed a coalition in 1982 to promote the acceptance by government of a national environmental strategy.[6]

In a similar vein to the OECD report, a need for appropriate institutional arrangements for environmental administration and planning emerged as the focus of their strategy (RFBPS & others, 1982). But they proposed a model for institutional reform which then must have been seen as very radical and which had either not been anticipated, or implicitly rejected, by the OECD panel of experts. They identified a need for two major structures in environmental administration: a nature conservancy; and a ministry to administer water and soil, and town and country planning legislation, as well as environmental health. The proposed strategy envisaged three major reforms:

- *the separation of central government environment-related responsibilities, between a nature conservancy to manage Crown-owned natural lands on the one hand, and an environment planning ministry to regulate the use of other resources such as air, water and production lands on the other.*

- *the creation of relatively autonomous profit-oriented commissions or cor-*

porations to undertake mostly exotic timber production and farm land development on a commercial basis and without hidden subsidies given hitherto to promote regional development objectives.

✗ • *the creation of an environmental ombudsman appointed by Parliament as a public advocate and auditor of environmental impact reports, as proposed earlier by the Environmental Council (Environmental Council, 1981).*

Despite its apparently radical stance, and compared to the OECD proposals for institutional reform, this model eventually emerged as more tenable and capable of drawing sufficient political support for environmental restructuring.

The 1984 Labour Election Manifesto

Prior to 1978, there were only marginal differences evident in the thinking and actions of the two main political parties concerning environmental administration issues. This is not surprising, given the historically important role of the government as a developer. Thus, it was a Labour administration which signed a *carte blanche* agreement with a multi-national consortium in 1960 to build a power station dependent on water from two glacial lakes, in a highly scenic South Island national park. Subsequently, during the late 1970s, controversial large-scale hydro projects on the upper Clutha river were sanctioned by a National government. Labour was by then opposed to such single-purpose projects. While Labour's 1978 and 1981 election manifestos recognised the significance of institutional reforms relating to environmental planning, the party's impact was constrained by its role as an opposition party. The National government was at this stage preoccupied with its "Think Big" development strategy and the constitutionally controversial empowering legislation for the Clyde hydro dam. Its 1981 manifesto did not accord major significance to the environment as an election issue. Both the political parties tended to leave to the officials the task of designing environmental planning statutes, so that there was, surprisingly, very little political input.[7]

Therefore, it is only since the eve of the 1984 election that one can say that the "greening" of the political process has begun in New Zealand. It was Labour, rather than National, who perceived the possible electoral benefits from adopting environmental concerns as a major component of its election manifesto (Cullen 1983; NZ Labour Party 1984a, b and c; NZ National Party 1984). National had been the governing party since 1975 and, with the eventual demise of the "Think Big" strategy in 1983, found itself caught in a crisis of confidence on the eve of the 1984 election.

The 1984 Labour Party manifesto did not state policy objectives explicitly and focussed on the machinery of government for achieving its implicit policy objectives. Nor did it anticipate a radical change in the traditional role of government as a major developer, to anything like the extent that has transpired. It envisaged a shift in that role, moving from its long-time emphasis on development or resource exploitation, towards integrating this role with the ideals of conservation. The manifesto reiterated, as a basic principle, the need for bio-physical and social considerations to be taken into account at the earliest possible opportunity in all decision-making processes. The existing planning processes were deemed too fragmented and complicated, and environmental administration too weak for that purpose. For this reason, Labour made a commitment to develop a new system of environmental administration to reflect these particular objectives and to review the environmental planning legislation.

Above all, the manifesto also spelt out specific policies on the configuration of the anticipated institutional reforms. The first proposal was to establish a ministry for the environment with two major functions: planning, and nature conservation. Such an ambitious proposal for a relatively large department, which amalgamated the environmental aspects of all land-use departments in central government, appeared similar to the third option contained in the OECD report.[8] The reasons why Labour chose this particular option, instead of the 1982 strategy of the environmental groups, are not clear. An independent conservation agency, devoid of a commercial development function, may have been perceived by the party hierarchy as "locking up" natural resources, and thus deemed politically unpopular. Bringing together all the resource management functions within one agency was seen as the most appropriate way to ensure that the policies were co-ordinated.

The second proposal was to create the office of the Parliamentary Commissioner for the Environment. This proposal was derived from the recommendation of the Environmental Council (Environmental Council, 1981) and the environmental groups. It amounted to giving statutory recognition to the Commission for the Environment; but, whereas this body was accountable only to Cabinet, the Commissioner, as an officer of parliament, would be accountable more publicly to that body. The environmental ombudsman role of the Parliamentary Commissioner was expected to include the task of auditing environmental impact reports.

These policies, it is said, were drafted in close consultation with the environmental groups (NFAC, 1987).

Initial Responses of the Fourth Labour Government

The task of implementing the above policies proved far from straightforward after Labour took office in August 1984. A great deal of controversy ensued over the constitution and functions of the proposed agencies. The most crucial institutional reform policies, in fact, were reformulated during the implementation phase; decisions were made following deliberations within and between government departments and the Cabinet, and consultations and negotiations with groups who had a vested interest in the outcomes. To a certain extent, this collaboration was to be expected, bearing in mind that Labour had made its policy commitments whilst still in opposition, presumably not having had adequate opportunity to discuss them with interested parties, particularly government officials. The election pledges still served to ensure that the topic of environmental reforms stayed high on the Cabinet agenda, in competition with a great number of other pressing issues.

The government convened a Task Group of officials in November 1984, to examine the procedure for and implications of implementing its election policies on planning and the environment (State Services Commission, 1984).[9] The shortcomings of the existing system were identified by the Task Group, and described in the same vein as the findings of the OECD panel and the New Zealand Conservation Strategy's recommendations. Yet, the Task Group's recommendations to the Cabinet departed from Labour's policies for the radical rationalisation of environmental functions as contained in the election manifesto. The Task Group also proved singularly unsuccessful in harnessing substantial support within or outside government. One can only speculate on the degree to which its recommendations were motivated by a desire to protect the vested interests of the existing bureaucracy. Thus, whilst supporting the proposal for a parliamentary commissioner, the Task Group appeared to dismiss the option of a large environment ministry. Instead, it advocated the model of a relatively small environment ministry and a nature conservancy separate from this ministry. This was a reflection of the views of the State Services Commission. By that stage, the Commission had already decided that there were too many conflicts and contradictions inherent in Labour's 1984 manifesto proposals for a large environment ministry.

Nor did the Task Group appear to favour the creation of an autonomous nature conservancy. The separation of conservation and production functions was perceived by the Task Group as contrary to the overall objective of integrating conservation and development. The officials argued that the government strategy of integrating conservation and development was best achieved by each department individually, as indeed was already happening. The officials also sought to divert attention away from the extensive review and restructuring of existing government agencies needed to establish a nature conservancy. The Task Group therefore deferred the establishment of a nature conservancy.[10] The environmental groups saw this as an attempt to maintain the status quo, made on behalf of the development departments such as the Ministry of Works and Development and the New Zealand Forest Service. Much of the logic in the official opposition to the proposed new environment ministry recalled the events of 1972 when the Commission for the Environment was established.

Treasury also took exception to the Task Group report, but for different reasons. Having just convinced the Cabinet to implement radically liberal economic policies, that anticipated massive deregulation of the economy through the reduction of public sector intervention, Treasury perceived the proposed reforms in environmental policy as contradicting the key principles of economic policy: less government, less regulation, less centralisation and more of a free-market approach. The recommendations of the Task Group could lead to a shift in decision-making away from the preferences of consumers, as expressed by market mechanisms. The statutory and administrative planning processes were deemed undemocratic, since they were structured by officials and not by the economic interests of the participants. One Treasury objective was specifically to reduce public spending on environmental regulation. The Task Group expected the government to continue its role as a major land owner and developer.

In fact, Treasury was able to convince the Cabinet to reconsider its environmental reform strategy, on examination of the issues deemed fundamental to the role of government in the management of natural resources. It was thereby able to impose on the environmental administration review process its particular analytical framework, based on neo-classical economic principles, which was in line with its recent post-election briefing to the government (Treasury, 1984b). A number of other government agencies and their respective Ministers also perceived particular recommendations of the Task Group as a potential threat.[11]

Amongst the public, the strongest response to the Task Group deliberations issued from individuals and environmental lobby groups, many of whom saw it as an attempt by the bureaucrats to hijack Labour's environmental policies (NFAC, 1985a; Synergy Ltd, 1985). The environmental groups felt it was inappropriate to delay the establishment of a nature conservancy and were ultimately able to hold the new government to its promises. As an alternative to the Task Group report, the "Group of Six" (RFBPSNZ, FMC, NFAC, EDS, ECO and Greenpeace) reiterated their support for a strong conservation agency (Environment Administration Task Group, 1985). Surprisingly, the development groups, representing farming, mining and industrial interests, assumed a comparatively lower profile in the discussions at this stage. This was evident, for example, during the public forum convened in March 1985 by the government to discuss the Task Group recommendations. While the forum may appear to have been dominated by environmentalists, it also enabled the Environment Minister to marshal considerable political support for the concept of the proposed environment ministry as a "ministry in the middle".[12] But the search for an option which was broadly acceptable, and thus able to be implemented, proved to be far from over.

Environmental Administration Strategy Reformulated

Following the forum discussions and public submissions, the Working Party on Environmental Administration (WPEA) was convened to advise the Cabinet on the future shape of environmental administration. Its constitution was broader than that of the Task Group. It comprised, as well as officials, private members representing a spectrum of development, conservation, mining and Maori interests.[13]

The Working Party's report was more analytical and treated the issues in greater depth than the Task Group report (WPEA, 1985). More significantly, its analysis produced different policy conclusions. This reflected the considerable influence of advice from Treasury and the State Services Commission. The report aggravated dissension within the government. Treasury felt it was important to have in place administrative and legislative frameworks that accommodated the appropriate private incentives for individuals to make correct decisions about the environmental aspects of economic activity. To accomplish this, it was seen as important to define the appropriate role for government in resource planning and also to define the necessary institutional arrangements for that role to be performed.

The WPEA report focussed not only on the broad principles of environmental administration, but also on some quite detailed matters, including the allocation of functions between government departments. The major WPEA recommendations were firstly a proposal for an environment ministry with two key functions. One function was to establish and monitor resource allocation systems and processes to ensure that full and balanced account was taken of community values in the management of natural and physical resources.

The ministry's other main function would be to act as a national environmental planning agency, that would articulate the Crown's perception of where the balance of public interest lay, as opposed to the Crown's perception of its own interest as a resource owner and user. This would entail responsibility for administering the two key statutes (Town and Country Planning and Water and Soil Conservation). The ministry would also be responsible for devising national strategies for the control of pollution and toxic waste, and have oversight of other resource use statutes such as mining.[14]

The second major recommendation was a proposal for a separate nature conservancy, Heritage New Zealand. This conservancy would undertake the Crown's responsibilities to promote the preservation and protection of natural and historic heritage areas, and would manage other parts of the Crown estate which were leased, or for which the final use had not been determined. This proposal was an attempt to bring key conservation functions together in a single agency which acted for the Crown as "owner" of these resources. Underpinning this proposal was the idea of separating conservation and preservation objectives from production objectives. The establishment of a nature conservancy would involve the restructuring of a number of large government departments and signalled a major change in direction in environmental administration. A separate management agency (Land Development Corporation) was proposed to provide for the development of uncommitted public lands.

The final key recommendation was that a Parliamentary Commissioner for the Environment be established as the Parliament's watch-dog to ensure that government agencies did their job properly. The Commissioner was also to have a role in auditing projects expected to have a significant impact on the environment.

However, even though the recommendations were said to represent a broad consensus within the Working Party, the details were subject to wide-ranging differences of opinion. The Working Party did not initially prove effective in securing a commitment to its proposals within the Cabinet, the bureaucracy or the broader community. Despite efforts by the Minister for the Environment to consult widely, the Working Party recommendations instead aroused a great deal of controversy and political acrimony.[15]

As the WPEA report made its way to the Cabinet Policy Committee, and finally to Cabinet, the powerful government bureaucracies fought an all-out war to forestall such radical reforms. The Lands and Survey Department, the New Zealand Forest Service and the Ministry of Works and Development were forced to seek the support of their respective constituencies in the wider community to protect their vested interests. Opposition was most marked in the mining and timber industries and amongst some groups on the West Coast of the South Island (NFAC, 1985b). Because the same Cabinet Minister (the Hon. Koro Wetere) was then responsible for the lands, forestry and Maori portfolios, he was able to muster considerable support amongst development groups for his stand against restructuring his own departments.[16] This led him to present to the Cabinet Policy Committee an alternative proposal to the WPEA report, which envisaged only incremental change to the existing organisational arrangements.

Other government departments, in particular the Ministry of Works and Development and Treasury, were more concerned about the operational planning functions proposed for the environment ministry. In contrast to the WPEA, they sought to restrict its role to that of a "pure" policy agency that would act as an adviser, from a position of neutrality, on environmental aspects of the institutional arrangements for resource allocation to ensure that full and balanced account was taken of all appropriate values. They sought to convince the Cabinet Policy Committee to reject the concept of the environment ministry as a national environmental planning agency, responsible for administering statutes governing the allocation and use of resources.[17] Many officials also shared the view, advocated by the Ministry of Works and Development, that the separation of the above "national interest" component of environmental planning from the Crown property servicing function of Works and Development was impractical. The underlying motive of Works and Development may have been to protect its planning and water and soil functions, while Treasury appears to have adopted a position based on its economic ideology. Both agencies had strong ministerial advocates in Cabinet, while the local government and catchment authority associations and the Federated Farmers came out as close allies of the Ministry of Works and Development.

Cabinet Decisions

Confronted with such intense polarisation of views amongst its officials, as well as in the wider political constituency, the Cabinet Policy Committee found itself in a hiatus. The State Services Commission was directed by the Cabinet to assist Ministers with further consultations with interested parties and, in yet another effort to resolve departmental conflicts, to convene an officials committee to re-examine the proposals relating to the proposed allocation of functions. A number of government departments, including the Forest Service, which had hitherto been on the fringe of these deliberations, were now part of the official working parties, under the umbrella of the Officials Steering Committee. An environmental secretariat was established in the State Services Commission to oversee this exercise.

The officials desperately sought political direction from the CPC on the separation of production and protection functions, as a means of integrating conservation and development in the public policy process. The alternative was to simply realign some of the existing departmental machinery, with improved independent oversight, as proposed by the Minister of Maori Affairs, Lands and Forests. The CPC, in turn, sought direction from the Cabinet. Some Cabinet members were concerned that the government may be seen to be "locking up" natural resources and not sufficiently responsive to the interests of the productive sector. The Cabinet found it difficult to resolve the contentious issues confronting it.

It was at this stage that a small group of Cabinet members, with the aid of Treasury officials, were able to successfully obtain Cabinet consent, almost surreptitiously, for their much wider-ranging corporatisation agenda. Thus, when the Cabinet decision was finally made in September 1985 to establish an environmental administration structure broadly along the lines proposed by the WPEA, it precipitated an even more fundamental and contentious policy decision to restructure the state sector, which ultimately led to the corporatisation of all production and several service delivery functions. It has been alleged that the initial Cabinet decision to corporatise the functions of the New Zealand Forest Service and Lands and Survey was made on the basis of a Treasury report, with little discussion and no prior consultation within the Cabinet.[18]

Treasury and the State Services Commission were instrumental in setting the broad agenda for state sector restructuring. The principles on which these reforms were based concerned the relation between Ministers and their heads of departments, the clarification of commercial and non-commercial objectives, and monitoring and accountability procedures (Clark and Sinclair, 1986; Dean, 1987). As part of these changes, nine state-owned trading companies were subsequently created under the State Owned Enterprises Act 1986, including four primarily natural resource corporations: electricity, coal, land and forests.[19] What began as a relatively limited reorganisation of environmental administration ended up as the biggest upheaval in the history of the public sector, affecting over 60,000 state servants.

The environmental administration structure agreed to by the Cabinet was as follows:

1) The Department of Conservation. The Cabinet rejected the WPEA's recommendation to create an agency called Heritage New Zealand, preferring instead to create a new government department with essentially similar functions. While significantly different in structure to the Heritage New Zealand proposal[20], it was a response to the same perceived need: to draw together the conservation-oriented elements of various departments to form a central body which could act as the focus and champion of conservation interests.

2) The Ministry for the Environment. The role of the proposed environment ministry was to be to advise the government on the allocative systems and processes under which decisions on the use of natural resources were made, to ensure that all appropriate values were taken into account. To the disappointment of the Environment Minister (the Hon. Russell Marshall), the Cabinet decided against giving the environment ministry direct responsibility for administering town and country, and water and soil planning statutes. The reason given for this was the need to review planning legislation before making a final decision on the allocation of these particular functions. The decision appeared to leave the door open for reconsideration at a later date; but in fact the Ministry of Works and Development managed to obtain only a short-term reprieve.[21]

3) The office of the Parliamentary Commissioner for the Environment.

4) It was also agreed that the following separate and relatively autonomous corporations be established:

   i. a land development corporation having responsibility for land development and farm management by the Crown, and oversight on management of Crown leasehold land (subsequently named LandCorp);

   ii. a commercial forestry corporation (subsequently named ForestCorp); and

   iii. a neutral office of Survey and Land Information.

5) The Cabinet also agreed that different Ministers be responsible for environmental, conservation and development portfolios.

6) It was subsequently decided to establish a Ministry of Forestry to retain the Forest Service's scientific staff as a functional unit. In deference to lobbying by both Landcorp and DoC, a decision was also made to retain the Department of Lands beyond 1 April 1987, as a neutral body to administer the Crown's pastoral leasehold land.

The Enactment of Legislation

Drafting the appropriate legislation for the Environment and Conservation statutes was a reiterative process of consultation amongst officials, ministers and public interest groups.[22] In this respect, drafting the Conservation Act proved to be far more demanding than drafting the Environment Act.

The scope of the functions of the MfE and DoC continued to be a contentious issue even at this stage. Considerable difficulty was encountered because, at times, the directives by the ad hoc committee, based on official advice, were not necessarily consistent, or were interpreted differently or modified by the drafting team. Such difficulties were a reflection of continuing differences amongst Ministers and officials.[23] The following discussion will focus on the more important issues that arose during the law drafting process. It would be wrong to assume that these concerns have been entirely resolved in the promulgated legislation.

The Role of the Ministry for the Environment

The differences in perception amongst ministers and officials as to the extent to which the MfE should be involved in the human environment, and in community development issues, became manifest most clearly during the law drafting stage of their establishment. In contrast to the Environment Minister, the Hon. Russell Marshall, a number of his colleagues and the Treasury saw a national strategic planning role being inconsistent with a systems-oriented approach to the ministry's activities. A national planning role was also seen as infringing on the responsibilities of other agencies such as the Department of Internal Affairs.[24]

In contrast to earlier drafts of the Environment Bill, the system-monitoring function of the MfE has been given greater emphasis in the Environment Act. The "control" function for the ministry, to integrate conservation and development, originally envisaged in the Labour election manifesto and the environment forum, were not incorporated in the final legislation.

In the earlier drafts of the Environment Bill, the definition of the environment was virtually all-encompassing and it was argued that the MfE could advise on just about all aspects of public and private sector proposals. Treasury was concerned that the MfE might become a "ministry of everything" and thus possibly challenge its own hegemony.

The Environment Act reflects attempts to constrain the role of the MfE by restricting the usage of the term "environment" in the Act. It was argued that, because conceptually the term is very wide, and because there were already various agencies in the machinery of government with specialised expertise in various sectors of the environment, it was essential for the MfE not to focus on these wide-ranging perceptions but, instead, to focus on the points where they relate to the use of natural and physical resources. The Act limits the MfE's policy role to the consideration of "external costs" of decisions relating to natural and physical resources. For this reason, references in the

Bill to the term "environment" in a number of clauses were replaced with the phrase "all natural and physical resources."

The Role of the Parliamentary Commissioner for the Environment

Compared to the provisions of the Environment Act, the powers of the PCE proposed in the earlier drafts of the Environment Bill were very extensive, more akin to those of a judiciary. The PCE had the authority to obtain information, to hold an inquiry into virtually any matter, and to recover costs from the proponent of a proposal. As a consequence, it was felt there was no incentive for the Commissioner to be selective in the number of proposals he or she might choose to investigate. The PCE could also report on any matter before Parliament, regardless of whether invited to do so or not. In the final draft of the Act that was passed, it was decided that the powers of the PCE should be much more closely subject to the authority of Parliament. The powers of the Parliamentary Commissioner to audit environment impact reports were also omitted from the Act. In hindsight, had it not been a feature of the Labour party's 1984 environment manifesto, it is doubtful if New Zealand would have ever had a PCE.

The Needs of Future Generations

The Environment Minister was keen to include in the long title of the Environment Act a reference to the needs of future generations. Such a provision was deemed essential to enable the MfE and the PCE to consider the conservation of resources, based on the concept of sustainability, as part of their mandate.

Treasury argued that such a recommendation was beyond the scope of the drafting instructions. Apparently, this issue had been debated at length in earlier Cabinet Policy Committee meetings in November 1985, and there was an explicit decision to leave out any reference to the needs of future generations. Eventually, the Environment Minister was able to convince the Cabinet to accept his recommendation.

The Role of DoC

While the Conservation Act puts primary emphasis on managing formally protected areas for their intrinsic worth, the earlier drafts of the Bill gave equal prominence to recreation, tourism and a range of other uses, even including logging. This caused considerable alarm amongst conservationists. The Conservation Bill was subject to major debate and was subsequently changed during the enactment process, as a result of the lobbying and submissions made by the various interest groups and the Nature Conservation Council, supported by Treasury advice.

The earlier drafts of the Bill defined the term "conservation" to include utilisation. The objectives of the Conservation Department, as initially defined, were also conflicting. This was a reflection of the confusion about whether the department's role should be as a conservancy of natural and historic resources or whether it should be an agency responsible for promoting multiple utilisation of these resources. The draft Bill prepared by officials in the DoC Establishment Unit tended towards the second model, which envisaged the Department using selected parts of the Crown's estate for production, as well as for preservation and protection. This came about as a result of the influence of the former developmental agency officials now employed in the DoC Establishment Unit, with additional influence from some Ministers and the private sector. This would have allowed DoC to act as a multiple-objective department, in a similar way to its predecessors.

The word "utility" was removed from the definition of conservation in the Act; hence utilisation was no longer central to DoC's functions. DoC was also not required to "manage for productive purposes" the resources vested in it. Instead, the concept of stewardship was introduced, defined as "the management of a resource so that its inherent character is largely retained." The stewardship concept aims to hold resources in their existing state to provide options for future generations. As defined, it allows DoC to control pastoral leases for low-intensity grazing, but excludes high-impact operations.

However, the environmental lobby was less successful in reducing the requirement for DoC to be self-funding as far as possible. While Treasury officials saw this as necessary, the recreational and other interest groups saw it as an attempt to curb free recreational access to public land. It has also made DoC vulnerable to political pressure from those wanting to exploit its resources.

The Allocation of Land

The re-organisation of environmental administration necessitated the transfer of certain land to DoC. This was relatively straightforward for land with primarily single-purpose uses, such as national parks, protected indigenous forests and wildlife areas. The Conservation Act provided for DoC to administer the legislation governing these uses. However, for unalienated rural Crown land and state forests, the situation was more complex and resulted in considerable public controversy. In both cases, only some of the land could be allocated to DoC. Land being farmed or used for commercial forestry had to be transferred to the new corporations when they were set up. Cabinet chose to do this by ministerial decisions rather than by legislation. This allocation exercise became extremely controversial and protracted, partly because of disagreements between officials and a lack of political direction.

Decisions had to be made as to which resources should be regarded as predominantly productive or exploitable, and which should be regarded as resources to be preserved or conserved in the public interest. As a resolution of some long-standing conflicts, the results of this exercise were historic. The most significant amongst them was the debate on the administrative future of Crown pastoral lands in the South Island high country, constituting some 2.7

million ha or ten percent of the New Zealand land area.[25] Alongside these issues there were debates on the role of DoC in the management of coastal zones and coastal waters, in the matter of public access to public conservation lands and in the future administration of marginal access strips along waterways. Ultimately, the realisation by the new corporations that they would have to achieve a rate of return on the assets they acquired, tempered their interest in the marginal lands.

Wider Implications

In contrast to the situation prior to 1984, the recent changes in the role of central government in environmental administration have been fundamental rather than incremental. They have certainly gone well beyond what was anticipated by many observers in 1984. An important attribute of the new institutional framework is that it is philosophically congruent with the unprecedented recent change of course in New Zealand's development, a change of course which was steered by the fourth Labour government without a political mandate or public discussion.

As I have shown, the environmental reform process was based on economic as well as environmental objectives and their negotiation was characterised by intense bureaucratic and political conflict. A major outcome of restructuring has been a separation of potentially conflicting objectives, notably between conservation and development, making conflicts in decision-making more visible.

But there are still areas of overlapping jurisdiction in the new structure; both at the policy level and the management level, conflict has not been entirely eliminated. For example, high country pastoral leases, which cover large areas of the South Island, are a continual source of conflict between DoC (which, acting as a Crown agent, has responsibility for nature conservation), LandCorp (which is responsible for management oversight) and the lessees themselves, who tend to favour productive use of the land (NZPC,1989). Marginal strips of land also continue to cause confusion. ElectriCorp sees a potential conflict in the management of lake levels where the marginal strips are controlled by DoC. The status of publicly owned land with no clear commercial or conservation values remains unclear. The tenure of water rights held by ElectriCorp also raises a number of questions, which must ultimately be resolved either through the political process or by the Courts.

The principle of separating the production and conservation objectives of central government has been widely supported. From a spatial perspective, however, the implementation of this approach to environmental management has entailed drawing rigid boundaries between production and conservation land resources. An inevitable consequence of this is that the potential for promoting the multiple utilisation of resources in large areas of New Zealand does not exist to the same extent as it did before 1984.

These environmental reforms have been achieved as part of a much wider-ranging economic restructuring exercise, which has had a significant impact on New Zealand society and lifestyles. The more immediate consequences have manifested themselves in the social dislocation of many rural communities and through high sustained levels of unemployment. The longer-term consequences, in changing the character of New Zealand society, are likely to be more subtle. Resources previously owned by the Crown, such as forests, have been privatised, as the Crown has divested itself not only of direct management responsibilities, but also of the ownership of large sections of Crown estate. The energy crisis of 1992 has brought home to many people the implications of corporatisation and privatisation.

As I have shown, major political hurdles had to be overcome during the process of implementing the new administrative structures. One significant issue was the recognition of Maori rights. An amendment made in 1985 to the Treaty of Waitangi Act 1975 has had and will continue to have significant implications for environmental administration in New Zealand. The amendment provides for the Waitangi Tribunal to hear applications from Maori claiming to be prejudicially affected by any law enacted since 6 February 1840 (whether or not still in force) or from any Act of the Crown since the same date. Previously the Tribunal could consider only claims in respect of laws currently in force, and Crown actions dating from 10 October 1975. Subsequent events have shown that the loss of rights in respect of land and other natural resources forms the basis of many claims. The Crown was required by the Court of Appeal to reach an agreement with Maori interests in 1987 about the transfer of certain assets to State-owned Enterprises (SOEs). This decision was put into legislation in 1988.[26] Following the privatisation of selected SOEs, the resumptive powers of the Crown have been retained. These issues still need to be resolved.

Concluding Comments

One has to question to what extent the recent changes in the role of central government in environmental administration have been justified. It is difficult to answer this question unequivocally. Today few New Zealanders would have regrets about the demise of the former state development bureaucracy: the Ministry of Works and Development, the Forest Service and the Lands and Survey Department. However, the devolution of the ownership as well as the management of large parts of the national estate to the private sector is likely to be perceived as unwarranted.

Seen from a longer-term perspective, while the state has abandoned its historically important role as a developer, the recent reforms have reaffirmed the foundations of New Zealand society as a property-owning democracy. Thus, not only has the state stepped back from its role as a developer, but decision-making as to the end use of resources has been devolved to market forces so that the role of the private corporate sector has been strengthened. Commercial objectives now direct the management of resources formerly owned by the Crown, save for the ministerial influence on the corporate plans of the SOEs. This line of accountability has been broken by the progressive sale of state assets to private interests.

Environmental objectives have to be pursued within the context of a free-market economy. The justification for public intervention to achieve environmental objectives is perceived from a restrictive, residual point of view. The fundamental tenet which has underpinned the environmental philosophy of the Labour and National governments since 1984 is that the role of the state should be restricted primarily to correcting market failures. From a wider social perspective, changes such as economic deregulation and privatisation will lead to increased conflict between different interest groups over who should benefit from the use of the environment and the wealth or welfare derived from its use. It remains to be seen how the state will respond to such conflicts.

Administrative reorganisation by itself will not necessarily lead to better decision-making from an environmental perspective. It could be argued that an allegedly "neutral" role on the part of the government towards the environment, which eschews consideration of the end use of resources, will constrain its commitment to respond to environmental issues effectively. For example, it is difficult to see how the objective of sustainability in the Environment Act can be addressed realistically by the government without the consideration of how resources such as land, minerals and forests are utilised. This has been made apparent in the recent policy initiatives relating to the management of fishery resources (Memon and Cullen, 1992), the current legislative proposals relating to protecting indigenous forests (Memon and Wilson, 1992) and the proposals on sustainable agriculture (MAF,1991).

During the last few years, there has been a move towards negotiating voluntary accords through mediation between development and conservation groups. This has been seen as a means to promote a more balanced approach to the management of indigenous forests in New Zealand, and to address long-standing conflicts over their use. This method of environmental mediation to resolve conflicts offers a number of advantages. It reduces the need for judicial intervention, with its unavoidable rigidities, and replaces confrontation with flexible negotiation. One may see more frequent application of these approaches in New Zealand than has so far been the case. But the long term success of environmental mediation is predicated on an equitable distribution of political power between the negotiating parties.

4

Local and Regional Government Restructuring

Introduction

Within the framework of a two-tier unitary style of government, environmental planning has progressively evolved since the 1930s as one of the more significant functions of local government in New Zealand. These functions have encompassed responsibilities for land use planning by territorial local authorities, for water and soil planning by catchment authorities and for regional planning by metropolitan authorities and their successors, United and Regional Councils. There were also a number of other ad hoc authorities, such as Harbour Boards, that undertook planning-related functions. Nevertheless, the recognition that environmental planning is more appropriately undertaken by local rather than central government has come about very reluctantly in New Zealand, as has the recognition that inadequate institutional arrangements have been a significant constraint on the effectiveness of local government in this respect. Such constraints were wide-ranging, including the fragmented and overlapping jurisdiction of local government,[1] inadequate funding and statutory powers, a lack of political and professional capability and problems of intergovernmental relationships (Memon, 1991). Until the recent local government and resource management reforms, there were limited attempts by successive Local Government Commissions to address these concerns, but these attempts were only marginally successful. On the one hand, central government deliberately denied a substantive environmental planning role to local government, in order to protect its own vested interests as the largest developer in the country; but on the other hand, local government itself, dominated by parochial vested interests, did not demonstrate a strong proclivity towards undertaking such a role with enthusiasm and commitment (Memon, 1989). Thus, from a theoretical as well as a practical perspective, the potential effectiveness of the recent reforms in developing effective institutional arrangements for environmental planning is an important issue.

Compared to the National Party, the Labour Party has traditionally demonstrated a greater commitment to local government reform and, to a lesser extent, to the related questions of administrative responsiveness in the provision of services, to be achieved through the decentralisation of power and resources from central government. During the second term of the fourth Labour government, these issues acquired considerable political prominence.

Far-reaching and fundamental changes have been implemented in this sphere in the wake of the recent economic reforms and restructuring of the state sector, and in a manner complementary to the environmental administration and planning reforms. Such reform has been a complex undertaking, with many interrelated facets to it. It is a significant political achievement when seen within the wider historical context of the previous attempts to reform local government, dating back to the first Local Government Commission appointed in 1946.

These policy initiatives have important implications for the future of local and regional government and environmental planning in New Zealand. Local government reforms were motivated primarily by economic objectives and functional planning considerations, rather than as a commitment to devolution. The potential effectiveness of the reform process has been compromised by the ad hoc and disjointed manner in which the reform policy has been formulated and implemented. Aspects of the reform process have not been particularly well conceived and implemented because of inadequate political direction, research and consultation. The National government that followed Labour into power in 1990 lacked a commitment to important aspects of Labour's local government reform programme, despite its favourable attitude to other components of Labour's environmental reforms. This lack of commitment has created a lingering air of uncertainty with respect to the future of regional councils.

Initial Responses of the Fourth Labour Government

The reform of local government, and the devolution of power to the regions, were policies in the Labour Party's manifesto for the 1984 parliamentary election (Labour Party, 1984a and 1984b; Burke, 1985).[2] Even though a very determined and aggressive approach to restructuring government machinery was foreshadowed in the manifesto, as a means to improve efficiency and accountability (Treasury, 1984), the government, on assuming office, did not assign as much importance to local government reform as it did, for instance, to economic restructuring and the reform of central government administration.

The attitude of the incoming Labour administration in its dealings with local government proved to be ambivalent, presumably because of the difficulty it had experienced in attempting to implement the 1974 Local Government Act during its previous term. More significantly, caution was dictated, and priorities re-ordered, by the financial crisis with which it was immediately confronted on assuming office. Local government reform was, in fact, put on the 'back burner' for the first three years, during which period the more urgently perceived economic restructuring policies were negotiated and implemented.

The sixth Local Government Commission, appointed by the National government in April 1978, remained in office until March 1985. However, on account of legislative constraints, it proved to be a largely ineffectual organisation, and essentially served to maintain the status quo (Welch, 1989). The impact of the Commission on the shape of New Zealand local government was limited to developing a structure of United and Regional Councils, albeit now swept away, to undertake the function of regional planning and to co-ordinate the provision of infrastructure services in the metropolitan regions.

The incoming Labour government chose not to opt for far-reaching changes to the jurisdiction of the seventh Local Government Commission, appointed in April 1985. Consequently, the Local Government Amendment Act 1985 did not make a clean break with existing practices, apart from a change in the local polling provisions. The polling provisions were altered to facilitate the amalgamation of contiguous territorial local bodies – a move which advantaged the bigger urban authorities. This change notwithstanding, the powers of the new Commission were limited to tinkering with the local government system, and were designed to enable only those reorganisation schemes which had the consent of affected local authorities to proceed.

The Commission, nevertheless, embarked on its mission with a degree of zeal, adopting a relatively aggressive stance which came to be seen by some as verging on arrogance. From a tactical point of view, the Commission made a number of mistakes which came to prove very costly, as it soon found out. Rather than formulate a broad strategy to guide its activities, the Commission decided to negotiate locally acceptable proposals on a one-to-one basis for each area. The former alternative was not adopted because "of the almost total rejection of the grand plan strategy of an earlier commission" (Elwood, 1986).

Partly because of the constraints imposed by the legislation, no consideration could be given to other, equally important aspects of institutional arrangements for local and regional government. Instead, the Commission identified boundary rationalisation through amalgamation as its most important goal. It also appeared to have misinterpreted, as being the view of the government, that boundary rationalisation in large cities needed to be undertaken first and foremost. It is quite likely that neither the Commission nor the government had taken on board the concept of regional government. Thus, during the first two to three years of its operation, the Commission chose to direct its energy towards creating larger urban authorities through the amalgamation of adjoining units of local government.

While the Commission had the power to undertake investigations, the financial and personnel resources made available to it were constrained. This left it vulnerable to the criticism that the proposals it initiated were poorly prepared. There was a groundswell of opposition to the perceived intent of the Commission, particularly from the smaller, typically suburban boroughs, and from those counties deemed economically inefficient by the Commission merely because of their size of operation. Consequently, many such authorities showed little or no hesitation in taking advantage of the statutory requirements laid out in the Act to forestall the deliberations of the Commission.

Despite growing frustration on the part of the Commission, it did make limited progress during this period, largely on account of the consent of participating local authorities. Fourteen amalgamations took place involving 33 territorial authorities, reported to be the largest number of reorganisations in the history of any Commission. At the regional level, very little change took place.

Above all, the experience of the seventh Commission's first three years underlines the invidious situation into which it had been placed, as a consequence of there not being a clearly thought-out rationale for restructuring local government. The Commission in effect was being forced to operate in a policy vacuum. The jurisdiction given to the Commission was inadequate to address wider policy issues pertaining to the philosophy and objectives of local and regional governance, or to the relationship between central and local government. It was apparent that Brian Elwood, the Chairman of the Local Government Commission, along with one or more members of that Commission, appeared to subscribe to a unitary view of local government, arising from their past personal experiences in local government politics and their perceived misgivings about the effectiveness of United and Regional councils. The Commission was criticised for appearing to promote the creation of large unitary metropolitan authorities almost as an act of faith, without having considered critically the merits of other ways of improving the efficiency and effectiveness of local government. If such intentions on the Commission's part had tacit government support, they were tantamount to a reversal of government policy, given the series of previous policy decisions to establish these agencies.

The Policy Development Strategy

One can only speculate on the motives which ultimately prompted the Cabinet, during its second term of office, to raise the issue of local government reform to near the top of its policy agenda. Regional authority approaches to the Minister of Local Government, Hon. Michael Bassett, with pressure, perhaps, from a frustrated Local Government Commission and the deliberations of one or more working parties, may have combined to force the adoption of a more forthright policy stance by the Minister and his Cabinet colleagues.[3] The involvement of officials, particularly from Treasury and the State Services Commission, has had a significant impact on the shaping of policy, but such advice appears to have been tempered by more pragmatic political considerations.[4] Rightly or wrongly, the fourth Labour administration perceived local government reform as an opportunity to establish a stronger Labour foothold in Town Halls. The views of the Local Government Commissioners also appear to have had a significant bearing on the outcome of the reform proposals. Finally, the Local Government Association was also an active participant as a lobby group in influencing the direction of the recent reforms. It can be argued that ultimately its tacit support was critical in ensuring successful implementation of these reforms.

A statement by the Minister of Local Government on a policy development strategy for local and regional government was appended to a controversial economic policy package endorsed by the Cabinet on 17 December 1987. This heralded the most far-reaching structural changes in the history of local government in New Zealand. A number of features of this strategy are worth emphasising.

Compared to previous initiatives, it was holistic in its approach. In the past, central government's plans for the reform of local government had tended to address interrelated policy issues such as its structure, functions, organisation, finance and accountability, in an isolated fashion. An attempt was now being made to integrate an assessment of these issues in a way which covered all classes of local authorities, including territorial and regional authorities and special-purpose bodies.

From a political point of view, an important feature of the strategy was that it represented an extension of the economic ideology that had come to characterise the wide-ranging economic and state sector reforms in the period after 1984. Local government reform proposals were thus expected to reinforce the central economic policy goals of the Labour administration. Local government constituted a significant part of the economy in terms of expenditure, employment and the output of goods and services. The government's desire to reform local government was therefore a logical progression from the state sector management and accountability reforms. Its primary intention was to ensure that local and regional authorities could perform their wide range of policy, service delivery and commercial trading functions effectively and efficiently in an unrestrained, competitive economic environment.

Contrary to common belief, this strategy did not appear out of the blue. It was instead precipitated by a number of official reviews that had been under way for some time. Apart from the Commission's reorganisation activities specifically relating to boundaries, a wide range of other related reviews were also in progress that affected local government. These dealt with local government's trading activities, granting of the Power of General Competence to permit greater autonomy in its functions, revenue sharing with central government, accounting procedures, resource management statutes and the role of regional councils. A somewhat belated attempt was now being made to co-ordinate the different strands through more coherent political direction. This was odd, in a sense, because such political direction logically ought to have preceded the official reviews. Seen from a policy development perspective, it typified the incremental manner in which aspects of the strategy had evolved since 1984, within a fragmented and overburdened policy-making environment.

The timing of the reforms was an important consideration of the Labour administration. It was essential to complete the review of the local government sector in order to enable new units of local government to be elected at the triennial 1989 local authority elections. An implicit objective was to complete the process before the 1990 general election. Fear of a National government undoing the reforms may have been a factor in the haste. The National Party did not support radical changes in the organisation of the local government.

In many respects, this policy directive served to secure the hitherto tenuous future for regional councils, by providing a firm statement of government policy. The Commission was henceforth forced to recognise, and make provision for, regional councils in its deliberations (Local Government Commission, 1988a).

The Review of Local and Regional Government

Completed within a remarkably short time, the review of local and regional government was divided into two overlapping phases: the formulation of policy and its implementation. The first phase was completed by July 1988. This was followed by amendments to the Local Government Act, requiring the Commission to establish the new structure for local and regional government by mid-1989 and to make legislative provision for the new statutory basis under which these authorities were to operate.[5]

The task of policy formulation was co-ordinated by the Officials Co-ordinating Committee on Local Government, comprising representatives from the Department of Internal Affairs, the Ministry for the Environment, the Local Government Commission, the State Services Commission and Treasury. To ensure co-ordination with the parallel review of resource management planning legislation, this committee was asked to report directly to the Cabinet Committee on Reform of Local Government and Resource Management Statutes, chaired by the Minister for the Environment, Hon. Geoffrey Palmer.

Public response to a widely circulated discussion document on the reform of local and regional government was seen as a key contribution to the development of the policy framework (The Officials Co-ordinating Committee on Local Government, 1988a). This document's stated purpose was to elicit views on the range of options open to the government pertaining to the future shape and direction of sub-national government in New Zealand. Unfortunately, this document did not explicitly state government intentions in this regard. As one might have expected, the response to the discussion document was dominated by submissions from local, regional and special-purpose bodies. In comparison, there was a limited response from central government agencies and the general public.

The views expressed were noteworthy for both their similarities and differences (The Bridgeport Group, 1988). Generally speaking, the government's declared intention to carry out the review and implement reforms was supported in principle, but there was considerable criticism of the discussion document: many people questioned whether it was sufficiently comprehensive, its apparent ahistorical, "Treasury" bias, and the paucity of time allowed for submissions. What was perhaps more serious was the doubt cast on the ultimate objectives of the government in pursuing reform, since the elaborate discussion-document exercise appeared to be a token effort on the part of the Officials Co-ordinating Committee. In fact, the focus of many of the criticisms was the proposed Local Government Bill then before Parliament, rather than the discussion document itself. The proposed legislation sought to make radical changes to the procedures for instituting reform. It prescribed the broad structure of local government without having provided an adequate opportunity for consultation with, and comment by, the authorities affected. The Bill also left it to the discretion of the Commission and the Cabinet to make the decisions on the delineation of the new units. Ideally, one would have expected the analysis and consideration of submissions made to the Committee to precede the introduction of this important Bill.

The Minister of Local Government was forced to seek a compromise. Following the submissions on the discussion document, further consultations took place between the Local Government Association, a number of other national interest groups and the officials and members of the Cabinet committee. These talks related to the provisions to be observed by the Commission when preparing reorganisation schemes (Bassett, 1988a and 1988b). As a consequence of fuller discussion, the Local Government Amendment Act (No.3) 1988 spelt out a relatively more acceptable government policy.

The Policy Framework to Guide Restructuring

The Local Government Amendment Act (No.2) 1989 recognised the purposes of local government for the first time,[6] while the Local Government Amendment Act (No.3) 1988, directed the Commission to prepare final reorganisation schemes by June 1989. There were to be two principal classes of directly elected, multi-purpose authorities: district (or territorial) councils and regional councils. These councils were to assume the functions of all existing territorial administrations and a number of special-purpose authorities.[7]

The Local Government Amendment Act (No.2) 1989 prescribed the main functions of regional councils, while leaving it to the discretion of the Commission to allocate other functions between regional and territorial authorities. To achieve the latter objective, as well as to delineate regional and district boundaries, the Commission was now required to give specific consideration to criteria designed to achieve economic rationality in the functioning of local and regional government. These criteria included: transparency of objectives, competitive neutrality, internalisation of externalities (or downstream effects) and competition in the provision of services, as well as taking into account local and regional community values and interests.

The underlying rationale for allocating functions has been based on the principle of the separation of policy, service delivery and trading functions. In order to avoid conflict between the policy and service delivery roles, the former was seen as the primary role of regional councils while the latter the role of district councils. Even where functional activities were allocated to regional councils, there was an expectation that they will set the policy environment for the particular function but contract with the private sector or with the district councils for the delivery of a particular service. Trading functions were to be placed at arm's length from local and regional government, through corporatisation or privatisation.

The specific functions allocated to the regional councils were: water and soil management, flood control, regional planning, civil defence, maritime planning, a responsibility for the destruction of pests and noxious plants, and the planning and funding of land transport services.[8] It was in response to the emphasis anticipated in the Resource Management Act on regional resource planning, that the boundaries of regional councils were defined on the basis of major water catchments rather than on a socio-economic basis. Difficulties in undertaking the planning function can be anticipated in those regions where the hydrological boundaries are not broadly congruent with the socio-economic hinterland boundaries of the dominant urban centres. The Act defined the boundaries of district councils on the basis of communities of interest, thus doing away with the long-standing separation between urban (cities, boroughs) and rural (counties) in territorial local government in New Zealand. While this should prove beneficial from a planning perspective, particularly in the urban fringe, a lack of congruence between district and regional boundaries has created problems in areas such as North Otago, where the catchment boundary cuts across the socio-economic hinterland of the urban service centre. This may make it difficult for regional councils to cultivate the support of local inhabitants.

The rationale for delegating environmental planning functions to regional and district councils has been based primarily on the economic premise that environmental planning should be carried out at the point where the required information is available and where the incentives to get the plan right are the greatest. Issues related to resource use, in terms of its environmental impact, vary according to locality; regional and district councils were thus seen as the most appropriate spatial jurisdiction for environmental planning. However, the role of regional councils was seen as particularly important in the new structure because of the emphasis on addressing environmental pollution in the proposed Resource Management Act. In the case of pollution, the receiving media of air, water and land have interrelated effects which extend beyond the jurisdictions of single territorial local authorities. In some instances, these effects correspond to river catchments. The decentralisation of environmental planning has also been justified, since decision-making has been brought closer to those affected by decisions. Elected council members will have to live with the consequences of their decisions and be held accountable for them. Regional and district councils were also perceived as the most appropriate agencies to administer environmental assessment procedures.

Figure 4.1 Regional and territorial authority boundaries, October 1989

1 Far North
2 Whangarei
3 Kaipara
4 Rodney
5 North Shore City
6 Auckland
7 Waitakere City
8 Manukau City
9 Papakura
10 Franklin
11 Thames-Coromandel
12 Hauraki
13 Waikato
14 Matamata-Piako
15 Hamilton City
16 Tauranga
17 Western Bay of Plenty
18 Waipa
19 Otorohanga
20 South Waikato
21 Rotorua
22 Kawerau
23 Whakatane
24 Opotiki
25 Gisborne
26 Waitomo
27 Taupo
28 Wairoa
29 New Plymouth
30 Stratford
31 Ruapehu
32 Hastings
33 South Taranaki

34 Wanganui
35 Rangitikei
36 Napier City
37 Central Hawke's Bay
38 Manawatu
39 Palmerston North City
40 Horowhenua
41 Tararua
42 Kapiti Coast
43 Masterton
44 Porirua City
45 Upper Hutt City
46 Carterton
47 Wellington City
48 Lower Hutt City
49 South Wairarapa
50 Tasman
51 Nelson City
52 Marlborough
53 Buller
54 Kaikoura

55 Grey
56 Hurunui
57 Westland
58 Selwyn
59 Waimakariri
60 Christchurch City
61 Banks Peninsula
62 Ashburton
63 Mackenzie
64 Timaru
65 Waimate
66 Queenstown-Lakes
67 Central Otago
68 Waitaki
69 Dunedin City
70 Southland
71 Gore
72 Clutha
73 Invercargill
74 Chatham Islands

Unitary Authority

Table 4.1: Numbers and types of local authorities before and after June 1989 reforms

	Before	After
Regional Authorities		
Regional Councils	3	13
United Councils	19	0
TOTAL	22	13
Territorial Authorities	217	73
Special Purpose Authorities		
Catchment Boards	17	0
Harbour Boards	15	1
Land Drainage/River Boards	27	0
Noxious Plants Authorities	92	0
Pest Destruction Boards	61	0
Reserve Boards	176	0
Miscellaneous	78	6
TOTAL	466	7

NOTE: As a result of the changes made in July 1992 by the National government, the Nelson-Marlborough Regional Council has been abolished. The Nelson City Council, the Marlborough District Council and the Tasman District Council have been designated as unitary authorities.

The range of functions for which district councils were responsible was not altered significantly.

Policy Outcomes

The final schemes for the reorganisation of local government were issued in June 1989, less than a year after the enactment of the Local Government Amendment Act. They contained what was described by the Commissioner as a "form of local government which did both what the legislation required, and [what] was the best possible compromise for everyone involved" (*Southland Times*, 13 June 1989). The Commission confirmed its original proposals for the establishment of 14 regions to be governed by 13 regional councils, and for Gisborne to have a district council without a separate regional council. Local territorial government comprised 14 city and 60 district councils (Figure 4.1). The Gisborne District Council was designated as a unitary authority, with the functions, duties and powers of both a regional council and a territorial authority. The number of territorial and regional authorities and ad hoc boards was reduced from about 700 to 93 (Table 4.1). The new structure came into being in November 1989.

A number of comments may be made regarding the attributes of the above policy outcome.

The Commission was by no means sympathetic to the wishes of the gov-

Figure 4.2 The Commission's model of the local government system

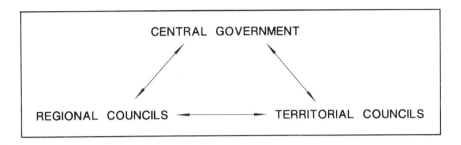

ernment to create regional councils. If the Act had been flexible, it is possible that the Commission may have instead preferred the establishment of large unitary authorities having the combined functions, duties and powers of a regional council and a territorial authority. That was the Commission's stated preference. But in seeking to achieve this objective, it was constrained by the terms of the Act as an expression of the Labour government's commitment to regional councils. Only in exceptional circumstances did the Act permit the Commission to establish unitary authorities. The large urban-based local authorities may have had the tacit approval of the Commission when canvassing this particular option. The Cabinet and the Commission got a very clear message from the smaller and rural councils that they were strongly opposed to the unitary authority model, so that the Gisborne District Council was in the end the only unitary authority created by the Commission.

The adopted framework comprising regional and district councils represented a trade-off between the conflicting wishes of Cabinet and the Commission. While requiring it to make provision for regional and district councils, the Act gave the Commission the discretionary responsibility to make a fundamental decision about the relationship between regional and territorial local government. Using this power, the Commission endeavoured to limit the jurisdiction of regional councils in favour of large district councils. It adopted the view that "regional and territorial units should be seen as components of the system of local government and not different levels of government"; its model identified "regional and territorial government as complementary parts of a single system" (Figure 4.2). Such a choice was justified by the Commission as likely to "ensure better public understanding and acceptance of the overall local government system..." (Elwood, 1988).

While one can appreciate the logic underlying this choice, such a framework is a poor compromise, because the opportunity to create an effective regional tier of government has been bypassed. The relationship between district and regional councils is not very clear-cut and has emerged as a source of continuing controversy. Following its election commitment, the National Government established a Working Group to report on the future options for regional councils in March 1991. On the basis of the group's recommendations (Working Party on the Future of Regional Councils, 1991) and advice from its officials, the Minister for Local Government, Hon. W. Cooper, recommended that regional councils be abolished and their functions transferred to resource management boards.[9] This proposal would have essentially stripped regional councils of all functions other than those under the Resource Management Act. The proposal was also supported by some environmentalists who felt that regional councils lacked a strong commitment to environmental values. The Minister was not successful on this occasion but subsequently he was able to push through amendments to the local government legislation to promote the unitary authority alternative. The Nelson-Marlborough Regional Council was abolished in July 1992 and its functions were assumed by three district councils which were designated as unitary authorities. The Minister continues to lobby for the abolition of regional councils.

At the local level, the Commission's long-standing predilection for large district councils cannot be sustained in terms of the alleged financial benefits from economies of scale. Logically, if economic principles had been the sole consideration in restructuring territorial local government, then the emphasis ought to have been on developing an appropriate institutional environment that permitted market signals to operate efficiently. Under that alternative, it would have been logical to concentrate on permitting existing communities to evaluate options and make policy choices for the delivery of services, instead of creating large bureaucracies. The implementation of such choices could be contracted to organisations deemed most competitive. However, the possible electoral advantages perceived by Cabinet in large district councils made them a more desirable option politically.

The establishment of large district councils has implications for the interrelationship between district and regional councils. With respect to resource planning, for instance, it is already apparent that the more powerful district councils do not have much sympathy for regional policies perceived to disadvantage the vested interests of the district councils. Regional councils are finding it difficult to establish an electoral constituency within such an organisational environment. This has implications for their viability, given the fact that the National government does not favour the allocation of service delivery and social advocacy functions to regional councils. The recent experiences of the Auckland Regional Council and the Wellington Regional Council have been quite instructive in demonstrating the reluctance of ratepayers to support organisations which do not have the high public profile that is commonly associated with the delivery of services.

It is possible that the establishment of large district councils may be accompanied by the centralisation of decision-making in planning and related activities, and by reduced access to services, particularly if district councils prove unwilling to share power with community boards. It is already apparent that the effectiveness of community boards in promoting public participation in decision-making will be limited if they are constricted to an advisory role. Likewise, the role of local service centres is presently limited to acting as a convenient contact point between the community and the full council, because of a lack of delegated powers.

Finally, the requirement to separate the regulatory, service delivery and trading functions of government could have a far-reaching impact on the fabric of local government, including the possible privatisation of some of its functions and assets. The corporatisation of local government services may have a number of negative impacts, including the loss of jobs, a reduction in equal employment opportunities, a reluctance to honour the Treaty of Waitangi, cutbacks in services and an increase in prices, as well as a restriction in the ability of councils to purchase goods from local suppliers. Services may come to be provided by organisations outside the full control of a council, such as a council company or private sector contractors. The enforced contracting-out of local government services may also lead to a domination of the contracts for functions such as waste management and road maintenance by large companies, including multi-nationals.

Wider Implications

The implementation of local government reforms, as envisaged by the Labour government in December 1987, was only partially completed. Labour's policy initiatives relating to funding, Power of General Competence and Maori participation appear to have fallen into abeyance with the National government that followed it into office in 1990 (Officials Co-ordinating Committee on Local Government, 1988b; Synergy Applied Research Ltd., 1989; Working Party on Regional Government Funding, 1990; Department of Internal Affairs, 1990; Officials Co-ordinating Committee on Local Government, 1989; The Bridgeport Group, 1990). The future constitution of regional councils is still uncertain.

The recent changes in the organisation of local government, along with parallel reforms in resource management statutes, appear to have been motivated by a number of economic and related functional planning considerations rather than through a commitment to devolution. Foremost amongst these considerations is the desire for efficiency in the public sector. This has been coupled with what is seen as an economically more rational allocation of environmental and related functions to the different levels of government. The larger, allegedly leaner and more efficient amalgamated local authorities are expected to cost ratepayers less. They are also expected to encourage economic growth by minimising obstructions to business interests and by streamlining environmental consent procedures. There was a common perception that environmental laws administered by local government were fragmented, overlapping and inconsistent, and that they were an obstruction to development. In addition to streamlining decision-making processes, and possibly reducing the extent of local government activity, the aim of these reforms has been to decrease expenditure on services by charging for them whenever feasible, and by putting as many activities as possible onto a commercial basis.

The fundamental issue is the hidden cost of such apparent or real benefits, in relation to the future autonomy of local government. While the recently established territorial authorities and regional councils may come to exercise their planning and other functions in a more corporate and cohesive fashion as a consequence of the reform process, they have at the same time been brought more closely under the dominance of central government. These reforms have enabled central government to force local government to comply with its overall economic policy objectives. Central government was able to accomplish this task with relative ease and with relatively limited public debate and consultation. At the same time, the ability of localities and regions to respond to the detrimental social impacts of central government economic policies has been reduced.

Concluding Comments

An air of uncertainty continues to prevail on the local government scene, for a number of reasons. A number of the important objectives of the reform programme have been abandoned, particularly the issue of local government funding. This is already constraining the ability of district and regional councils to undertake their responsibilities, including environmental planning.

Moreover, the present (1993) National government is equivocal about the future of regional councils. Recent amendments to local government legislation have further clipped the powers of regional councils to address wider issues of socio-economic significance. While the unitary model is politically more acceptable in some localities, the ability of unitary authorities to separate environmental policy and regulatory functions from service delivery functions has been recently questioned on the basis of the experience of the Gisborne District Council (Office of the Parliamentary Commissioner, 1990). Further structural reforms at the regional level cannot be ruled out as a possibility. Even though the enactment of the Resource Management Act has been based on the assumption of a strong regional tier of government to undertake planning functions, the existence of regional councils will continue to be challenged by local interests. The National party has traditionally been sympathetic to such concerns.

The picture is comparatively clearer at the local territorial level of government. The political future of these authorities appears secure. The number of territorial local authorities has been reduced and several of them have a bigger population and area base; but it is too early to judge if amalgamation has improved their political and professional capability to respond to local needs and issues. Accompanying a consideration of these councils' efficiency is the question of the accessibility of local people to local government decision-making. This is likely to be an important issue in the larger territorial local authorities, such as the City of Dunedin, which comprise an amalgamation of urban and rural interests.

Apart from some exceptions, the spatial jurisdictions of the city and district councils have been defined on the basis of their functional hinterlands. From a planning perspective, this is a more satisfactory situation than the historical fragmentation of local government along an urban-rural divide. Nevertheless, the ability of these new entities to subsume the conflicts and traditional differences in values that exist between rural and urban communities remains to be seen. Incremental boundary changes, based on a clearer definition of perceived communities of interest, are a possibility in situations where such divisions prove difficult to heal.

5

Reform of Environmental Planning Legislation

Introduction

The Resource Management Act 1991 (henceforth the Resource Management Act or the Act) provides a statutory framework for a relatively more holistic and integrated approach to environmental planning for the first time in New Zealand. It replaces a large number of separate and in some respects inconsistent and overlapping statutes concerned with the use of resources.[1]

The Act is a response to the perceived inadequacies of the legislation that had preceded it and which had grown over the years without a clear and consistent guiding philosophy. While the Act was was a Labour government initiative, its enactment by the National government in June 1991 may be seen to reflect a broad consensus within New Zealand society for a strengthened commitment to maintain and improve environmental quality.

But the Act does more than streamline and integrate previously existing statutes. Its constitution is the outcome of quite a lengthy and critical review. In conjunction with the restructuring of the state sector and of local and regional government, and underpinned by a libertarian ideology, the Act has been expected to bring about significant changes in the approach to the management of New Zealand's environment. It restricts the scope of environmental planning to that of a regulatory activity, to be undertaken principally at a sub-national level by regional and district councils. Consequently, even though sustainable management is the guiding principle of the Act, its ambit is limited chiefly to empowering district and regional councils to mitigate undesireable effects of human activities on the environment. It also provides a framework for allocating common property resources including water, air, coastal marine waters and geothermal energy. The ability to address wider urban and rural community planning concerns, such as the provision of adequate housing, transportation and employment, are excluded from the purview of this legislation.

Despite its relatively limited scope, and even though it did not have the status of a full-scale political issue such as the reorganisation of the state sector, the Act proved to be a difficult piece of legislation to pass through Parliament, taking nearly two years to enact. Although very much a product of the fourth Labour government, it also bears the imprint of the 1990 National administration. Party politics has weakened the potential effectiveness of this legislation and made it vulnerable to further political intervention.

In order to assess the significance of this statute as a vehicle to maintain and improve the quality of New Zealand's environment, it is necessary to understand the forces that have been instrumental in shaping the form and content of the Act.

The Prelude to the post-1984 Reforms.

In common with many other countries, environmental planning legislation in New Zealand had evolved in a piecemeal fashion over a relatively long period of time, as I outlined in chapter 2. As specific environmental concerns gathered sufficient political momentum to warrant public action, the state tended to respond by enacting legislation it deemed appropriate for that particular purpose. For example, over the years it has sought to regulate urban and rural land use and subdivision, soil erosion, water and air pollution, urban renewal and mining. Such changes often led to grafting new arrangements onto the old. Hence, the legislative framework that came into being was characterised by problems of fragmentation, overlap, complexity, procedural inconsistency and a degree of ambivalence and bias in the values underlying it. Even though central government was a major developer, it absolved itself from such legislative constraints. The Environmental Protection and Enhancement Procedures, conceived as a substitute for inadequate planning procedures relating to central government projects, were only marginally successful in containing undesirable impacts on the environment.

Statutory planning increasingly became a target of public dissatisfaction during the 1970s and the 1980s. Development interest groups complained about problems arising from the bureaucratic hurdles they encountered when seeking multiple consents from several different central and local agencies. They complained of an inflexibility of planning schemes, too liberal public participation provisions in the decision-making process, and the delaying tactics employed by some community groups. Planning was perceived by many developers as unwarranted intervention in the market place. But there were also environmental organisations and Maori people who were critical of the inadequate recognition of environmental and Maori values in relation to economic considerations; of adversarial decision-making procedures; unaffordable hearing costs; lack of access to information; and the excessive discretionary powers accorded to central government bureaucrats and local councils.

Before the 1980s there had been periodic attempts to respond to some of the perceived shortcomings in the environmental planning legislation, but such initiatives tended to be limited in scope by the particular agencies coordinating such reviews. The Ministry of Works and Development, for instance, held the responsiblity to review land use and water resource legislation, as did the Department of Lands and Survey with respect to public land statutes. Quite often, these reviews were captured by the the resource users such as the timber and mining industries and the professional interest groups. For these reasons, the legislative changes that took place tended to be limited in scope.[2] A move by the National Government to improve the situation, by enacting the National Development Act in 1979, increased the scope for political and administrative discretion and created further uncertainty for the participants. Many of these concerns were canvassed by the OECD panel in 1980 and improvements were recommended (OECD, 1980). The proposed New Zealand Conservation strategy similarly emphasised the importance of effective legislation to encourage the integration of conservation and development (NCC, 1981).

Initial Responses of the Fourth Labour Government

Seen as an integral component of its broader environmental and local government reform strategies, there were two essential objectives underpinning Labour's election pledge to review and consolidate the environmental planning legislation: to enable adequate consideration of environmental values in the public policy process at all levels of government; and, related to this, to devolve decision-making to a stronger tier of regional government (N.Z Labour Party, 1984).[3] However, a piecemeal approach characterised its implementing of this pledge during the first term, as the reforms of the central government environmental bureaucracy were a more important preoccupation. It was only after 1987 that the Labour government was able to design and implement a cohesive and concerted strategy, under close political direction, to comprehensively review environmental planning and local government.

An important factor that led to the postponement of the review of environmental planning legislation until 1987 was the pressure by Treasury and the environmental groups to address first those concerns relating to the activities of the existing central government agencies who acted as managers of natural resources. Initially, the Task Group of Officials, convened in 1984 to advise the new government on the implementation of its environmental strategy, concerned itself mainly with the reform of the planning processes, within the wider inter-governmental context.[4] It identified changes to existing decision-making processes at national, regional and local levels – changes which would complement the proposed formation of a Ministry for the Environment – as a key requirement to implement the new government's philosophy on environmental management. But the environmental groups and the Working Party on Environmental Administration (Environmental Administration Task Group, 1985; WPEA, 1985), with the support of Treasury, successfully redefined the debate to direct attention to restructuring the environmental bureaucracy of central government.

Unresolved Policy Issues

The pressure for a more comprehensive and fundamental review of the environmental planning legislation and related resource statutes, compared to what may have been envisaged by the Task Group, also became clearly manifest during the negotiations on the restructuring of environmental administration. Underpinning this pressure was a desire to ensure compliance of the planning statutes with the rapidly changing direction of the relationship between the state and New Zealand society. Thus, the need for a radical review of the environmental planning legislation became increasingly apparent during the debate on state sector restructuring from 1984 to 1986. The policy decisions relating to the provisions of the proposed Environment Act and the Conservation Act, as well as the wider questions arising from the proposals by the Task Group to review the Planning Act, also made it necessary to undertake such a review. The issues that arose during the policy development process at this stage comprised three interwoven strands:

i. Legislative status for the environmental impact assessment procedures.

The Environment Minister, Hon. Russell Marshall, supported by the Commission for the Environment and environmental groups, was a strong advocate within the Cabinet for giving statutory recognition to the environmental impact assessment (EIA) procedures within the framework of the proposed Environment Act. It was envisaged that the MfE would administer environmental assessment procedures while the PCE's office would be accorded the role of an environmental audit agency. But major impediments to Cabinet acceptance of these recommendations ensued from Treasury and a number of other government departments, including the Ministry of Works and Development. Their arguments were quite compelling and exposed deep-seated differences within government ranks relating to wider policy issues.

At the most fundamental level, the appropriateness of EIA procedures as a form of central government intervention in a market-led economy was questioned, as was the role of the MfE in administering these procedures. The Commission for the Environment wished to see the new Ministry directly involved in deciding how the procedures should be applied to particular proposals and which proposals needed a full environmental audit, and in assisting developers to comply with the procedures. Other departments saw the procedures being more appropriately administered by local government, with the role of the new Ministry explicitly limited to monitoring the effectiveness of the procedures. The justification for environmental assessment procedures, as an additional requirement to the statutory planning process, was also debated. It appeared more logical to integrate these procedures into the planning process so that proposals had only one consent process to comply with.[5] The officials were unable to resolve these differences within the given timeframe. Consequently, the proposed procedures were omitted from the Environment Act 1986.

ii. Devolution of decision-making on environmental planning to regional government, as envisaged in the 1984 election manifesto and supported by the Task Group.

Once again, it became apparent that before this policy could be implemented, a number of unresolved issues associated with regional government and the regional planning process needed to be adequately addressed. As I point out in chapter 4, Treasury had earlier questioned the benefits of the planning function of United and Regional Councils, which it regarded as complex, lengthy and an impediment to economic change. Also unclear was the role of the Crown, particularly the extent to which it could be bound by regional scheme policies and its participation in regional planning in a deregulated economic environment. Cabinet needed to consider the appropriate relationship between central and sub-national government, as a precursor to devolving decision-making to the regions.

iii. The role of local government in land-use planning.
This debate related to intervention by local government, through the planning process, in an area viewed by some Cabinet members, officials and powerful pressure groups in the private sector as more efficiently dealt with by private choice, through the mechanisms of private property rights. Critics of the relative costs and benefits of statutory planning had become increasingly more vocal (for example Brown, Copeland and Co. Ltd., 1987). Developers, Cabinet Ministers with development portfolios, and the Economic Development Commission complained about the delays, inflexibility and costs imposed by statutory planning and the alleged detrimental implications for economic growth and job creation (EDC, 1987).[6]

The advice of officials to the Cabinet was polarised. In contrast to the MoW&D officials (reflecting the views of the planning and legal professions), who saw local government planning as a participatory and facilitative approach towards resolving land-use conflicts, Treasury officials deemed it politically undemocratic and economically unwarranted. They advocated individual negotiation and the use of economic instruments based on tradeable property rights to achieve good environmental outcomes.

In the event, during its first term, the fourth Labour government was unable to resolve many of these policy issues so as to enable the review of the planning statutes to make much headway. Given the differences within Cabinet, as well as amongst officials, it proved difficult to reach a satisfactory consensus on these issues. The government, as it was running out of time to enact legislation to implement Cabinet decisions on the creation of the new Ministry for the Environment, was compelled to defer substantive action on the review of the planning process.[7]

The Resource Management Law Reform as a Policy Initiative
The resource management law reform (henceforth RMLR) project was conceived immediately after the 1987 election. It led to the enactment of the Resource Management Act 1991, which formed a framework for apportioning environmental planning responsibilities between central, regional and local

government agencies, and established appropriate decision-making procedures for allocating and resolving conflicts over resource use.

As a policy initiative, the RMLR project was only partially anticipated in Labour's 1987 election manifesto (N.Z Labour Party, 1987). The manifesto made a commitment to review all existing natural resource statutes, but beyond this, the scope of the anticipated reforms was not made explicit – a reflection of uncertainty within Labour's ranks. For instance, with respect to the proposed review of the Town and Country Planning Act, the manifesto did not state whether the objective was to streamline and strengthen environmental protection, or to sweep away existing controls on land development, as "Rogernomics" had already done in other areas. Such uncertainty was symptomatic of the deep divisions that had emerged within the government in relation to economic liberalisation and the role of the state in protecting the environment in a deregulated market economy.

In spite of this, the RMLR initiative was designed, put into place and completed within a relatively short time. This achievement was made possible by a number of factors. Foremost amongst these was the strong commitment of the new Prime Minister, Rt. Hon. Geoffrey Palmer, who also held the environment portfolio, to rationalise what he discerned as fragmented, overlapping and complex statutes (Palmer, 1987; Palmer, 1990). Even though the RMLR project was politically driven, the MfE officials played a key role in conceiving the project and steering it to a successful completion. The elevated status of the MfE enabled it to obtain, with the support of Treasury, Cabinet approval and resources for the project. The decision to finally abolish the MoW&D and allocate its land and water planning policy functions to the MfE, was instrumental in removing political opposition to, and providing funding for, the RMLR project.

The Review Process

The RMLR exercise was directed by a small Core Group in the MfE, which reported to the Cabinet Committee on Reform of Local Government and Resource Management Statutes (henceforth, the Cabinet Committee).[8] While the review of the resource statutes was orchestrated by the Core Group, the Act reflects the input of a wide range of contributors: officials, politicians, and the public, including pressure groups.

The political objective of the Labour government was to complete the substantive analysis ready for enacting legislation before the 1990 election. Cabinet Ministers' perspective of the RMLR exercise, when it was begun, was quite limited. The negative public reaction to the National Development Act passed in 1979 by the National government to implement its "Think Big" strategy had made them particularly aware of the significance of public participation in decision-making. They saw the RMLR primarily as a means to streamline and rationalise the tangled web of statutes, and their appreciation of the more complex substantive and procedural issues was then limited. The consideration of these latter issues was principally the input of the bureaucrats: in particular, the MfE, Treasury, DoC and Commerce officials and consultants.

The Core Group took a leading role in co-ordinating the review process and analysing and recommending policy options. It had a wide-ranging mandate, and in contrast to the traditional interdepartmental process for policy development, it was able to adopt a more concerted approach to the task.[9] The Core Group made extensive use of consultants and task groups, rather than relying on the more conventional interdepartmental committee approach to policy development. The Environment Minister did not trust the conventional approach, with its tendency to perpetuate the status quo and vested departmental interests.

The role of the MfE as the agency responsible for this review, and its close working relationship with Ministers, were crucial to the success of the RMLR. Treasury was particularly powerful and would have captured the RMLR process totally if a less influential agency had been in the lead. Other departments, not represented on the Core Group, also had their particular concerns to promote, but at times perceived the Core Group as a barrier in this respect.[10]

The Act is as much a product of a conventional, theoretical economic analysis of resource management issues, as of political direction and negotiation. The review, intellectually structured by the Core Group within the school of institutional economics, was concerned with addressing the problem of environmental externality in the context of property rights arrangements (or more generally, institutional arrangements). The objective was to identify property right arrangements that would produce an efficient allocation of economic goods and bads (Bromley, 1988). During the course of the review, analysis of resource ownership and use rights was thus accorded a high priority.[11]

The clear specification of property rights, seen as tantamount to ownership rights, was deemed an efficient way to improve environmental outcomes. This also provided the context for the consideration of Maori claims to resources under the Treaty of Waitangi, of the definition of sustainability as a policy objective, and of the potential for using economic instruments (such as tradeable development and water rights) for resource management.

Treasury's overriding objective throughout the exercise was to limit the scope of the proposed Act as a means of controlling externalities, by providing clear property rights to natural resources. It was critical of the broader purposes of the proposed legislation, such as sustainability and the needs of future generations, which it regarded as being based on vague values and which it thought could therefore lead to arbitrary decisions by the Planning Tribunal. Contrary to the MfE, Treasury was determined to resist any presumption in favour of environmental control, and was opposed to the notion that economic activity should be constrained in order to promote sustainable development. Treasury argued that such a presumption was inconsistent with economic efficiency, and that the protection of the environment should take its place alongside other objectives and should be given no special status.

The Core Group was forced to work in an uncertain policy environment, on account of the possible implications of reforms in related areas such as local government and coastal legislation. These uncertainties compounded the difficulties experienced in obtaining a concensus within the group. Fortunately for the MfE, during the second term of the fourth Labour government, the advocates of the Treasury viewpoint in Cabinet were not as politically influential as before. On the basis of its analysis of fundamental issues relating to the purposes, objectives and priorities for reform and the role of government in resource management (MfE, 1988a), the Core Group identified a pivotal role for regional government in resource planning. It was then able to formulate a comprehensive and integrated law reform proposal as a basis for the drafting of the new law (MfE, 1988b). The responsibilities of different levels of government, as therein defined, were derived from an assessment of wide-ranging, substantive and procedural issues (MfE, 1988c).

The Core Group subsequently played an important role in translating the review findings into policy proposals for the Cabinet Committee.[12] Cumulatively, these proposals became the basis of the provisions of the proposed resource management statute and of instructions to the law drafters.[13] Towards the end of 1989, there was further discussion and fine-tuning of the draft Bill, jointly by the Cabinet Committee, the Cabinet Economic Development and Employment Committee, and the Cabinet Legislation Committee, in response to departmental comments and comments by independent reviewers.

This iterative process continued until the Select Committee stage. While the input of the pressure groups had been important all along in the policy development process, the role of these groups became most clearly dominant during the select committee stage, immediately prior to and after the 1990 general election, while the input of the officials was, in some respects, marginalised.

The Role of the Pressure Groups

Besides the politicians and the bureaucrats, a diversity of pressure groups, with a major stake in the outcome of the review, played a very significant role in shaping the evolution of the Resource Management Act. The Core Group members were subject to considerable lobbying by representatives of interest groups during the review process. At the same time, the Core Group also made a considerable effort to seek a wider public input into the review process.

The environmental groups played an influential role throughout the review process; to a lesser extent, the input of professional groups, such as lawyers and planners, was also apparent. By comparison, there was less incentive for the representatives of the corporate sector, such as the Business Round Table, or those representing the individual resource sectors, to be involved in a positive fashion during the earlier stages of the review. They marshalled their forces later, when the draft Bill was taking shape; it was then that they became aware of the extent of political commitment to it.

Throughout the review process, the environmental groups operated in a very dedicated and organised fashion, especially in their relations with Cabinet Ministers. The environmental groups were initially uncertain about the underlying objectives of the RMLR policy initiative. Some of them saw it as a desire by Cabinet to devolve central government's environmental functions to local and regional councils, which were deemed to be more development oriented. Nevertheless, by the stage of preparation of the draft Bill and its subsequent consideration by the Select Committee, a small group of influential environmental advocates had developed a close working relationship with the Ministers of Environment and Conservation as well as, to a lesser extent, Treasury officials.[14]

By comparison, the response of the various industry groups tended to be reactive. For example, the approach of the mining industry was old-fashioned: to try and forestall any attempts to improve environmental legislation. The initial responses of the Business Round Table were also critical of the RMLR process and characterised by hostility to the environmental lobby. However, as I shall show, this attitude changed markedly during the final negotiations, prior to the enactment of the legislation in 1991.

Because of a lack of time and internal dissension within its ranks during its final days in office in 1990, Labour was unable to pass the Act. The Round Table and the Maruia Society appear to have influenced to a very significant extent the approach of the incoming National government to the Bill. The Round Table, concerned by the apparent "green bias" of the Bill, was influential in having the National party withhold support for its enactment into law just before the 1990 election. At the same time, the Round Table now appeared to regard the environmental cause as legitimate and recognised a need to come to terms with the environmental movement, rather than to oppose it. The National Party agreed to subject the Bill to peer review before enacting it (Review Group, 1991).

The Resource Management Act
Many of the concerns about environmental planning in New Zealand, raised by the panel of OECD experts in 1980, have been addressed in the Resource Management Act. The rest of this chapter will examine the key features of this legislation.

The Act creates rational and streamlined procedures for decision-making for environmental planning and provides an integrated focus on natural resources (land, air, water, geothermal and mineral). Despite its name, it is essentially a planning instrument, not an operational code. It highlights the significance of policy formulation as a means for making decisions within the public sector. The central purpose of the Act is defined in terms of the principle of sustainability. The Act recognises that government has an important role in environmental planning and defines a hierarchical, three-tier planning structure (Table 5.1). This hierarchy is based on the assumption that decisions should be made as close as possible to the appropriate level of community of interest where the effects and benefits accrue. While central government's principal role is to oversee and monitor the Act, it also retains direct management responsibility for the allocation of Crown-owned mineral, energy and coastal resources, and the control of hazardous substances.[15] It also has a key role in setting technical standards, such as for air and water quality, which is binding on all plans and consents. Central government can take over the consideration of a proposal which raises matters of national significance, in order to make a decision about it at a national level.

Most of the responsibility for identifying issues, developing policy responses and implementing and monitoring these responses has been delegated to local authorities. National policy statements and standards are expected to guide regional and district councils, and disputes are settled by the Planning Tribunals. Regional councils have direct responsibility for soil, water and geothermal resources and pollution control. They share coastal management

Table 5.1: Functions by levels of government

Central Government

– Overview role
– Developing policies for managing resources
– Performance and quality standards
– Mineral allocation
– Aspects of coastal management
– Management of toxic wastes, explosives, other hazardous substances

Regional Councils

– Overview/co-ordination role: regional resource policy statements; regional plans (optional)
– Water and soil management
– Management of geothermal resources
– Natural hazards mitigation/planning
– Regional aspects of hazardous substances
– Pollution management and air pollution control
– Aspects of coastal managemen

Territorial Councils

– District plans
– Control of land-use and subdivision
– Noise control
– Control for natural hazards avoidance and mitigation
– Local control of hazardous substances use

with central government. District councils have the primary responsibility for land-use management and noise control. Rights and obligations of the various parties are more clearly defined and the decision-making procedures for the different resources are consistent. The Act provides for penalties and systems of enforcement to ensure that the law is upheld, as well as granting liberal provisions for public participation. It also signifies the government's objective that developers face prices which reflect full environmental costs.

The Act can also be expected to bring about other far-reaching changes in the practice of environmental planning, as a reflection of its libertarian under-pinnings that are as significant as the improvements to its rationale. In order to appreciate this, it is important to highlight the differences in the assumptions on which the Act is based, compared to those of the statutes it has replaced.

Even though, as discussed below, sustainable resource management is the central purpose of the Act, its structure reflects a determination on the part of the government for a more open and competitive economy, a move away from state participation in promoting economic growth, and towards a decentralised administration of regulatory systems and the use of economic instruments to achieve good environmental outcomes.

The Act constitutes a radical departure from the parallel legislative provisions it has replaced, in a number of important respects. It concentrates on regulating the impact of human activities on the environment rather than regulating the activities *per se*. As a deliberate change in legislative approach, it includes wider and stronger powers to manage environmental impacts. In some respects, though, depending on the attitude of local authorities, its provisions could prove less protective of the environment than previous planning law. This is because the Act is much less prescriptive: within very wide boundaries, people can do what they like, so long as they do not harm the environment.

Virtually all environmental standards and guide-lines from earlier legislation have been discarded in the Act. The only minimum standards provided are for water use classification. It is up to the MfE and individual local authorities to promulgate appropriate environmental standards as a basis for regulating environmental impacts and promoting sustainability.

The Act constitutes a radical change in the basic objectives of the land-use planning system. This system, which had evolved since 1926, made provision for opportunities for development and the direction and control of that development. Land-use planning was an essential tool for promoting development and regulating its effects. The positive statutory obligation on local authorities to create opportunities for development in a controlled way has been removed, and been replaced by a requirement to promote the sustainable management of resources.

Finally, the Act is neutral with respect to competition between economic and environmental goals. It is primarily a law designed to control externalities. In this respect, the Act marks a significant change from preceding legislation, in that decision-makers are not expected to make the trade-offs in promoting the wise or beneficial use of resources that were formerly required.

Environmental Objectives

The promotion of the sustainable management of natural and physical resources is the overriding objective of the Act. The use of the term sustainable management, rather than development, is intended to cover the concepts of use, development and protection. This is seen to be in accord with the government's apparently neutral stance with respect to resource allocation decisions.

The recent origins of sustainability as an environmental policy objective may be traced back to the World Conservation Strategy (IUCN, 1980), which was endorsed by the New Zealand government and adopted by the Labour party in its 1984 and 1987 election manifestos. More recently, the principle of sustainable development was strongly advocated in the Brundtland report, *Our Common Future* (WCED, 1987). It encompasses ecocentric as well as anthropocentric considerations, as I shall show.

The WCED report defines sustainable development quite widely as "development that meets the needs of the present without compromising the ability of future generations to meet their needs" (WCED, 1987, p.43). Sustainability is thus a value-based concept: it is the moral imperative of accepting intergenerational equity as an overriding goal in the public policy process. It seeks to satisfy the reasonable material and non-material needs of society indefinitely. To achieve intergenerational equity means that the actions of the current generation should not substantially limit the options available to future generations. Decision-making agencies have therefore to ensure that resources are not harnessed beyond the carrying capacity of the bio-physical systems of which they are a part. The above definition implies that development should be compatible with the continued functioning of these essential ecological processes.

But what is equally important is that the sustainability concept, as defined in the Brundtland report, also implies that at any one particular time the reasonable needs of all humans should be met. Such a notion of intragenerational equity raises important implications in terms of the socio-economic constraints on the access to resources by different sections of the community, particularly in a property-owning democracy. From a more limited perspective, it implies that during the decision-making process, the actions of a particular developer or group should not substantially limit the options available to other individuals or groups. Thus, an important attribute of a sustainable proposal is that it has a fairly broad measure of social acceptability.

The principal conclusions of the WCED report have been endorsed by the New Zealand government, and a number of recent policy initiatives have sought to recognise it. The Resource Management Act is the most far-reaching in this respect. However, the concept of sustainable management of natural and physical resources, as defined in Section 5 of the Act (see Appendix 2) and discussed below, has a much more limited focus than the definition in the Brundtland report. It is a delicately worded definition, based on extensive consultation and negotiation amongst the development and environmental groups, the bureaucrats and the successive Labour and National governments. The Act specifically defines three constraints on the use, development and protection of resources which are necessary to achieve sustainable management of these resources: the needs of future generations; the need to safeguard the life-supporting capacity of ecosystems; and the mitigation of detrimental environmental impacts.

The definition of sustainable management in the Act falls short of giving precedence to environmental protection objectives over other objectives. The inclusion of such provisions in the Act would have entailed constraining economic activity to ensure sustainability of bio-physical systems. Any such presumption for environmental control, advocated by some environmental groups, was opposed by Treasury and developers as inconsistent with economic efficiency. Furthermore, as a non-renewable resource, mining is excluded from consideration under the sustainability clause, except in respect to the effects arising from mining activity.

The extent to which the sustainability clause provides a satisfactory guiding philosophy for comprehensive and integrated environmental planning will become more apparent with greater experience in implementing the Act. In view of the potential implications of this clause in influencing the direction of environmental planning practice, its interpretation is likely to be subject to considerable discussion and litigation. As has been already pointed out, the objective of promoting sustainable management, as defined in the Act, is capable of variable interpretation (Fisher, 1991). Thus, depending on the relative emphasis put on the word 'while' in Section 5 of the Act, the bio-physical and intergenerational equity constraints on managing the use, development and protection of natural and physical resources stated in clauses (a), (b) and (c), can carry more or less weight compared to the objective of enabling people and communities to provide for their social, economic and cultural well-being.

It is also clear that, even if the Courts choose to adopt a very strong ecocentric stance, the decision-making process of district and regional councils will entail a balancing exercise between social, economic, cultural and bio-physical values. In order to put into operation the three constraints on development activity stated in Section 5, district and regional councils need to define environmental standards. However, environmental standards are only relative. Given the resilience of ecosystems to change, the notion of an environmental bottom-line is questionable. District and regional councils could therefore be expected to have considerable latitude in setting such standards, depending not only on bio-physical considerations but also on local socio-economic conditions and aspirations. Hence, the debate about environmental issues in the district and regional planning process is likely to reflect the plurality of prevailing values and conflicts of interest.

Following the definition of sustainable management as its central purpose, the Act lists "Matters of National Importance" (Section 6). These relate primarily to the quality of the natural environment and the recognition of Maori values; the list reflects the objective of the government to protect both the environment and the relationship of the Maori people with their taonga. All policies, plans and consent decisions made under the Act are obliged to recognise and provide for these "Matters of National Importance".

Section 6 is modelled on the parallel provisions of the former Town and Country Planning Act, thus providing a link with some of the case law. It could be argued that, in some ways, this section is likely to be as important in influencing the resolution of environmental conflicts as the preceding clause on sustainable management. The Act specifies a number of other principles which need to be taken into account as appropriate (Section 7). These principles also cover environmental values, including those relating to the physical (built) environment, such as amenity and heritage values.

Given the place of sustainable management as a purpose, and the related Sections 6 and 7, planning under the Resource Management Act is concerned with achieving primarily natural resource objectives. The extent to which the Act provides a satisfactory planning instrument for the more diverse planning needs in urban areas remains to be seen.

Treaty Issues

The Treaty of Waitangi was expected to be a central issue in the resource statutes review when the review commenced. Given the analytical approach adopted for the review, it was believed that resource management issues were intertwined with ownership questions. In particular, Maori claims to the ownership of the resources under the Treaty of Waitangi had implications for the expected changes in the ownership of resources and the granting of consents, such as water rights. While the Maori people supported this initiative to address long-standing grievances, they were deeply concerned that if the existing functions of central government were devolved to sub-national government, there may not be a corresponding responsibility to devolve the Crowns's obligation to honour the Treaty.

The analysis of ownership options for natural resources (water, minerals, geothermal, petroleum) was, as I indicated earlier, a major concern during the review. Considerable work was done, examining the advantages and disadvantages of changing the existing ownership patterns, such as the vesting of mineral rights solely in the surface owner or the Crown, and the practice of selling water rights in perpetuity (MfE, 1988c). However, before any significant changes in ownership patterns could occur, the full resolution of fun-

damental Treaty issues was required. There also needed to be some procedure for recognising the Treaty in the proposed Act.

It soon became apparent during the review process that some sections of
the Maori community considered it undesirable for the review to attempt to
deal with fundamental ownership issues. Recognizing that the RMLR had
major implications for the management and control of their taonga, they were
concerned that there was insufficient Maori influence over the review procedure, since consultation was not equivalent to direct involvement. The Core
Group having subsequently encountered considerable hostility, its initial expectations, to address ownership issues, did not prove politically and socially
feasible in the context of the RMLR exercise.[16]

Consequently, a decision was made by the Cabinet not to deal with issues
of Maori ownership within the RMLR exercise. The resolution of the Treaty's
implications for resource ownership had to be addressed outside the context
of the review. Attention was therefore now given to ways of increasing Maori
participation in decision-making within the framework of the proposed Act.

To what extent has the Resource Management Act achieved this limited
objective? The Act is much stronger in recognising Maori interests than its
predecessors, and provides guidance on achieving meaningful consultation,
particularly at the local and regional level. In the past, it had been the actions
of local authorities that were frequently contrary to the Treaty, as revealed in
notable cases reported by the Tribunal, including aspects of the Motonui,
Kaituna, Manukau and Orakei claims. Thus, there are several points in the
Act at which attention is directed to Maori concerns, with the intention of
promoting a closer dialogue on issues of mutual concern. A local authority,
for instance, can transfer its resource management functions and powers to
an iwi authority. Legislation was introduced into the House in 1990 by the
Labour Government to create runanga, or Maori councils, based on traditional tribal structures. The iwi runanga were to be the official representatives
of the tangata whenua, akin to local government, to manage resources in
their own right. The National government that came to power in 1990, however, decided against enacting the proposed legislation. Iwi management plans
do not place any statutory obligation on resource management agencies, and
the role of iwi may thus have been marginalised.

The Maori expectation was that the Resource Management Act would ac-
knowledge te tino rangatiratanga under the Treaty. That is, it would recognise that the iwi is a legitimate entity on account of its mana whenua status
recognised in the Treaty. Yet, the Act delegates to central government agencies and regional councils the authority to allocate Crown-owned resources,
without even provisionally acknowledging Maori ownership of resources. The
government has sidestepped the ownership issue for the time being. As a
consequence of these decisions, ownership vested in the Crown could be
divested to a third party, thus possibly prejudicing obligations to the Maori
people under the Treaty.

National Policies

Despite its apparent commitment to devolution, central government has retained a number of important functions under the Act and its role is now defined in statute. One of its primary responsibilities is developing national policies (Table 9.1). These policies should provide much-needed guidance to local authorities when they are exercising powers and functions over resources of national significance, or making decisions having nationally significant implications. Provision is also made for a Ministerial "call-in" procedure for development proposals of national significance. There was considerable discussion during the review process as to whether this was a legitimate role for central government in the deregulated state sector environment. On the one hand, economists were concerned that national policy statements could lead to the centralisation of decision-making and an unwarranted intervention by central government, like the National Development Act. On the other hand, at the local and regional level, and amongst environmental groups, there was growing uncertainty that central government might find it convenient to devolve all responsibility for environmental management to local government. The bigger environmental groups were concerned that central government might withdraw as a participant from the planning process. They find it easier to lobby central government than regional and local government.

Coastal planning is given particular prominence in the Act. This was a deliberate political decision, reflecting the strong national interest in the conservation values of the coast, and in use of the Crown conservation estate. The Act assigns to the Department of Conservation a major role in preparing national coastal policy statements. This provision could be criticised as according special status to the coast, since responsibility for managing other resources has been delegated to the regional and district councils. The Minister of Conservation also has the ultimate authority to approve regional coastal plans and consents for "restricted coastal activities", and the ability to overturn Planning Tribunal's recommendations. There are other areas where policy guidance should be provided by central government on resources such as soils, wetlands and resources having implications for the Treaty of Waitangi.[17]

The special consideration given to coastal planning in the Act reflects the input of DoC to the review process. As a national conservation estate management agency with a major responsibility for granting consents under the former Harbours Act, DoC was given a mandate in 1987 to undertake a review of the coastal legislation, parallel to the RMLR review. The Core Group was keen to link the two reviews but DoC officials were concerned that this would weaken coastal protection as a consequence of the "free market" influences within the Core Group. They were also concerned that the proposed Resource Management Act might devolve coastal planning to regional government. DoC saw the main objective of the Coastal Legislation Review as the protection of the natural qualities and intrinsic values of the coastline, and anticipated a separate coastal statute based on this premise. However, DoC found it difficult to secure enough support in Cabinet, partly because of sensitive Maori owner-ship issues relating to the foreshore and sea bed.

Consequently, the Coastal Review became incorporated within the RMLR process. The challenge for DoC now was to ensure that the Act made appropriate provision for recognising and providing protection for the conservation values of the coastline. It has been successful in this respect.[18]

However, in hindsight, the Act has failed to resolve the difficulties associated with coastal management. These centre upon the conflict between the role of the Minister of Conservation as an advocate for conservation, his role as an allocator of space in the coastal zone, and his role in the regulatory process affecting coastal activity. The satisfactory resolution of coastal management problems will not be possible until issues of ownership and the administration of unallocated Crown estate are resolved. Creating the necessary property rights is seen by Treasury and developers as essential to address these issues. But, for the time being, the government has refrained from this because of the potential conflict between the environmental groups and industrial interests.

Mineral and Energy Resources

The provisions of the Crown Minerals Act 1991 were developed within the context of the RMLR process. The final decision to enact these provisions as a separate statute was made at a late stage in the process, as a political concession to the mining lobby, and as a reflection of Treasury advice. The reason for this was to separate the regulatory issues associated with mining as an activity, from the allocation issues associated with Crown ownership of minerals. The Crown Minerals Act is concerned with central government's role in mineral allocation, and health, safety, pricing and taxation in relation to mining. It also sets out the rights of landowners (including Ministers of the Crown) to refuse consent to mining activities on their land. It recognises that central government should continue to have responsibility for the allocation of Crown-owned mineral and energy resources, but that local government should deal with the externalities of mining activities in the same way that it does with other land and water use activities under the Resource Management Act.

In many respects, mining proved to be one of the most contentious issues to resolve during the RMLR process. The origins of the difficulty can be traced to long-standing conflicts between the mining industry and the environmental groups in regions with significant conservation values such as the Coromandel. In its 1984 manifesto, the Labour Party made a commitment to review the mining legislation for this reason, and the Mining Legislation Review team reported in 1987 (Interdepartmental Committee on the review of Mining Legislation, 1987). It addressed wide-ranging and differing views in the mining and energy sectors and emphasised the need for a more in-depth investigation and the co-ordination of the review with the parallel reviews of the planning, and water and soil legislation.

Given the responsibilities of the Ministry of Commerce in administering mining and energy legislation, its officials were disappointed at being excluded from membership of the Core Group. The Ministry of Commerce was concerned about the special character of exploration for energy and mineral resources, fearing that the application of environmental controls that did not recognize that difference might impose further barriers to mining activities. Its view was that the functions of central government that specifically related to energy and mineral resources should not be provided for in a resource management statute that would be administered by the MfE. Instead it suggested that these functions should be contained in a separate Act administered by the Minister of Energy. However, in a situation that was parallel to DoC's experience with coastal management, it did not receive much support for its views, at that stage, within the Core Group or the Cabinet Committee.

During the RMLR process, the debate on mining was dominated by ownership issues relating to minerals and to the rights of the land owners. It was concerned particularly with the implications of the Treaty of Waitangi and of any rearrangement of ownership to parties other than the Crown in regard to Crown-owned minerals. This proved to be a very difficult issue to resolve, so that in the end any changes to the existing legislative provisions with respect to ownership of mineral and energy resources were excluded from the review. Nevertheless, the influence of Treasury and some environmental groups in seeking property rights, and a market in these rights, has become a significant feature of the Crown Minerals Act. The most important aspect is that the Act gives to surface owners a veto over the exercise of non-petroleum mineral rights, because of the conservation benefits of having land-owner title to minerals. The land-owner consent provision went through many changes, and the eventual decision to retain it was a political one.[19]

Regional and District Planning

The scope of central government participation in the environmental planning process is limited to allocating Crown-owned resources and protecting the national interest, both in terms of a strategic policy role and for specific issues whose impact may extend beyond the boundary of a particular region. The task of preparing more detailed policies, plans and rules, as a framework for granting consent and enforcing the rules, has been devolved to regional and district councils (Table 9.1). In the past, local authorities often did not take environmental effects fully into account because statutes did not explicitly require this. The Act has remedied this situation.

During the earlier stages of the RMLR process, there was considerable political uncertainty regarding the expected role of local government in environmental planning. The Cabinet and Treasury did not appear very sympathetic to the idea of local government intervention in the development process. Having deregulated other factors of production, including labour and capital, land was the next obvious target for deregulation. Even the Core Group appeared to advocate a strongly reduced role for government in resource management, in favour of market mechanisms (MfE, 1988a). A concerted effort was made to advocate a pricing approach to resources such as water, and to address externality issues by negotiation and tradeable property rights. But this was found to be costly, cumbersome and difficult, quite apart from the possible implications on the Treaty of Waitangi of changes to the ownership of water resources. More recently, however, the National government has emphasised its preference for economic instruments as a means to achieve environmental objectives.

The impact of these influences is reflected in the circumscribed scope of district and regional planning. Environmental planning under the Act is seen as being essentially market led, and limited in scope to addressing the negative environmental effects of development proposals. To do this effectively, strategic planning is essential in identifying priorities, goals and objectives as a basis for decision-making. This is essentially the role of regional policy statements, which provide a framework for regional and district plans.

As I emphasized earlier, the Act gives primacy to natural resources. As a consequence of this, the integrating role of regional councils, whose jurisdiction has been defined on a catchment basis, has emerged as pivotal in the local government planning system. Because the role of territorial local authorities in land-use planning is cast within this hierarchical structure, the direction of district planning is also likely to acquire a limited focus in relation to the urban environment.

The Act has substantially reduced the justification for separate environmental impact assessment procedures.[20] Environmental groups might have preferred to see these retained at the central government level, as well as preferring greater involvement by the Parliamentary Commissioner for the Environment in auditing impact reports. As a reflection of the Act's emphasis on the analysis of effects, the requirement for environmental impact reporting is now integrated into the planning process. This places a much bigger onus on all levels of government to adequately assess the anticipated effects of policies, plans and projects.

The Planning Tribunal

Because of the lack of adequate policy direction by central government in the past, the Planning Tribunal was at times forced to make policy decisions – a role it did not feel comfortable with. The role of the Tribunal has also been a cause of concern to environmental groups because they perceive it as being too development oriented, and even hostile to their interests. The Act has, nevertheless, extended the powers and responsibilities of the Planning Tribunal.

Given that the fundamental objective of the Act is to promote sustainable management, it is inevitable that it will raise questions about the end-use of resources and require that choices be made between which resources are to be used and which are to be conserved. Major issues of this kind may be dealt with by the Minister for the Environment under the "call in" procedures, but this is unlikely to happen very often. Many of these questions will have to be resolved by the Tribunal through the appeal mechanisms provided in the Act, unless there is an adequate policy direction by the central government. It is likely that, even more so than in the past, the Planning Tribunal could become involved in policy issues and become a de facto policy-making agency.

Concluding Comments

To what extent does the Resource Management Act provide an adequate framework for the protection of the New Zealand environment? Environmental objectives are given statutory recognition in the Act. Compared to the preceding legislation, the Act has a clearer guiding philosophy and, in keeping with a long-term historical trend during the course of this century, its enactment may have led to a marginal increase in favour of public rights over rights of the individual. This signifies a progressive change in public values relating to the environment and an increasing acceptance of the environmental movement.

But the environmental objectives enshrined in the Act have to be achieved within a political economy dominated by a libertarian ideology. Environmental planning is seen as being essentially market-led, where collective decisions are taken only to cope with private decisions. Compared to the preceding legislation, the restraints on public intervention in a property-owning democracy are now more clearly defined and circumscribed in the Resource Management Act.

The agenda of Treasury was to minimise all restraints on the utilisation of New Zealand's resources. This objective was supported by a number of Cabinet Ministers in the fourth Labour government as well as by many developers and was a dominating theme during the RMLR process, even though the argument has only been partially won by the advocates of a free market economy. While the Resource Management Act may be seen to represent a political compromise between the environmental and development lobby groups, the Act does not necessarily constitute the end of this policy debate. It is quite likely that the gains that have been achieved by the environmental movement will be challenged in the wider arena of electoral politics, as well as through the Courts.

The environmental objectives of the Resource Management Act are primarily natural resource objectives. The Act is seen as a means of addressing externality problems and related issues. Socio-economic environmental objectives are excluded from the scope of the Act. Such a natural and physical resource bias in the Act is a consequence of the concerns motivating the environmental lobby as much as the neo-classical economic ideology that pervades official thinking. There appears to have been a retreat from the broader community development objectives implicit in the preceding statutes, such as the Town and Country Planning legislation. The needs and objectives of community development are seen as more appropriately addressed within the ambit of the annual planning provisions of local government legislation. But the extent to which this proves feasible remains to be seen. Partly on account of pressure from central government, local authorities are being forced to limit expenditure, including their investment in the urban environment, that is undertaken to promote community well-being.[21]

Despite its limited environmental objectives, the effective implementation of the Resource Management Act depends on access to adequate information by district and regional councils. The ability to identify and address the environmental effects of development, to judge the adequacy of impact reports, and to formulate performance standards and monitor their effectiveness, assumes a political commitment to allocate ratepayers' resources for this purpose. These aspects have received marginal consideration during the review process.

Finally, the public participation provisions have been considerably strengthened in the Act. Nevertheless, issues related to Maori participation, in terms of Maori ownership and management rights under the Treaty of Waitangi, are unresolved. Contrary to earlier anticipations, a role for the iwi runanga as a relatively autonomous local authority that manages its own resources has not eventuated.

6

Environmental Quango Reforms

Introduction
Quasi-autonomous non-governmental organisations (quangos) constitute the third component of environmental administration in New Zealand, and complement the roles of central and sub-national government. In broad terms, quangos may be defined as organisations established by the government which are not departments. By the 1980s, there was a range of such agencies which served the government in an advisory capacity and in some instances also performed specialised policy and management functions. Ideally, quangos can play a useful role in the policy process by devolving decision-making, promoting public participation and, more generally, providing an oversight of the activities of public agencies. But their effectiveness can be hampered by fragmented and overlapping jurisdictions, a lack of accountability and an inability to influence decision-making.

This chapter will examine the process of restructuring environmental quangos parallel to, and consequent upon, the reform initiatives discussed in the preceding chapters. The main theme which emerges in this analysis is that the quango restructuring process was driven primarily by considerations of efficiency and accountability rather than as a commitment to devolve decision-making and promote public participation. Moreover, the focus of the restructuring process was biased towards nature conservation quangos. The need for an environmental quango which provides a public platform to articulate and examine urban and socio-economic environmental issues has been suppressed.

The Antecedents to Quango Restructuring
Beginning with the OECD report in 1980, the environmental quangos were subject to a series of reviews and recommendations for restructuring during the course of the 1980s. The reforms anticipated in the earlier reviews tended to be limited in scope, with marginal changes proposed to the existing quangos. As a consequence of the radical reorganisation of the state sector in 1986, it became imperative to widen the scope of the environmental quango review. This became even more apparent when parallel reviews of local and regional government and of resource management statutes commenced in 1987.

A number of factors have prompted the proposals for the restructuring of environmental quangos. The many problems perceived included a lack of accountability to Parliament and the public, an absence of clearly defined functions, an overlap with other government bodies, effectiveness in achieving results, as well as the costs involved in supporting extra-governmental agencies. Such concerns were not necessarily limited to environmental quangos. While recognising their important role in promoting citizen involvement in the public policy process (Task Force, 1976), critics have periodically questioned the need for the large number of quangos in existence. For instance, there were an estimated 1,268 quangos in 1978, many of which were deemed unnecessary (Palmer, 1987).

Table 6.1. Environmental quangos, 1984.

---

1 Councils, Committees etc. primarily advisory, with sustained environmental interests.

Clean Air Council
Environmental Council
Fauna Protection Advisory Committee
Freshwater Fisheries Advisory Council
Nature Conservation Council
State Forest Park Advisory Committees
State Forest Scientific Reserves Advisory Committee
Toxic Substances Board

2 Councils, Committees etc. with management functions and substantial environmental interests.

Agricultural Pests Destruction Council
Beautiful New Zealand
Guardians of the Lakes
Indigenous Forest Timber Advisory Committee
Land Settlement Board
National Parks and Reserves Authority
National Water and Soil Conservation Authority
NZ Council for Recreation and Sport
NZ Forestry Council
NZ Historic Places Trust
NZ Walkways Commission
QE II National Trust

3 Councils, Committees etc. primarily advisory, with interests mainly outside the environmental area.

Advisory Committee on Women's Affairs
Energy Advisory Committee
National Research Advisory Council
NZ Maori Council
NZ Planning Council
NZ Tourism Council
Social Advisory Council

(Source: State Services Commission (1984), p.41.)

With specific reference to environmental quangos, a wide variety of government appointed councils, committees and authorities had been established by different governments to advise on an extensive range of environmental matters (Table 6.1).

The activities of these organisations tended to focus on single aspects of the environment, and their effectiveness was limited by a lack of direct input into the decision-making process. The origins of some environmental quangos may be traced as far back as the 1870s when they were created as a vehicle to assist central government in decision making, following the abolition of the provincial system of government. Hence, agencies such as the Land Boards played a useful role in helping the government to achieve its objectives of promoting settlement and development. In contrast to this, the Scenery Preservation Commission, the first nature conservation quango established at the beginning of this century under the Scenery Preservation Act 1903, sought to provide protection for scenic areas. At a regional level, acclimatisation societies for many decades played an important role in the management of recreational freshwater fisheries and of game birds.

Environmental quangos have became more prominent since the 1960s, as a general reflection of the growing public awareness of environmental values. They were also seen as a means to promote greater public involvement in the decision-making process; it was hoped they might help resolve conflicts over the allocation and management of natural resources. In this respect, the most prominent agencies have been the National Parks Authority created in 1952, the Nature Conservation Council created in 1962, the National Water and Soil Conservation Authority created in 1967, and the Environmental Council, which came into being in 1970.[1]

The National Parks Authority and the individual National Park boards were created under the National Parks Act 1952. The enabling Act made provision for the nomination of members by the Federated Mountain Clubs of New Zealand, by the Royal Forest and Bird Protection Society and by the Royal Society of New Zealand, as well as for representatives of the bureaucracy. The primary objectives of the Authority and the boards were advisory as well as executive. They were given significant executive powers since, prior to the 1970s, the Department of Lands and Survey had limited professional expertise in the management of National Parks and reserves (DoC, 1988). This situation changed with the increase of professional expertise within the Department. The National Parks Act 1980 rationalised the park management structure by according to the National Parks and Reserves Authority and the boards the role of policy formulation and the supervision of the implementation of these policies by the Department. The responsibility for the oversight of day-to-day management was transferred to the Department. This relationship was described as a partnership between, on the one hand, the Authority and the boards, largely appointed on the basis of public nomination, and the Minister and his Department on the other (National Parks and Reserves Authority, 1983).[2]

The circumstances leading to the establishment of the National Water and Soil Conservation Authority (NWASCA), the Nature Conservation Council, and the Environmental Council have been discussed in chapter 2. Comparable to the National Parks Authority, the NWASCA was given significant executive powers, but its constitution provided for formal representation by a much wider range of interests. In contrast to these two agencies, the functions of the Nature Conservation Council and the Environmental Council were primarily advisory. Appointments to these latter agencies were made on the basis of personal merit rather than of interest group representation.

The first generation of reviews on environmental administration, at the beginning of the 1980s, stressed the importance of environmental quangos in terms of the independent advice they gave, as well as their role as an educator and public critic (OECD, 1980; NCC, 1981; RFBPSNZ et.al., 1982). However, overlap between these various bodies was perceived as a particular concern. Hence, one of the recommendations of the OECD assessment of environmental administration was to re-examine the objectives of, and the relationship between, the environmental quangos, with the intention of rationalising and strengthening the framework for external advice to the government on environmental matters (OECD, 1980). Noting the need for a strong, independent, high-level source of such advice, it proposed the option of amalgamating the Nature Conservation Council and the Environmental Council. While emphasising a need for strong links with non-governmental environmental groups, it cautioned against representation by government departments on such an agency, in order to protect its independence.[3]

However, no action was taken by the National government to rationalise the environmental quangos. Given its frustration with the growing public opposition to the "Think Big" strategy, the government is unlikely to have had much sympathy with proposals to promote greater public scrutiny of its activities.

Approach of the Fourth Labour Government
The Fourth Labour government adopted a different stance, more in tune with the OECD review and the New Zealand Conservation Strategy. As part of its broader environmental strategy, it had earlier made an election commitment to rationalise the diverse and overlapping environmental quangos and to create an Environmental and Conservation Council as a single, strong source of advice. It had also proposed investigating the combination of heritage protection quangos into a New Zealand Heritage Trust (NZ Labour Party, 1984). The National Party election policies made no comparable reference to the issue of advisory agencies (NZ National Party, 1984).

A Working Party was convened by the government in 1984 to review the role of advisory councils (SSC, 1984).[4] The Working Party chose to concentrate on three of the existing agencies: the Environmental Council, the Nature Conservation Council and the Planning Council, exploring ways to strengthen these and establish links between them. While reiterating earlier concerns regarding the overlap between environmental quangos, it also raised an issue that had not hitherto been taken on board: a tendency by these agencies to emphasise the rural rather than the urban environment, and to give greater prominence to the bio-physical aspects rather than to the social, cultural and economic aspects of environmental concerns. It was critical of an implicit "environment protection" bias in the activities of advisory agencies and, in keeping with the Labour government's environmental strategy, it saw the need to widen the scope of environmental advice to consider wider policy issues relating to the sustainable utilisation of resources. It therefore recommended the formation of an agency with a broad mandate concerned with resource management issues at a policy level. It perceived the New Zealand Planning Council as the vehicle for integrating the proposed agency into a broader advisory structure, and as the means to achieve an integration of conservation with development values. The role of the proposed advisory agency was seen to complement that of the Ministry for the Environment.

While this proposal was supported by several environmental groups, there was an understandable reluctance to see the Nature Conservation Council (NCC) merged with the Environmental Council to create a new integrated body (Environment Forum Secretariat, 1985). The NCC was perceived as a valuable field-oriented watchdog, specifically concerned with nature conservation. Instead, the option of merging the NCC with the National Parks and Reserves Authority (which itself was proposed to be broadened to a National Parks and Protected Areas Commission) was deemed more acceptable. The Commission concept was mooted following the earlier 1982 proposal by the National government to merge the Lands and Survey Department and the NZFS.

The Quango Review Process

The Environment Forum did not make specific recommendations with respect to the roles of different environmental quangos. The wider implications for the future of these agencies only became apparent once the restructured departmental framework for environmental administration had been negotiated. As discussed in chapter 3, this highly controversial issue was not resolved until the end of 1985, following the recommendations of the Working Party on Environmental Administration (WPEA) (WPEA, 1985). Final decisions on the appropriate structure of advisory agencies to complement the new departmental structure were not made until during 1988 and 1989.

The WPEA report served as a policy guide to assess the role of environmental quangos within the broader central government bureaucracy. It envisaged a rationalised tier of advisory bodies, independent of government departments, as an important component of the institutional structure. The functions proposed for these advisory bodies were:

- to provide for formal community involvement in the resource management decision-making process at the national and local levels;
- to oversee and monitor the implementation of policies and plans by resource users and managers; and
- to articulate to the government the concerns and aspirations of the community (WPEA, 1985).

While emphasising community involvement at the national and regional levels in all aspects of decision-making, the WPEA report also drew particular attention to the needs of Maori people. It was deemed appropriate that the role of officials on such agencies was restricted to speaking rights only. An attempt was made to limit the management powers of quangos, concentrating instead on their functions to provide advice to Ministers, who had the final say.

Based on these considerations, the WPEA report proposed a rationalised quango structure to complement the new departmental operation. This consisted of:

(1) a Council for Environmental Quality (CEQ), associated with the Ministry for the Environment and the Parliamentary Commission for the Environment, and linked to the Planning Council through an Environmental Monitoring Group. It was tantamount to a newly strengthened Environmental Council, its principal roles being to give advice and monitor the quality of the environment;

(2) a number of other advisory bodies that would be associated with Heritage New Zealand (subsequently renamed DoC):

   i) A combined National Parks and Nature Conservation Commission (NPNCC) to replace the National Parks and Reserves Authority (NPRA) and the NCC. This organisation would oversee the policy and management responsibilities of DoC.

   ii) A Crown Estate Commission, replacing the existing Land Settlement Board, which would act as the channel through which the future use of land and other resources held under the stewardship of DoC could be considered. It would ensure that the views of the community on the future of the uncommitted Crown estate were brought to the attention of the government in an integrated form. It would also oversee the management of the uncommitted Crown estate to ensure that preservation and development interests were successfully integrated.

   iii) The Fauna Protection Advisory Council and the New Zealand Walkways Commission to remain in existence but with the possibility of being incorporated or associated with other bodies.

   iv) A body of Rangatira Kaitiaki (Resource Guardians) to be established where special circumstances were deemed to exist.

v) The Queen Elizabeth II National Trust and the Historic Places Trust to be serviced by DoC.

vi) The Minister of Internal Affairs's responsibility for Acclimatisation Societies to be transferred to the Minister of Conservation.

It was envisaged that the two proposed national environmental advisory bodies, the NPNCC and the CEC, would be supported in the regions by a regional structure, corresponding to the then existing regional bodies: the NPRA and the Land Settlement Board, which the new quangos were intended to replace.[5]

While the Cabinet in September 1985 approved the restructuring of government departments recommended by WPEA, it directed a working party of officials to report on the quangos needed to support the new departmental structure.[6]

The officials reiterated a number of the recommendations of the WPEA. Such views were articulated more coherently within the evolving pattern of state sector reforms. The changes recommended reflected the fact that, under the new departmental structure, many of the specific areas of concern addressed by existing advisory bodies would become the primary functions of either the MfE or DoC. Officials endorsed the view of the WPEA that the primary function of quangos was to provide advice to Ministers, and that they therefore should not have executive powers which would duplicate the management and decision-making responsibilities of Ministers and Departments. For reasons of public accountability, the final approval of policy was seen to rest with the Minister, as did the responsibility for any policy's operational efficiency and effectiveness. The Minister was also responsible for the funding of the Departments in implementing these policies. It was emphasised that decisions on controversial matters must be taken at the political level. This stance implied a significant change in the powers of some existing quangos.

However, the quango structure recommended by the officials departed in some respects from the WPEA proposals. Nor were officials unanimous in their recommendations. Thus, Treasury officials did not see the necessity for an advisory body on environmental policy to assist the MfE, whereas a number of other officials perceived the need for such a quango, modelled on the New Zealand Planning Council.

The relationship between the quangos and DoC was a more important area of official concern.[7] There were two schools of thought: that all "protective" or "trusteeship" quangos be under the umbrella of a parent quango organisation or, alternatively, that the existing advisory bodies be directly linked to the operation of DoC. The Labour Party's Environmental Policy for 1987 favoured the first option. It anticipated that all protected public lands would come under the guardianship of the National Parks and Reserves Authority, which would be expanded to give a greater role to the nominees of conservation and recreational organisations.

The appropriate structure to support the conservation functions of DoC was seen to comprise three types of quangos: recreation and protection quangos concerned with the lands and waters of the Crown; quangos concerned with the conservation of natural and historic resources on private property; and fish and game management quangos.

With respect to the first category, two options were proposed: a single quango – the New Zealand Conservation Commission – with a system of regional commissions; or two separate quangos, one addressing matters concerned with land and water, and another focussing on wildlife. The first option was favoured by a majority of the officials.

The second category related to conservation on private lands and involved the three existing quangos which addressed these concerns: the New Zealand Historic Places Trust, the Queen Elizabeth II National Trust, and the New Zealand Walkways Commission. Officials were once again divided in their recommendations, which ranged from making the existing bodies responsible to the Minister of Conservation, with no change to their statutory functions, to suggesting amalgamation of the Queen Elizabeth II Trust and the Walkways Commission to establish a Queen Elizabeth II Countryside Commission. The latter was the favoured option. In other respects, the officials supported the recommendations of the WPEA relating to the Crown Estate Commission, Rangatira Kaitiaki, and the retention of specialist technical or scientific advisory committees.

The future status and role of Acclimatisation Societies was also an important area of concern for the officials. The societies performed a role and exercised statutory powers under both the Wildlife Act 1953, and the Fisheries Act 1983, that were substantially different from those of other quangos.[8] In particular, they had powers to collect fees, employ staff and manage the game and fresh water fisheries within their district boundaries.

The Acclimatisation Societies were accountable to two different departments for the management and conservation of the gamebirds and freshwater fisheries within each district. The executive powers of the Societies for the management of gamebirds and freshwater fisheries were out of step with the new approaches to the management of resources owned by the Crown. They were also not in accord with the generally agreed role and powers of quangos. Even though officials were divided on the effectiveness of the Societies and their performance of their management responsibilities, they agreed on the need for the amalgamation and rationalisation of existing districts. But they were unable to reach firm conclusions on the future role and status of the Acclimatisation Societies. Three options were proposed: to transfer the executive powers of Acclimatisation Societies to DoC and make the Societies become advisory bodies within the quango structure approved by Ministers;

that the Acclimatisation Societies should continue with strengthened powers and functions for the management of gamebirds and recreational freshwater fish; or that the State Services Commission should be directed to co-ordinate a review of the Acclimatisation Society movement.

Public submissions were invited separately on the future of the Environmental Council and the conservation and heritage protection quangos (Environmental Council, 1987; DoC, 1987; DoC, 1988). Wide-ranging changes were envisaged. Even excluding Acclimatisation Societies, it was suggested that about half of the remaining 85 environmental quangos be terminated. Of those that would survive, half would be only small regional committees of the Historic Places Trust. Once again, the conservation and heritage protection quangos seemed more highly valued by the public than the Environmental Council. In some respects, the Environmental Council was perceived to have become redundant within the new environmental bureaucracy.

But even as the final decisions were being made by Cabinet on restructuring the above quangos, the scope of the review process was extended to include the quangos for noxious plants and hazardous substances, the Clean Air Council, the Toxic Substances Board and the Agricultural Pest Destruction Council. The intention was to identify the functions of these agencies which could be reassigned to government departments or delegated to regional or local government. This move was a consequence of the decisions made in December 1987 to embark on a review of local government and resource management statutes.

Policy Outcomes

The Conservation Law Reform Act 1990 has created a much more rationalised quango system that complements the role of DoC as a national conservation agency. This system is made up of three components: the New Zealand Conservation Authority, the heritage protection quangos and the fish and game councils.

The New Zealand Conservation Authority has been created as a comprehensive and integrated national conservation body, having taken over the responsibilities of a number of former special-purpose protection and recreation quangos.[9] The Authority has brought together the administrative responsibilities for seven Acts of Parliament: the National Parks, Marine Reserves, Marine Mammals Protection, Wildlife, Animal Control, Nature Conservation Council and Walkways Acts. It has been given the power to prepare and approve statements of general policy for National Parks. But in respect of all other protected areas, the Authority's function is limited to advising the Minister on statements of general policy. The Authority is also required to consider any view expressed by the Minister.

When final decisions were being made on the role and constitution of the Authority, the most controversial issue was the balance between the powers granted to the Authority and those retained by the Minister of Conservation

Figure 6.1 The Conservation Boards

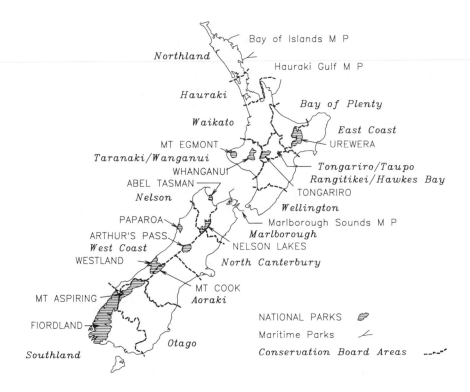

Northland

Bay of Islands M P

Hauraki Gulf M P

Hauraki

Bay of Plenty

Waikato

East Coast

MT EGMONT

UREWERA

Taranaki/Wanganui

WHANGANUI

Tongariro/Taupo

ABEL TASMAN

Rangitikei/Hawkes Bay

Nelson

TONGARIRO

Wellington

PAPAROA

Marlborough Sounds M P

ARTHUR'S PASS

Marlborough

West Coast

NELSON LAKES

WESTLAND

North Canterbury

MT COOK

MT ASPIRING

Aoraki

FIORDLAND

NATIONAL PARKS

Maritime Parks

Otago

Conservation Board Areas

Southland

and DoC. The environmental groups wanted the Authority to have wider powers so as to oversee the actions of DoC, as a means of increasing DoC's accountability to them. From their perspective, it was important to monitor the activities of DoC, which was perceived as a large, unwieldy organisation, with a monopoly on the provision of conservation services. With the support of the opposition party, some of the environmental groups advocated the alternative concept of an autonomous National Trust, as a platform for power sharing with the public, but this proved unacceptable to the government. The environmental groups also sought a wide-ranging mandate for the Authority to oversee all the policy and management activities of DoC. The government sought to limit the role of the Authority to advising the Minister on general policy rather than approving the statements of general policy.[10]

The role of the Conservation Authority is complemented by 19 regionally based Conservation Boards (Figure 6.1). Their boundaries reflect those of the DoC conservancies, with minor deviations to ensure that major protected areas lie within the jurisdiction of only one conservation board. The territorial network of the boards is expected to enable a holistic approach towards the management of all protected areas, promoting their integrity and identity. The hierarchical structure of the Conservation Authority and the regional boards complements the two-tiered resource planning system established within DoC: formulation of general policies at the national level, of conservation strategies at the regional level, and of more detailed plans for areas of special significance.[11] The conservation strategies are approved by the Authority and the plans by the Boards. To balance these powers, the Minister approves general policy (except National Park policy) after considering comments from the Authority.

It proved more difficult to rationalise the quangos related to conservation on private lands. Instead of establishing an integrated national heritage protection quango concerned with the conservation of private natural and historic resources, and comparable to the Conservation Authority, the government decided to retain the Historic Places Trust and the Queen Elizabeth II National Trust. These quangos have advisory as well as executive powers.[12] The Walkways Commission was abolished.

Finally, a new set-up for fish and game councils was created, comprising a national council and associated regional councils (Figure 6.2).

The government has refrained from setting up a separate quango to advise

Figure 6.2 The Fish and Game Councils

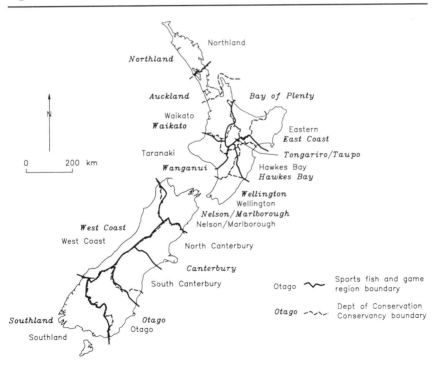

on environmental policy. The Ministry for the Environment and Treasury were opposed to the proposal for a Council for Environmental Quality, recommended earlier by WPEA. Unlike the NCC, the Environmental Council lacked a statute; it was formally disestablished in April 1988 without too much resistance.

The Cabinet decision to abolish the National Water and Soil Conservation Authority (NWASCA) was made swiftly, apparently without much deliberation, in December 1987, along with the decision to terminate the largest and most powerful of the bureaucracies, the Ministry of Works and Development. A year later, in December 1988, the Cabinet decided to abolish the Agricultural Pest Destruction Council and re-allocate its functions to regional councils. Decisions on the future of the Clean Air Council and of the advisory bodies concerned with pollution and hazardous substances have been considered as part of the process of Resource Management Law Reform. The Resource Management Act 1991 makes provision for a Hazardous Substances Control Commission, yet to be established.

The Crown Estate Commission proposal also proved to be politically unviable. Instead, a Lands Department was created to retain the Crown-owned pastoral leasehold land in a neutral department. More recently this function has been transferred to the Commissioner of Crown Lands, and the Lands Department disestablished.

Concluding Comments

Over a period of many years, special-purpose environmental advisory bodies were created by the government in response to emerging problems and needs. As a consequence, the activities of these agencies were characterised by their fragmented and somewhat overlapping jurisdictions, a lack of accountability and, in some instances, their capture by special-interest groups.

While the 1984 Labour Party election manifesto recognised many of these problems, Labour envisaged making only limited changes to rationalise the structure of the environmental quangos. The anticipated reforms were primarily directed at building closer links between the Environmental Council, the NCC and the NZPC. These anticipated reforms were by far exceeded by the comprehensive restructuring of the quangos that actually eventuated. These reforms became inevitable, initially as a consequence of the restructuring of the state sector, and then of the subsequent reform of local government and the resource management statutes. The review process was principally aimed at clarifying the accountability and status of quangos and reducing expenditure on them.

The environmental groups have also played an important role in directing the thrust of the review process. While to a large extent sympathetic to the quango review exercise and its outcomes, they may ideally have wished to see even more radical changes in the constitution of the quangos. These changes would have been based on the concept of an autonomous National

Trust whose principal function would have been to manage the large conservation estate. For the time being, this has proved to be politically unacceptable.

While the reforms have been wide-ranging, it would appear that particular attention has been concentrated on the conservation quangos associated with DoC. Comparatively, a lower priority has been accorded by the environmental groups to the need to oversee the activities of the MfE. This may be a reflection of the importance of DoC from their point of view, of its range of functions as a national heritage management agency, and of concerns relating to its accountability. Until its abolition in 1991 as a cost-saving measure, it was anticipated that the New Zealand Planning Council would carry the responsibility for the broader social, cultural and economic aspects of environmental policy, including concerns relating to the urban environment. In view of the fact that over 80 percent of New Zealanders live in urban areas, and considering the rising public concern regarding urban environmental issues such as transportation and housing, an advisory agency to provide a forum for articulating and promoting these concerns is essential. Such an organisation should be linked to the MfE and provide an impetus for the Ministry to address these issues.

7

Looking Forward

Where to From Here?

One may be accused of sensationalism by suggesting that New Zealand faces an environmental crisis. But there is no denying that, as in many other parts of the world, there are significant environmental problems in this country. While the physical and climatic attributes of New Zealand make much of it susceptible to environmental hazards such as land slips, cyclones, floods, droughts and earthquakes, the current environmental dilemma reflects, rather, the cumulative impact of human activities on the environment, both rural and urban. The origins of some problems may be traced back to the beginnings of Polynesian settlement during the pre-colonial period. Most have become exacerbated with the development of a pastoral-based export economy and of urbanisation during the course of the twentieth century. These changes increased the scale and complexity of the environment's transformation, which was seen as something essential and unavoidable in New Zealand's development. The state has played a central role in promoting many of these changes to achieve its wider political objectives and, more specifically, in acting as a major development agent in its own right. The developmental role of the state was apparent in the ideological bias towards promoting the utilisation of resources, which was always inherent in the institutional arrangements for environmental administration and planning.

This institutional framework has been radically reformed. The recent developments in environmental policy have been consistent with a remarkable and deliberate change of course in the direction of the country's development, from a highly protected economy to one open to market forces. The environmental reforms have been dominated by a libertarian doctrine based on a belief in the ability of market forces and of the public sector bureaucracy to accommodate environmental demands.

While these reforms were, to a large extent, conceived and implemented by the Labour administration during the period 1984 to 1990, they have been largely supported by the National government that succeeded it, with only relatively minor changes. It is therefore very likely that these reforms have set the context for environmental management for at least the next three to four decades. In time, one must ask questions as to the extent to which the fourth Labour administration's policies marked a significant turning-point in environmental administration and planning, from the pioneering mentality of promoting growth and utilisation of resources, to one which accommodates a growing concern for environmental quality and sustainable development. One must also ask whether these environmental and planning reforms will be as effective as anticipated. The answers to these two questions will continue to be debated for some considerable time.

A feature of the evolution of environmental administration since 1984 has been the restructuring of the authoritarian agencies that previously carried out resource management functions, to achieve a mix of commercial, conservation and environmental quality objectives. The old organisations were able to divert resources to special interest groups and ignore the external costs of resource exploitation. New organisations have now been established to achieve single-purpose objectives, more explicitly defined. One could argue that the reorganisation of the state sector has removed one of the major causes of environmental maladministration in this country. Likewise, the resource management and local government reforms have rationalised the allocation of environmental planning functions between different levels of government, and the planning procedures are more clearly orchestrated and focussed. The number of environmental quangos has been reduced and their respective jurisdictions more clearly defined. Over all, these changes complement one another. Seen within the confines of a political economy based on capitalism, they provide a better opportunity for addressing environmental problems and concerns, compared to the situation that existed prior to 1984. A more open economy, unfettered by production subsidies and import controls, will also be environmentally beneficial; for example, by lessening the use of chemicals in production and taking pressure off the need to develop marginal land.

At the same time, the deregulation of the economy and the dismantling of the welfare state have potentially exacerbated the environmental crisis in New Zealand. Recently, New Zealand has become increasingly linked to the economic systems of the countries on the Pacific rim – a trend which has been reinforced by the New Right policies of the recent Labour and National administrations. The pressures on New Zealand to be competitive within the global arena will continue to be a major constraint on its ability to pursue environmental objectives in a free-market economy. The conflicts and choices between resource utilisation options, which mean balancing the relative significance of economic growth with environmental considerations, will be as acute in the metropolitan as in the provincial and rural regions of New Zealand.

It would be foolhardy to hope that the recent environmental reforms provide the answers to the environmental dilemmas facing New Zealand. Indeed, this is far from the case. Fundamental issues and assumptions remain unquestioned, such as the merits of continuous economic growth and increasing consumption, in a predominantly individualistic society that continues to subscribe strongly to materialistic values. The recent environmental reforms are based on an optimistic world view: that a secure and competitive economic niche for New Zealand in the global system will make the task of making choices between the different options for utilising and managing resources easier, with a minimum of governmental intervention. The validity of this assumption is questionable. A comparative international advantage in the production of agricultural commodities and other natural resources may be to New Zealand's economic benefit in the short term. This is why, for instance, New Zealand is strongly in favour of the removal of barriers to international trade – a view displayed in its continuing concern about the GATT negotiations. But, from a longer term perspective, the current economic activities – and the lifestyles dependent on them – may not be sustainable.

While the recent environmental reforms have been innovative, it is important to recognise that the fourth Labour government's approach towards environmental restructuring in New Zealand has been instrumental rather than normative. The restructuring has been primarily concerned with the organisational considerations and decision-making procedures for managing resources, its objectives based on the New Right ideology. The resource management law reform process has been guided by procedural concerns whose scope has been limited to reducing the detrimental impacts of human activities; incidentally, it has also been concerned with conflict resolution through greater public participation and mediation. Because of the ideological premises on which the environmental administration and planning legislation are based, there may be limitations in their ability to promote sustainable development objectives. Attempts to improve organisational and statutory decision-making processes can go some way towards promoting appropriate resource utilisation policies. But it can be argued that those pre-occupied with such matters run the risk of ignoring the more fundamental questions relating to the causes of environmental problems: the political and economic context of decision-making about resource allocation. The existing social structures and relationships, based on the tenets of private property ownership, have been perpetuated and reinforced through a continuing belief in the virtues of privatisation; this process has led inexorably to a dismantling of the public estate. Public intervention is sanctioned, as in the past, only to minimise the undesirable downstream consequences of individual and corporate decision-making.

The fundamental issues relating to the causes of environmental problems and conflicts have been ignored or played down. From an environmental perspective, the gains that have been made are limited and the dilemma of integrating conservation values with economic growth is far from resolved. The extent to which the sustainable development ethic can be achieved within the paradigm that has guided the recent environmental reforms will be limited primarily to functional considerations such as minimising adverse impacts.

Achieving the sustainable development of resource-based activities in New Zealand, such as agriculture, tourism, forestry and manufacturing, is a much bigger challenge. This demands a critical examination of the existing activities and practices from a bio-physical as well as a social and economic perspective. A more responsive and democratic approach towards sustainability is predicated on a significant realignment of the direction of development in New Zealand.

This can be achieved through a progressive transformation to technologies that facilitate equitable economic growth while reducing environmental pressures. Growth is necessary to meet basic human needs. It should be based on an agricultural sector which requires the low use of commercial fertilisers, pesticides and energy. Emphasis needs to be placed on the importance of the longer-term health of the supporting ecological and social systems which help to maintain a viable rural sector. Much broader criteria than those based upon economics and the "user pays" principle are needed to promote sustainable agriculture (Dahlberg, 1990). As part of a national environmental strategy, it may be necessary to re-allocate land and other resources away from their present uses in situations where these are not sustainable.

Industry and transportation should be transformed from materials-intensive, high-throughput processes to those that rely on raw materials with low environmental costs, use materials with greater efficiency, generate little waste and recycle residues. Long-term integrated planning is needed to achieve this kind of sustainability. A better scientific and social understanding is necessary of the processes of environmental change and methods of resource use appropriate to New Zealand.

Greater community control could be achieved through the devolution of power and decision-making to localities including iwi and hapu groups. The planning system should enable local and regional communities to aspire towards the above normative goals and objectives, as well as to anticipate and manage the environmental effects of economic growth.

Changes in our lifestyles should preferably proceed concurrently with technological shifts. This requires a critical re-examination of the cultural underpinnings of current western lifestyles, a movement towards less materialism and individualism, and an acceptance of the "virtue of enoughness" (Sachs, 1989). It is important also to recognise that environmental issues in New Zealand are inextricably linked with those in the rest of the world. Environmental problems are a major global concern. It is also clear that solutions to global environmental threats such as atmospheric warming and air pollution cannot be adequately addressed without satisfying the basic needs of the less privileged inhabitants of the earth.

The environmental administration and planning reforms discussed in this book have been ambitious in conception and achievement. It would be surprising if similar reforms could be achieved in other western countries with comparable ease. This may be a reflection of a number of factors, including the relatively small size of New Zealand, the simplicity of its political system, and the absence of strongly vested political and economic interests on a scale comparable to countries such as the United Kingdom, Canada or Australia.

Accepting that we live in an imperfect world, the post-1984 reform initiatives should not be dismissed as merely symbolic or placebo policies. But, I shall argue, the current institutional structure is constrained in significant respects.

The Ministry for the Environment

The fundamental challenge for the Ministry for the Environment (MfE) is to ensure that functional economic considerations do not override environmental objectives in the public policy process. During the time since its creation, the Ministry has been relatively more successful than the Department of Conservation in establishing a role for itself within the central government bureaucracy. Having successfully accomplished the task of reforming resource management statutes, it has developed policy proposals relating to hazardous substances, pollution control and waste management, and to global environmental issues including the Antarctic, climate change and ozone depletion. In view of the increasing domestic and global significance of the environment as a social concern, the Ministry can expect to be accorded considerable status within the public sector's decision-making process in its role as a control agency, akin to Treasury and the State Services Commission. But the stance that has been adopted by the MfE as a participant in this process is open to question.

A degree of ambiguity which is inherent in the Ministry's role may constrain its effectiveness. This is a reflection of the conflicting forces which have influenced the constitution of the Ministry within the confines of the Environment Act 1986. The source of the difficulty arises from a potential conflict between the environmental advocacy role of the Ministry and its role in integrating conservation and development. As I pointed out earlier, the MfE has adopted the concept of neutrality as the *modus operandi* for its activities: a position that enables it (as the "Ministry in the middle") to balance the values of others in relation to the environment and the use of natural resources. The Ministry has adopted this accommodating stance primarily in view of the concerns of the development lobby. Developers did not wish to see the planning functions undertaken by an apparently environmentally oriented Ministry. Consequently, the MfE has tended to place greater emphasis on the procedural aspects of decision-making rather than act as a strong advocate of the substantive environmental objective of sustainable development.

One may argue that the Ministry's stance is not congruent with a proper interpretation of the Environment Act, nor does it constitute the basis for sufficient action to promote sustainable development. The Act requires the MfE to implement the Act by ensuring that in the management of natural and physical resources, full and balanced account is taken of:
i)   the intrinsic values of ecosystems; and
ii) all values which are placed by individuals and groups on the quality of the environment; and
iii) the principles of the Treaty of Waitangi; and

iv) the sustainability of natural and physical resources; and

v) the needs of future generations.

The above objectives, encompassed in the long title to the Act, are capable of variable interpretation in terms of their inter-relationship and relative ranking. Nevertheless, seen as the expression of the fundamental principles of a national environmental policy, these substantive and procedural objectives are expected to guide the Ministry when it is assessing and advising the Cabinet on policies and programmes relating to the management of natural and physical resources. This should enable the Cabinet to be the final arbiter of the often contrasting values put by different groups on the environment.

An equally important concern about the MfE as a participant in the public policy process, is its apparently limited ability to address environmental issues associated with changes such as new technology or disinvestment, or with changes in the provision of community services such as health and housing. Social concerns generally seem to have been downgraded in importance by central government, and the Ministry has been forced into a much narrower role than envisaged earlier in 1984. The mandate of the MfE under the Environment Act is limited to assessing the social impacts of only resource-use proposals. The Act also implies that the solutions to all environmental problems must lie in the intelligent management of natural and physical resources. This constitutes a limited and selective perception of, and response to, environmental problems. It reflects the neoclassical economic paradigm and the particular interests of the environmental groups which have governed the formulation of the Act.

The MfE should accord social goals equal status with predominantly biophysical goals. It should do this by assessing the impacts on communities of departmental policies and programmes, and co-ordinate strategies for mitigating the adverse effects of such policies on community wellbeing. There is no central government agency currently charged with these tasks. The MfE has so far distanced itself from such a role.

The MfE should have the mandate to advise the government on all aspects of the development process from a broad environmental perspective. The formulation of a national environmental strategy could provide the basis for a more comprehensive approach towards the environment by the MfE than has been possible hitherto. The Ministry should develop the capability to bring social, economic and ecological factors together into a common analytical framework, with sustainable development as the normative basis for an environmental strategy. This would enable the MfE to exercise its control function more effectively, as a counterweight to Treasury. One may argue from a pragmatic stance that an accumulation of specific environmental policies developed by the MfE incrementally over a number of years could be collectively described as a national strategy, but the drawback of this approach is that it is partial in its scope.

A national environmental strategy should have a strong regional dimension; its formulation and implementation should be predicated upon a responsive structure of strong multifunctional regional and local authorities. The MfE should act in partnership with regional and territorial government, community organisations, pressure groups and the corporate sector, in exploring issues and setting priorities.

The Department of Conservation

From an environmental perspective, the formation of the Department of Conservation (DoC) has been a major achievement, consolidating the management of all the heritage resources under one umbrella. DoC administers nearly 30 percent of New Zealand's land area, some 8 million hectares, almost half of it formally protected as reserves or National Parks. The Conservation Act 1987 gives DoC a statutory conservation management and advocacy role such as has never been allowed for in the history of public administration in New Zealand.

But in many respects, DoC has had a more difficult task establishing itself than the other two recently created central government environmental agencies. The difficulty can be attributed to a number of different factors. In the initial years of its operation, DoC experienced major hurdles in developing a unified structure and philosophy, for it brought together a wide range of conservation activities and people with different experiences and values. DoC was staffed almost entirely from the pre-existing departments, including the Department of Lands and Survey, the Forest Service and the Wildlife Service, which generally followed different ethics in relation to natural resource management. Internal frictions amongst inherited staff from departments that traditionally were competitive (especially Lands and the Forest Service) has taken longer to resolve than may have been expected when DoC was created.

Partly as a reflection of such difficulties, the Department was reorganised three times between 1987 and 1991 and had four directors-general within the same period. Its problems have raised fundamental questions about whether there is any coherent view about the appropriate role for DoC.

The problems facing DoC also stem from the influence of two different sources of pressure for environmental reorganisation, which only coincided prior to the new department's creation in April 1987: the environmentalists and Treasury. Since then, the objectives of the two groups with respect to DoC have differed, which in turn has made it difficult for the department to set priorities. DoC has been hampered by budgetary constraints, being given a cost recovery target of 20 percent of its expenditure to be achieved by 1991. However, its sources of potential revenue are limited. The need to earn an increasing proportion of its annual budget from its own resources has caused public resentment amongst some recreational user groups, especially over considerably increased hut fees and a range of other charges. The continual reduction of its staff and funding have not improved the department's ability to deal effectively with some of its major responsibilities, such as controlling possums and weeds.

More importantly, the funding constraints have put pressure on DoC to be less restrictive towards tourism development, commercial concessions and other uses of resources on public lands. In the face of such pressures from developers, DoC has sought to adopt a strong conservation stance for which it has been criticised, even though this is consistent with the enabling Act. Until now DoC has placed an overriding importance on "conservation" purposes, as defined in the Act, in relation to permitting other uses of Crown land. Continual cost-cutting may compromise the government's commitment to establish a strong conservation agency. Evidently, the initial expectations that led to the creation of the department are too ambitious in the present economic climate.

In view of the considerable pressure on DoC to be self-funding, conservation and recreational groups are keen to improve DoC's accountability to environmental interests, and for DoC to give pre-eminence to protection values. For this reason, the concept of a nature conservation trust, as an alternative to DoC, may have a considerable measure of support amongst them. However, it is not clear how such a non-profit organisation could relieve the financial burden on the public sector, in the absence of alternative sources of funding. Privatisation is a further alternative that had been mooted, but this is not likely to receive public support.

The Parliamentary Commissioner for the Environment

The appointment in 1987 of Helen Hughes as the Parliamentary Commissioner for the Environment (PCE) in New Zealand was unique. No other country with a Westminster system of government has a comparable officer who is an appointee of Parliament. In theory, the Parliamentary Commissioner serves as a check on the executive branch of the government. Potentially, this is an important appointment because New Zealand does not have a second chamber.

It is appropriate to describe the current activities of the PCE in terms of two roles: as an environmental auditor, and as an ombudsman. During the last few years, the latter task has come to be accorded greater prominence even though it is only an advisory function. Nevertheless it gives the office a higher public profile and enables the Commissioner to exercise subtle pressure.

Prior to its establishment, and as recently as 1986, the principal rationale for the position of the PCE was perceived in terms of its proposed environmental audit function. But this has not materialised to the extent envisaged earlier, for two main reasons. Initially, in 1984, it was expected that the PCE would have a major role in auditing impact reports relating to the proposed policies and programmes of central government. The corporatisation of the state sector has reduced that particular requirement. The Commissioner is also disadvantaged in terms of not being made aware of proposed policies and programmes early enough to exercise meaningful influence. This is because the position is not part of the executive branch of government. Consequently, the Commissioner has audited very few impact reports during the last few years.

The Commissioner has also been denied a direct role as an actor in the statutory decision-making process in local and regional planning under the Resource Management Act. During the resource management review process of 1988-89, the Commissioner was understandably cautious about proposals to devolve the primary responsibility for environmental impact assessment to the regional councils. With the support of the environmental lobby groups, she advocated a role for the Commissioner in assessing the impact of major projects. In particular, she argued that there was a strong public perception that the Commissioner had an important role in reviewing the impact assessment reports prepared by proponents.

In the absence of such a role, there has been a deliberate shift in emphasis by the Commissioner towards the functions of adviser and information provider, to assist district and regional councils to prepare and audit impact reports. However, in this respect, the relative responsibilities of the PCE and regional MfE staff are unclear, because the MfE also expect to give advice on impact assessment. Given the enabling provisions of the Environment Act, the Parliamentary Commissioner anticipates a wider, proactive role in monitoring the effectiveness of the environmental planning and management functions of local government. This would entail combining an ombudsman function with an auditing role.

The office of the PCE is relatively small. The range of issues that have been investigated by Helen Hughes during the last few years include the environmental implications of the Treaty of Waitangi, the introduction of the myxomatosis virus, urban motorway proposals, sewage treatment and the effectiveness of unitary authorities. With limited resources and no regional offices, there is considerable pressure to ensure sensitivity to regional concerns. While one should not underestimate the potential significance of the position, there is uncertainty concerning the possible overlap of its functions with the MfE, with respect to monitoring the state of the environment and assessing the performance of central and local government in delivering environmentally sound outcomes.

Environmental Quangos
The environmental quangos' success in forming a sound partnership between the public and the government will depend on a number of factors. The quangos are reliant on the government departments they are associated with (primarily DoC) for funding and staff support for research investigations. In order not to compromise their independence, the challenge for the quangos is to avoid becoming an appendage of DoC.

A reduction in the number of environmental quangos has been achieved through the amalgamation and rationalisation of functions, a move generally perceived as desirable. However, a consequence of this has been an increased workload for some quangos. In particular, the New Zealand Conservation Authority's functions are wide-ranging, and there may be a possible loss of emphasis and attention to matters of detail. The quality of the quangos' membership will be an important factor in this respect.

The new framework of environmental quangos represents a compromise for the environmentalists. During the initial stages of the reform process they advocated a nature conservancy, equivalent to a public membership organisation with boards elected nationally and regionally, because a conservancy would be directly accountable to them. This was conceived as an alternative to a heritage ministry or department, which is only accountable through the election process. The conservancy model did not prove politically tenable and the decision was made in 1987 to establish DoC. In order to increase DoC's accountability to existing conservation and recreation organisations, the National Conservation Authority has been given powers to oversee the activities of DoC. However, following the recent abolition of the New Zealand Planning Council, there is no equivalent quango associated with the MfE concerned with the social dimension of environmental concerns, such as making cities more liveable. There is a manifest need for a broadly based environmental quango to provide a public forum for, and advise the MfE on, social and cultural issues associated with everyday urban life.

In its time, the Planning Council was also expected to play a wider role in monitoring and evaluating the outcomes of the environmental administration restructuring process (NZPC, 1989). One could argue that in a sense that kind of evaluation is done politically every three years at election time, but there remains a need for more formal monitoring and assessment.

Regional and District Councils

The economic and political environment within which local government operates in New Zealand, as well as the functions of local government itself, have been the subject of fundamental changes initiated by central government. Until 1987, the local government interest groups had been very successful in circumventing significant changes in the organisation and activities of local government. But the situation has changed radically as a consequence of events since 1987. Moreover, in contrast to many previous initiatives, the reforms are not limited to changing geographical boundaries but encompass wide-ranging, interrelated issues, including the structure, functions, organisation, finance and accountability of local government.

The recent policies for restructuring local government have emanated from two complementary directions. The map of New Zealand local government has been radically redrawn as a process of reforms that culminated in the establishment of district and regional councils. The Local Government Amendment Act (No.3) 1988 created this new framework of sub-national government and allocated important resource planning functions to it. Complementing this, the parallel review of resource management statutes and the enactment of the Resource Management Act 1991 has spelt out more precisely the nature of these functions and how they are to be administered within the wider inter-governmental context. The new institutional arrangements for environmental administration and planning at the local and regional level have brought about marked improvements. When seen within the broader historical context of previous attempts to reform local government and planning, one cannot underestimate the significance of these achievements. Nevertheless, the extent to which this structure is conceptually sound and workable is still questionable.

The potential effectiveness of the local government reform process has been compromised by the ad hoc and disjointed manner in which a number of important policies were formulated and implemented. In particular, reforms relating to the constitution of regional councils within the wider sub-national governmental context have not been particularly well conceived and implemented because of the absence of adequate political direction, research and consultation. Some related issues, such as the questions of Maori self-government and resource ownership, and the relationship of these to the policy issues discussed above, have proved to be too sensitive to address with any success. Yet these questions have important constitutional as well as practical implications for the institutional arrangements for sub-national government and its role in environmental planning.

Environmental planning is one of the major functions delegated to regional and district councils under the Resource Management Act 1991. Generally speaking, it is a more logical and coherent planning statute than its predecessors. However, this Act only partially addresses the need for environmental planning. Its essential concern is with property rights in relation to natural and physical resources, and the conditions under which these are to be exercised. The Act has reinforced the traditional New Zealand values of private property ownership. Environmental planning is seen as being essentially market led, where collective decisions are taken only to cope with the impact of private decisions.

The powers conferred on regional and district councils basically seek to achieve instrumental rationality in the management of the environment. These local bodies are not expected to promote normative goals and objectives, based on policies for utilisation of land, water and other resources, in their regions and districts. The allocation of such resources, and the related task of weighing competing uses (such as between power production and irrigation from a scarce water resource), are deemed to be achieved more efficiently in the market place. Public intervention in making such decisions is seen as generating economic inefficiencies. Such a planning set-up is a reflection of the wider conservative political and theoretical context within which the Act has been formulated.

Moreover, the environmental concerns that have risen to the top of the political agenda since 1984, and which are reflected in the Act, relate to the well-being of the bio-physical environment. Social planning concerns such as the provision of adequate housing, recreational facilities and access to services have been downgraded in importance. It needs to be emphasised that, in addition to addressing resource externality issues, environmental planning should also respond to community development needs and aspirations, and exercise a local and regional advocacy role. A strategic environmental planning function is necessary at the district and regional level in view of the rapid change that is characteristic of many communities, and which will intensify in the future. It should seek to anticipate such changes and identify and assess the opportunities for responding to them.

The strategic planning function has been omitted from the Resource Management Act on the assumption that this is more appropriately undertaken within the ambit of the annual planning provisions in the local government legislation, for example, by influencing policies on the delivery of health, housing and public transport services provided by public agencies. But the extent of such involvement is left to the discretion of individual local authorities in an environment of severe budget austerity. Moreover, as a consequence of corporatisation and privatisation, there is no obligation on the service delivery agencies to promote public participation in decision-making or to assess the local social and economic implications of their decisions.

Even within the limited context of managing natural and physical resources, the effectiveness of the Resource Management Act is by no means assured. As I intimated in chapter 5, considerable litigation challenging the Act's fundamental tenets can be expected in the future. The Act is also vulnerable to political pressure from development lobby groups who perceive, rightly or wrongly, that too much power has been given to local government to intervene, and that the views of the "free market" advocates were not accorded sufficient recognition in framing the legislation.

It is not altogether clear how effective the regional councils can be, given the political and financial constraints under which they will have to operate. Central government may have conveniently delegated tasks which are too demanding in terms of resources and capability. Given the high rates of unemployment in the provinces, regional councillors may find themselves under pressure from development lobby groups to adopt permissive environmental policies and standards.

The Maori Concerns
The considerations related to the Treaty of Waitangi have been a significant common thread in the formulation and implementation of the environmental administration and planning reforms examined in this book. The Maori have been a major stakeholder in the outcome of these reforms. From their particular perspective, the control of the ownership and management of increas-

ingly scarce resources, including land, air, water, geothermal energy, minerals and fisheries, has been at the heart of the recent debates and decisions regarding how such resources should be managed. The Treaty of Waitangi guaranteed to the Maori ownership of these resources and, by implication, a major say in their management.

The existence of the Waitangi Tribunal and, more particularly, the fact that its powers were widened by the fourth Labour government to consider claims dating from the signing of the Treaty of Waitangi in 1840, is a major reason why the Maori have been able to function as a significant pressure group. Moreover, claims brought by the Maori groups under the Treaty of Waitangi Act during the last decade have enabled a fledgling, and at times uneasy, alliance of Maori and environmental interests to emerge.

State sector restructuring posed a major threat to Maori interests because the state sought to devolve the ownership as well as management of natural resources. The Maori were forced to secure, through judicial channels, legislative safeguards to protect those iwi affected by the corporatisation and privatisation of government assets such as land and forests. The resource management and local government reform initiatives were likewise not successful in traversing wider constitutional issues relating to Maori ownership rights. Hence, the scope of the local government and resource management statutes is limited to recognising Maori values and increasing Maori participation in decision-making, within the workings of the new institutional arrangements. Proposed reforms to empower iwi authorities and increase iwi participation in local government decision-making have been abandoned. From the Maori perspective, this outcome may be expected to be regarded as only partially satisfactory, since the ownership and participation issues are closely intertwined.

The significance for the Maori of the environmental and local government reforms has been overshadowed by more recent events relating to the negotiations between the government and the Maori on fishery claims. However, a fundamental question that still needs to be addressed with respect to these reforms is the incorporation within central and local government decision-making of Maori cultural, spiritual and traditional beliefs related to the environment. It has been a dominant theme of the Waitangi Tribunal that what is needed is not an incorporation in the environmental legislation of Maori values and Treaty rights by reference only, but that these values and rights should permeate the laws, institutions and practices of New Zealand environmental administration and planning.

Appendix 1

Environment, Land Resources, Local Government & Maori Affairs Cabinet Portfolios 1984-1991

Lange Ministry 26.7.1984–24.8.1987
Hon. K.T. Wetere   Minister of Maori Affairs; Minister of Lands; Minister of Forests
Hon. Russell Marshall   Minister for the Environment (until 19.2.86); Minister for Conservation (19.2.86–24.8.87)
Hon. Dr. Michael Bassett   Minister of Local Government
Hon. R.J. Tizard   Minister of Energy
Hon. Fraser Colman   Minister of Works and Development
Hon. P.B. Goff   Minister for the Environment (19.2.86–24.8.87)
Hon. David Caygill   Minister of National Development

Changes consequent upon establishment of new State-owned Enterprises on 1 April 1987: K.T. Wetere ceased being Minister of Forests and Minister of Lands. He was appointed Minister of Forestry and Minister of Survey and Land Information and assumed responsibilities for Land Corporation and New Zealand Forestry Corporation. R.J. Tizard assumed responsibility for Electricity Corporation and Coal Corporation.

Lange Ministry 24.8.1987–14.8.1989.
Rt. Hon. David Lange   Minister for State-owned Enterprises (4.11.88–8.11.88)
Rt. Hon. G.W.R. Palmer   Minister for the Environment
Hon. Richard Prebble   Minister for State-owned Enterprises (until 4.11.88); Minister of Works and Development (until 5.11.88). Responsibility for Coal Corporation; Electricity Corporation; Land Corporation; NZ Forestry Corporation*
Hon. K.T. Wetere   Minister of Maori Affairs
Hon. Dr. M.E.R. Bassett   Minister of Local Government
Hon. Stan Rodger   Minister of State-owned Enterprises (8.11.88–14.8.89)
Hon. Peter Tapsell   Minister of Forestry; Minister of Lands; Minister of Survey & Land Information
Hon. Helen Clark   Minister of Conservation (until 30.1.89)
Hon. David Butcher   Minister of Energy
Hon. P.T.E. Woollaston   Minister of Conservation (30.1.89–14.8.89)
Hon. W.P. Jeffries   Minister of Works and Development (8.11.88–14.8.89)

Ministers Not in Cabinet:
Hon. Fran Wilde   Associate Minister of Conservation (until 8.11.88)
Hon. P.T.E. Woollaston   Minister Assisting the Deputy Prime Minister Rt. Hon. G.W.R. Palmer; Associate Minister for the Environment; Associate Minister of Conservation (until 30.1.89)

* On 4 November 1988 Mr. Prebble was dismissed and his responsibilities for State-owned Enterprises assumed by Mr. Lange until 8 November and appointment of Mr. Rodger.

Hon. Peter Neilson   Associate Minister for State-owned Enterprises; Associate Minister of Works and Development.
Hon W.P. Jeffries   Associate Minister for State-owned Enterprises (4.7.88–14.8.89)

Palmer/Moore Ministry 14.8.1989–2.11.90
Rt. Hon. Geoffrey   Palmer Minister for the Environment
Hon. Stan Rodger   Minister for State-owned Enterprises (until 9.2.90)
Hon. K.T.Wetere   Minister of Maori Affairs; Minister in Charge of Iwi Transition Authority
Hon. Dr. Michael Bassett   Minister of Local Government (until 9.2.90)
Hon. Peter Tapsell   Minister of Forestry (until 9.2.90); Minister of Lands; Minister of Survey and Land Information.
Hon. David Butcher   Minister of Energy
Hon. J.R. Sutton   Minister of Forestry (9.2.90–2.11.90)
Hon. Richard Prebble   Minister for State-owned Enterprises (9.2.90–2.11.90)

Ministers Not in Cabinet
Hon. Philip Woollaston   Minister of Conservation; Minister Assisting the Prime Minister (until 9.2.90); Minister of Local Government (9.2.90–2.11.90)
Hon. Peter Neilson   Minister of Works and Development; Associate Minister for State-owned Enterprises
Hon. P.F. Dunne   Associate Minister for the Environment (9.2.90–2.11.90)
Hon. Clive Matthewson   Minister for Energy (9.2.90–2.11.90); Associate Minister for State-owned Enterprises (9.3.9–2.11.90)
Hon. K. Shirley   Associate Minister of Forestry (9.2.90–211.90)

In addition: Mr. Rodger had responsibility for Coal Corporation of NZ Ltd., Electricity Corporation of NZ Ltd., Land Corporation Ltd. and NZ Forestry Corporation Ltd. until 9.2.90 when he was replaced by Mr. Prebble.

Bolger Ministry 2.11.90–
Hon. John Falloon   Minister of Forestry
Hon. Doug Kidd   Minister for State-owned Enterprises (until 3.10.91); Minister of Works and Development; Minister in Charge of the Iwi Transition Agency (2.10.91 onwards); Minister of Maori Affairs (2.10.91 onwards)
Hon. Simon Upton   Minister for the Environment (until 3.10.91)
Hon. Warren Cooper   Minister of Local Government
Hon. Rob Storey   Minister of Lands; Minister of Survey and Land Information; Minister for the Environment (3.10.91 onwards)
Hon. Winston Peters   Minister of Maori Affairs (until 2.10.91); Minister in Charge of the Iwi Transition Agency (until 2.10.91)
Hon. Denis Marshall   Minister of Conservation
Hon. John Luxton   Minister of Energy
Hon. M. McTigue   Minister for State-owned Enterprises (3.10.91 onwards): Minister for Works and Development (3.10.91 onwards)

In addition:
Mr. Kidd was responsible for Coal Corporation of NZ Ltd., Electricity Corporation of NZ Ltd., Land Corporation Ltd. and NZ Forestry Corporation.

Source:
Wood, G.A. (ed.) *Ministers and Members in the New Zealand Parliament. Part 1: NZ Ministries 1912-1987.* Dunedin, Tarkwode Press, 1987.
Wood, G.A. (ed.) *Supplement to Ministers and Members in the New Zealand Parliament. NZ Ministries 1987-1991.* Dunedin, Tarkwode Press, 1992.

Appendix 2

Sustainable management as defined in the Resource Management Act 1991:

5. Purpose–(1)The purpose of this Act is to promote the sustainable management of natural and physical resources.

(2) In this Act, "sustainable management" means managing the use, development, and protection of natural and physical resources in a way, or at a rate, which enables people and communities to provide for their social, economic, and cultural wellbeing and for their health and safety while –

(a) Sustaining the potential of natural and physical resources (excluding minerals) to meet the reasonably foreseeable needs of future generations; and

(b) Safeguarding the life-supporting capacity of air, water, soil, and ecosystems; and

(c) Avoiding, remedying, or mitigating any adverse effects of activities on the environment.

Source: Resource Management Act 1991, Section 5.

Notes

Chapter 2

1. From the beginning of New Zealand as a British colony, the ownership and use of land were closely controlled by the government. The area of land vested in the Crown in 1960 was well over 50 percent of New Zealand's total land area but the proportion was much higher for the South Island than the North Island. The area of land held under freehold title was 32.3 percent.

2. For example, in 1966/67, the Forest Service administered state forests covering 9,929,185 acres, or 15 percent of the total land area of New Zealand; the Lands and Survey Department was responsible for land development and farming on a total of 1,839,500 acres; $91.4 million were spent on electricity development and $70.6 million on roading; a chain of thirteen hotels was operated by the Tourist Hotel Corporation, and the Ministry of Works employed 572 professional engineers and 192 architects on a wide range of projects. The State employed about one in every five members of the labour force. It was by far the largest employer, and collectively the largest business concern in the country (Cleveland, 1972a).

3. Extensive state intervention in the New Zealand economy to promote public welfare dates back to the latter half of the nineteenth century, with the social experiments of the Liberal government which came to power in 1891. These early ventures in public enterprise have been described as "experiments in state socialism" because public enterprises were set up to counteract private sector monopolies, to provide competition and to protect the public interest. A subsequent major advance to the role of the state came with the election of the Labour government in 1935. It laid the foundations for the "welfare state" through policies such as a comprehensive social security system and state housing programmes (Jackson, 1988; Mascarenhas, 1982).

4. For example: Agricultural Pests Destruction Act 1967; Clean Air Act 1972; Coal Mines Act 1979; Electricity Act 1968; Geothermal Energy Act 1953; Harbours Act 1950; Housing Corporation Act 1974; Marine Farming Act 1971; Marine Pollution Act 1974; Toxic Substances Act 1979; Wildlife Act 1953.

5. The Ministry of Works became the Ministry of Works and Development in 1973, following the review of the Public Works Act 1928. The change in name was a recognition of the responsibility of the Ministry for development planning in relation to public works. The Town and Country Planning Branch became the Town and Country Planning Division in 1971. Planning was accorded higher status in the Ministry and the Chief Town Planner became the Director of Town and Country Planning. Following the reorganisation of the Ministry in 1983, the Town and Country Planning and the Water and Soil Divisions became Directorates.

6. The Authority comprised representatives of central government departments, territorial and ad hoc local bodies and user interest groups such as the Federated Farmers and the Dairy Board. It operated through two subsidiary councils: the Water Resources Council and the Soil Conservation and Rivers Control Council.

7. For instance, with increasing pressure from recreational and environmental lobby groups, the wild and scenic rivers amendment to the Water and Soil Conservation Act was introduced in 1981. It caused considerable friction between interest groups because of the

difficulty in interpreting the law and the narrow definition of water bodies, which did not include all wetlands.

8. Sponsored by the National Development Council, the Physical Environment Conference was described as "probably the most influential and prestigious gathering of its kind ever held in New Zealand". (O'Riordan, 1971, p.203). It included over 280 participants comprising academics, professionals, government officials and politicians.

9. The models of a single central government agency with overall administrative authority, such as the English Department of Environment, or a single agency with a specific environmental protection role, such as the United States's Environmental Protection Agency, were rejected.

10. In 1973, contrary to widespread opposition from officials, the Cabinet decided that all Environmental Impact Reports (EIRs) be made public before a decision is made. A second wave of pressure on the Commission for the Environment came in 1980, after it produced a critical audit of one of the first Think Big projects to face an environmental audit. The Prime Minister Rt. Hon. Robert Muldoon instigated a review of the role of the Commission, with a view to restricting it from commenting on social and economic aspects of projects, or on whether or not a project should proceed. The National Development Act was amended accordingly.

11. Between 1970 and 1988, the average energy intensity worldwide fell by 24 percent, while in New Zealand it rose by 31 percent. Of the OECD countries, only Turkey was a worse performer.

Chapter 3

1. The complementary framework of advisory councils associated with the new government departments is examined in Chapter 6.

2. These are:

a) The maintenance and restoration of ecosystems of importance, especially those supporting habitats or rare, threatened, or endangered species of flora or fauna;

b) Areas, landscapes, and structures of aesthetic, archaeological, cultural, historical, recreational, scenic, and scientific value;

c) Any land, water, sites, fishing grounds, or physical or cultural resources or interests associated with such areas, which are part of the heritage of the tangata whenua and which contribute to their well-being;

d) The effects on communities of people of -

(i) Actual or proposed changes to natural and physical resources;

(ii) The establishment or proposed establishment of new communities;

e) Whether any proposals, policies, or other matters, the consideration of which is within the Commissioner's functions, are likely to -

(i) Result in or increase pollution; or

(ii) Result in the occurrence, or increase the chances of occurrence, of natural hazards or hazardous substances; or

(iii) Result in the introduction of species or genotypes not previously present within New Zealand (including the territorial sea); or

(iv) Have features, the environmental effects of which are not certain, and the potential impact of which is such to warrant further investigation in order to determine the environmental impact of the proposal, policy, or other matter; or

(v) Result in the allocation or depletion of any natural or physical resources in such a way or at a rate that will prevent the renewal by natural processes of the resources or will not enable an orderly transition to other materials;

f) All reasonably foreseeable effects of any such proposal, policy, or other matter on the environment, whether adverse or beneficial, short term or long term, direct or indirect, or cumulative;

g) Alternative means or methods of implementing or providing for any such proposal, policy, or matter in all or any of its aspects, including the consideration, where appropriate, of alternative sites. [Environment Act, 1986, Section 17(a) to (g)]

3. The only other ministry charged with a comparable responsibility is the Ministry for Maori Affairs.

4. For instance, the authors were careful not to criticise the National government's "Think Big" strategy.

5. For instance, an attempt in 1983 by the Commission for Environment to gain statutory recognition under an Act of Parliament was aborted by other government departments weary of the Commission's auditing role (Gresham, 1983).

6. The environmental lobby comprised five main groups: the Royal Forest and Bird Protection Society, the Federation of Mountain Clubs of New Zealand, the Native Forest Action Council, the Environmental Defence Society, and the Environment and Conservation Organisations of New Zealand.

7. For example, the review of the 1953 Town and Country Planning Act, which commenced in 1972 under a Labour government but was enacted in 1977 by a National government, reflected, to a very large degree, an acceptance of the recommendations of professional advisers.

8. The manifesto was ambiguous with respect to the composition of the nature conservation function. It did not make clear whether the intention was, in fact, to separate the production functions from protection functions and, if so, how the production functions were to be administered.

9. The State Services Commission identified 21 departments as having a direct interest in environmental and planning issues. The Task Group comprised the Commissioner for the Environment, and officials of the Ministry of Works, the Environmental Council and the Department of Lands and Survey and was chaired by the State Services Commissioner.

10. Thus, it did not recommend, as a high priority, the administrative rationalisation of protected recreation and conservation areas in relation to the production functions of the Forestry and the Lands and Survey agencies, and for this reason did not adequately examine this particular issue.

11. The Ministry of Works and Development was the agency expected to be affected most immediately by the recommendation to transfer the town and country planning function to the proposed environment ministry. Hence, while supporting the concept of an environment ministry, it expressed strong opposition to the proposed transfer.

12. This implied a ministry responsible for the bringing together of views.

13. The officials came from the State Services Commission, the Commission for the Environment, the Ministry of Works and Development, Treasury and the Department of Lands and Survey.

14. The need to review these statutes, including the option of passing a single "umbrella" statute, was stressed in the report. Reform of the environmental planning legislation is discussed in chapter 5.

15. While its deliberations and recommendations were confidential until they had been considered by the Cabinet Policy Committee, the intensity of public interest and concern was evident from the very beginning. The Minister received deputations from the Municipal Association, Counties Association, Federated Farmers, Institute of Foresters, NWASCA, Catchment Authorities Association, Ministry of Works and Development, NZ Workers Union, Timber Workers Union and PSA. A number of these groups were given copies of the WPEA report in confidence, and may also have been given a right of consultation prior to the Cabinet Policy Committee meeting on 4 June 1985 when the report was tabled. There was intense lobbying and public media releases were made by both development and conservation groups even while the report was still confidential. Even then, the Minister was criticised for a lack of adequate public consultation with development interests and for deliberately having those interests under-represented in the Committee's findings. Subsequently, with the release of the WPEA report in June 1985 for public submissions, the Minister and the Parliamentary Under Secretary for the Environment undertook further extensive consultations on the report and received deputations from

many organisations. Meetings were held with department officials, local and regional councils, private sector interests, professional bodies, environmental groups and Maori groups. Over 1,200 submissions were received.

16. In response to complaints that the 1985 environment forum and the WPEA report had been biased towards conservation interests, the Minister of Forests hosted a meeting in August 1985 of nearly 80 interest groups associated with his three portfolios, including Federated Farmers, the Fruitgrowers Federation, Timber Industry Federation, Forest Owners Association, NZ Chamber of Commerce, NZ Manufacturers Federation, NZ Workers Union and NZ Timber Workers Union. Subsequently he met the Business Round Table representing the top twenty business firms.

17. The Minister of Works and Development argued that the WPEA report greatly exaggerated the efficacy of departmental changes as a means of setting new policies or creating a shift in emphasis, and greatly underestimated the ability of already existing departments to respond to clear policy directions from the government. Thus, many of the criticisms expressed by the WPEA and presented as justification for radical bureaucratic change were seen as no more than criticism of the previous government.

18. Cabinet decisions about the MfE and DoC were made first, as recommended by the CPC. The Cabinet then adopted the recommendations of a Treasury report, tabled at the same meeting, (contrary to conventional procedure), which advocated corporatisation of the residual functions of the N.Z Forest Service and Lands and Survey. The Hon. Richard Prebble, an Associate Minister of Finance, and Treasury acted unilaterally in this respect, in the absence of the Deputy Prime Minister, Hon. Geoffrey Palmer, and without the knowledge of the State Services Commission. Thus, according to one participant, in less than five minutes of Cabinet deliberation, the corporatisation exercise was begun, without any substantive analysis of the shape, structure and operations of the corporations.

19. More recently, since December 1987, the assets of some of these corporations have been, or are expected to be, privatised in order to reduce the public debt.

20. A department was judged to be more directly accountable to the Cabinet. The Heritage New Zealand proposal was more akin to a nature conservancy, a public membership organisation, with elected boards operating nationally and regionally.

21. The Cabinet decided in December 1987, immediately after the election, to abolish the Ministry and its arm, the NWASCA. Its policy functions relating to town and country planning and water and soil were transferred to the MfE while its commercial operations were corporatised. This initiative was related to the decision to undertake a comprehensive review of the planning and resource management statutes, under the direction of the Minister for the Environment Rt. Hon. G.W.R. Palmer.

22. An Ad Hoc Ministerial Committee on Environmental Legislation was convened to oversee the drafting and detailed implementation of the changes involved. Chaired by the Minister of State Services, it comprised the Minister for the Environment, the Minister for Lands, Forestry and Maori Affairs, and an Associate Minister of Finance. It reported to the Cabinet through the CPC.

23. As a reflection, to some extent, of a changed power balance within the Cabinet, the Ministers for the Environment and for Conservation and their officials may have ignored Treasury comments, even though that meant the final drafts departed from Cabinet's drafting instructions. Treasury complained about a lack of consultation during the final drafting stages of both the Bills, despite significant changes to the drafts.

24. Attempts by the Department of Social Welfare to include the responsibility to report on the social policy implications of resource use proposals as an MfE function were also opposed. The Environment Minister's proposal to have the Ministry called "the Ministry for the Environment and Community Development", to give a territorial focus to the activities of the Ministry, was not accepted because of Treasury concerns over the role of MfE in social planning. Likewise, Treasury was strongly opposed to making provision in the Environment Act for an environmental impact assessment role for MfE, as discussed in Chapter 9.

25. Some 600,000 ha of Crown land was eventually retrieved for DoC, largely by final Minis-

terial resolution, including some important conservation land.

26. The New Zealand Maori Council took the Crown to the Court of Appeal on the issue of whether, in allowing large sections of the Crown's estate to be essentially passed into private hands without providing for Maori claims, the Crown was acting consistently with the principles of the Treaty of Waitangi. The Court of Appeal found that it was not – and ordered the parties to reach an agreement to resolve the claims. The outcome was a Crown commitment to resume lands allocated by it to States-owned Enterprises if Maori claims were successful. The legislation passed in 1988 means that mining rights owned by the Coal Corporation, the power-station sites of ElectriCorp, farms and other lands held by LandCorp, and hilltop transmission sites of Telecom Corp all become potentially returnable to Maori if the Waitangi Tribunal finds claims for these lands to be valid.

Chapter 4

1. There were over 800 local authorities of various types in New Zealand, each with different boundaries, functions and administrative systems. As a result, their ability to effectively manage resources, to service communities, respond to local and regional needs and implement national policies was often compromised.
2. Admittedly, the manifesto focussed primarily on structural considerations and did not address related aspects such as finance and accountability.
3. This process brought an abrupt halt to the proceedings of the Commission and a change in its direction. Existing amalgamation plans were scrapped and the Commission went back to the drawing board.
4. The Minister of Local Government, Hon. Michael Bassett, was an Auckland City Councillor prior to 1972 and a keen advocate of local government reform for many years. He oversaw the recent reforms until he relinquished his portfolio in 1990.
5. The implementation comprised three components: the enactment of legislation from July 1988 onwards; structural changes undertaken by the Commission between July 1988 and June 1989; and facilitating the transition phase overseen by the National Transition Committee between July 1989 and March 1990.
6. As defined in the Act, the purposes of local government in New Zealand are to provide, at the appropriate levels of local government –
   (a) recognition of the existence of different communities in New Zealand;
   (b) recognition of the identities and values of those communities;
   (c) definition and enforcement of appropriate rights within those communities;
   (d) scope for communities to make choices between different kinds of local public facilities and services;
   (e) for the operation of trading undertakings of local authorities on a competitively neutral basis;
   (f) for the delivery of appropriate facilities and services on behalf of central government;
   (g) recognition of communities of interest;
   (h) for the efficient and effective exercise of the functions, duties, and powers of the components of local government;
   (i) for the effective participation of local persons in local government.
7. Initially, a very wide range of special purpose authorities were to be included in the reform process. However, soon after deciding that this should be so, the government decided to review separately the structure and functions of education boards, hospital and area health boards, electric power boards, regional employment advisory councils, regional development councils and licensing trusts. Therefore, these special-purpose and quasi-government agencies were excluded from the local government reform programme.
8. In addition, in Auckland and Wellington, they took over the following functions of the Auckland Regional Authority and Wellington Regional Council: bulk water supply, regional reserves and forestry, as well as sewerage and refuse disposal in Auckland.
9. It was proposed that the regional councils would dispose of their functions to other agencies, except those relating to the Resource Management Act, pest destruction, nox-

ious plants control, flood protection, and land drainage and harbours management (Office of the Minister of Local Government, 1991).

Chapter 5

1. Over 50 statutes have been repealed in whole or in part. The principal statutes repealed include the Town and Country Planning Act 1977, the Rivers Control and Soil Erosion Act 1941, the Water and Soil Conservation Act, 1967, Harbours Act 1950, Geothermal Energy Amendment Act 1957, Clean Air Act 1972, and the Noise Control Act 1982.
2. For example, the reviews of the Town and Country Planning Act 1953, the Water and Soil Conservation Act 1967, the National Parks Act 1952 and the mining legislation.
3. Once again, it is not entirely clear from the statements made in the 1981 and 1984 election manifestos how wide-ranging the proposed reviews were expected to be. It is unlikely that the major implications of this commitment had been thought through. Labour's major concerns related to mining, the National Development Act 1980, the water and soil legislation and the commitment of the Crown to the planning statutes.
4. In the view of the Task Group, in order to achieve the Labour Government's objective of the integration of conservation and development, it was essential to make changes to the process of decision-making at all levels of government and in the private sector. The main change which had to be made was to bring the key aspects of the environment – physical, biological and social – to bear on all stages of planning. Hence, the management of the planning process became a central part of its enquiry.
5. Treasury sought clearer objectives for the use of these procedures as an intervention instrument and saw the need to consider other options to meet these objectives. Other considerations were: the scope of information required by the procedures; a concern that this might, for example, encompass private profitability considerations, and whether the costs of these procedures were likely to exceed the benefits.
6. The Economic Development Commission was created by the Cabinet with a specific mandate to assist in the deregulation of the economy. Its report advocated an almost totally market-driven town planning system. It proposed fundamental changes, with the aim of facilitating development.
7. In such a politicised environment, the Ministry of Works and Development proved unsuccessful in keeping control of the proposed review of the Town and Country Planning Act. The Minister for National Development, Hon. David Caygill, and the Department of Trade and Industry took the initiative to do this review, in response to pressure from the Business Round Table, the Economic Development Commission, and the Treasury. The Minister appointed Tony Hearn to undertake this task (Hearn, 1987). However, Cabinet action on his recommendations was pre-empted by the birth of the Resource Management Law Reform project.
8. The Cabinet Committee was chaired by the Minister for the Environment, and comprised the Ministers of Local Government, Energy, Commerce, Finance (and a Deputy Minister), Conservation, Tourism, State Services and Maori Affairs. The Core Group, serviced by the MfE, was convened by a MfE official, and comprised a Treasury official, a MfE Maori issues adviser, and a lawyer practicing in the natural resources area. It played a key role in steering the project, in the context of intense interdepartmental rivalry.
9. Its terms of reference were defined as follows:
• to review in an integrated way the planning, water and soil, and the minerals legislation, the EIA procedures, and resource management statutes related to above.
• to undertake the reviews from a zero-based perspective, from which it should:
i) identify the objective and purpose of present legislation and areas of overlap;
ii) identify what natural and physical resource management objectives are desirable and for what reasons;
iii) identify options and proposals for implementing the purposes and objectives – including institutional and organisation matters such as desirable regulation regimes. The new legislation was expected to be ready for introduction in 1989.

10. Treasury was also of the opinion that the Cabinet Committee was "green" and not pre-pared to listen to Treasury views, which were ignored on some occasions.

11. The review considered the options for government with respect to ownership of, and the rights to use water, mineral, geothermal, petroleum, air and land resources. The issues considered were as follows: a.) the characteristics of the resource and its markets; b.) the implications of these characteristics for defining rights to the resources and the options for ownership or management of the resource; c.) the costs and benefits of the different ownership or management options identified and the costs of altering existing rights; d.) the role of government with respect to i) third party or spill-over effects and ii) public goods; e.) the appropriate level (i.e., national/regional/local) of government involvement where a role for government is identified.

12. Treasury representatives on the Core Group sometimes ended up with minority views. That split got bigger and bigger over time; eventually, the Core Group ran out of time and was forced to make decisions under a lot of pressure.

13. Translating ministerial decisions into law was the role of law drafters. Their role was very important, because their interpretations were, at times, quite different from those of Core Group officials or from Cabinet directives. Sometimes there was difficulty in interpreting Cabinet decisions.

14. The Minister for the Environment, Hon. Geoffrey Palmer, was at times unable to attend meetings of the Cabinet Committee and placed a great deal of reliance and trust on his colleague, Hon. P.T.E. Woollaston, who had close links with the environmental groups, and subsequently chaired the Select Committee hearings. Some say this gave undue access to the environmentalists.

15. The minerals allocation section of the Resource Management Bill was removed to be enacted separately as the Crown Minerals Act 1991, as discussed below.

16. The Core Group decided that continuing the Review could result in opposition from Maoridom and possible disruption at later stages of the Review. It had to identify an approach acceptable to Maori which was constructive rather than confrontational and fitted within the time frame.

17. Protection of indigenous forestry has been legislated in a separate statute.

18. It could be argued that, compared to the Harbours Act and the Marine Farming Act, the Resource Management Act will provide more effective protection for the coast. The Har-bours Act was cumbersome and made it difficult to prosecute offenders, while the Marine Farming Act was promotional in its objectives.

19. There is an override provision where access is in the national interest. In certain situa-tions, however, land owners have an absolute right of veto. These situations include land under indigenous forest cover, DoC land, land subject to conservation covenants, as well as the situations already exempt in previous legislation.

20. The EP&EP continue to apply to the works and the management policies of Government departments which may affect the environment, including proposed actions which are publicly funded, and to the granting by the Crown of all licences and permits which may have environmental implications and which are issued pursuant to the specified Acts.

21. Compared to the Resource Management Act, the Healthy Cities Project reflects more fittingly the social concerns of many New Zealand communities. The Healthy Cities project has been developed by the World Health Organisation and has been adopted by several New Zealand communities. Its objective is to promote a holistic approach to public health and urban planning.

Chapter 6

1. The role of the New Zealand Planning Council was also significant from an environmental perspective. The wide-ranging mandate of the New Zealand Planning Council created in 1977 was to advise the government on social and economic planning issues; the mandate was implicitly inclusive of social concerns.

2. While this relationship worked very well in practice, the Minister and the bureaucrats

sometimes sought to manipulate these quangos for their own ends.

3. While the New Zealand Conservation Strategy supported the proposed merger (NCC, 1981), the environmental groups favoured a retention of the status quo. They saw the proposed merger as diluting the potential influence of the NCC. The Environmental Council was also opposed to the proposed merger.

4. The Working Party comprised the Chairman of the Environmental Council, the Under-Secretary to the Minister for the Environment and a MoW&D official.

5. It was proposed that other advisory bodies and committees associated with the Department of Lands and Survey, and with other government departments involved in the transfer of responsibilities, should be associated with DoC and the Land Development and Management Corporation as was appropriate; this proposal was subject to a later review of their roles and functions.

6. The working party comprised officials from the Department of Lands and Survey, the Department of Internal Affairs, the New Zealand Forest Service, the Commission for the Environment and Treasury. It was chaired by the State Services Commission.

7. Two other parallel reviews were also concerned with the future of quangos related to DoC: the Protected Areas Legislation Review and the DoC Management Planning Task Force. Subsequently, the Minister of Conservation decided to exclude the consideration of public participation in planning from these two reviews. However, some of their ideas and recommendations were incorporated into the quango review exercise.

8. Their responsibilities included the preservation and conservation of New Zealand's indigenous and introduced wildlife, and of freshwater fisheries and their habitats.

9. The quangos abolished included the NPRA and National Parks Boards, the Forest Park Advisory Committees, the New Zealand Walkways Commission and District Committees, the NCC, the Fauna Protection Advisory Council and a number of other scientific advisory committees.

10. This was seen by the environmental groups as a step back from the National Parks Act 1980, which gave the National Parks and Reserves Authority the power to approve statements of general policy, having regard to the views of the Minister.

11. The Conservation Law Reform Act established a hierarchical planning system, with general policy and the National Park policy at the apex. The purpose of the regional conservation management strategies is to establish objectives for the integrated management of natural and historical resources administered by the Department. The functional plans include those for National Park management, conservation management, freshwater fisheries, and sports fish and game.

12. The Historic Places Trust has executive powers, some of which are regulatory in nature; and it has a community base in its over 23,000 fee-paying members. The same is true of the Queen Elizabeth II National Trust; although it does not have a regulatory role, it is in the main an executive body.

References

Chapter 1

Boston, J. and Holland, M. (eds.) *The Fourth Labour Government: Radical Politics in New Zealand.* Auckland, Oxford University Press, 1987.

Britton, S., Le Heron, R. and Pawson, E. (eds.) *Changing Places in New Zealand: A Geography of Restructuring.* Christchurch, New Zealand Geographical Society, 1992.

Caldwell, L.K. *Environment: A Challenge for Modern Society.* New York, Natural History Press, 1970.

Douglas, E. "The Maori", *Pacific Viewpoint,* Vol. 32(2), 1991, pp. 129-138.

Dryzek, J.S. "Designs for Environmental Discourse: The Greening of the Administrative State?", in Paehlke, R. and Torgerson, D. (eds.) *Managing Leviathan: Environmental Politics and the Administrative State.* Peterborough, Ontario, Broadview Press, 1990, pp. 97-111.

Emel, J. and Peet, R. "Resource Management and Natural Hazards" in Peet, R. and Thrift, N. (eds.) *New Models in Geography,* Vol.One. London, Unwin Hyman, 1989, pp. 49-76.

Fernie, J. and Pitkethly, A.S. *Resources: Environment and Policy.* London, Harper and Row, 1985.

Franklin, H. "New Zealand in the Eighties", *Pacific Viewpoint,* Vol. 32(2), 1991, pp. 119-120.

Glasby, G.P. "A Review of the Concept of Sustainable Management as Applied to New Zealand", *Journal of the Royal Society of New Zealand,* Vol. 21(2), 1991, pp. 61-81.

Gold, H. and Webster, A. *New Zealand Values Today.* Palmerston North, Massey University, 1990.

Hill, M. and Bramley, G. *Analysing Social Policy.* Oxford, Basil Blackwell, 1986.

Holland, M and Boston, J. (eds.) *The Fourth Labour Government: Politics and Policy in New Zealand.* Auckland, Oxford University Press, 1990.

Kivell, P.T. "Geography, Planning and Policymaking", in Kivell, P.T and Coppock, J.T. (eds.) *Geography, Planning and Policymaking.* Exeter, Geo Books, 1986.

Memon, P.A. and Cullen, R. "New Zealand Fisheries Policies and Maori", in Whitwell, J. and Thompson, M.A. (eds.) *Society and Culture: Economic Perspectives.* Wellington, New Zealand Association of Economists, 1991, pp. 77-87.

O'Riordan, T. "Institutions Affecting Environmental Policy", in Flowerdew, R.T.N. (ed.) *Institutions and Geographical Patterns.* London, Croom Helm, 1982, pp. 103-140.

O'Riordan, T. "The Challenge for Environmentalism" in Peet, R. and Thrift, N. (eds.) *op.cit.* pp. 77-102.

Park, C.C. "Environmental Policies in Perspective" in Park, C.C. (ed.) *Environmental Policies: An International Review.* London, Croom Helm, 1986.

Peet, R. "Introduction" in Peet, R. and Thrift, N. (eds.) *New Models in Geography,* Vol.One. London, Unwin Hyman, 1989. pp. 43-47.

Portney, P.R. (ed.) *Public Policies for Environmental Protection.* Washington, Resources for the Future, 1990.

Rees, J. *Natural Resources: Allocation, Economics and Policy.* London, Methuen, 1985.

Wildavsky, A. *Speaking Truth to Power: The Art and Craft of Policy Analysis.* Boston, Little Brown, 1979.

World Commission on Environment and Development. *Our Common Future.* Oxford, Oxford University Press, 1987.

Chapter 2

Anderson, A.G. (ed.) *The Land Our Future: Essays on Land Use and Conservation in New Zealand.* Auckland, Longman Paul, 1980.

Bartlett, R.V. "Comprehensive Environmental Decision Making: Can It Work ?" in Vig, N. and Kraft, M. (eds.) *Environmental Policy in the 1990s: Towards A New Agenda.* Washington D.C., Congressional Quarterly Press, 1990, pp. 235-254.

Buhrs, T. "The Co-ordination of Environmental Policy: An Unresolved Dilemma." Paper presented at the NZPSA Conference, University of Otago, Dunedin, May 1990.

Buhrs, T. Working Within Limits: The Role of the Commission for the Environment in Environmental Policy Development in New Zealand. Unpublished Ph.D. Thesis, University of Auckland, 1991.

Cameron, C. *Town and Country Planning. The Right Use and Development of Land. Planning Legislation and Administration in England and New Zealand: A Comparison.* Report prepared for the Ministry of Works. Wellington, 1947.

Cleveland, L. "The Major Agencies of Central Government in New Zealand", in Cleveland, L. and Robinson, A.D. (eds.) *Readings in New Zealand Government.* Wellington, A.H. & A.W. Reed, 1972a, pp. 20-64.

Cleveland, L. *The Anatomy of Influence: Pressure Groups and Politics in New Zealand.* Wellington: Hicks Smith & Sons, 1972b.

Commission of Inquiry into Housing. *Housing in New Zealand: Report of the Commission of Inquiry.* Wellington: Government Printer, 1971.

Commoner, B. *The Closing Circle.* London, J. Cape, 1972

Cox, J. "Organisation for National Development: Its Role in Post War Development", *People and Planning*, No.13, March 1980, pp. 19-21.

Cullingworth, J.B. *Town and Country Planning in Britain.* London, George Allen & Unwin, 1964.

Cumberland, K.B. "Man in Nature", *New Zealand Geographer*, Vol.17(2), 1961, pp.137-154.

Dryzek, J.S. "Designs for Environmental Discourse: The Greening of the Administrative State?", in Paehlke, R. and Torgerson, D. (eds.) *Managing Leviathan: Environmental Politics and the Administrative State.* Peterborough, Ontario, Broadview Press, 1990, pp. 97-111.

Franklin, S.H. *Trade, Growth and Anxiety: New Zealand Beyond the Welfare State.* Wellington, Methuen, 1978.

Gibbs, H.S. "Management of Land and Water Resources", in Johnston, R.J. (ed.) *Society and Environment in New Zealand.* Christchurch, Whitcombe & Tombs, 1974, pp. 170-184.

Gilbert, J.T.E. "Environmental Assessment in New Zealand", *The Northwest Environmental Journal*, Vol. 2(2), 1986, pp. 85-106.

Hawke, G.R. *Government in the New Zealand Economy.* Planning Paper No. 13. Wellington, New Zealand Planning Council, 1982.

Hawke, G.R. *The Making of New Zealand: An Economic History.* Cambridge, Cambridge University Press, 1985.

Hearn, T.J. "Riparian Rights and Sludge Channels: A Water Use Conflict in New Zealand, 1869-1921", *New Zealand Geographer*, Vol. 38(2), 1982, pp. 47-55.

Hearn, T.J. "Mining and Land: A Conflict Over Use 1858-1953", *New Zealand Law Journal*, August 1983, pp. 235-238.

Horsley, P. "Recent Resource Use Conflicts in New Zealand: Maori Perceptions and the Evolving Environmental Ethic", in Hay, P. Eckersley, R. and Holloway, G. (eds.) *Environmental Politics in Australia and New Zealand.* Occasional Paper 23, Centre for Environmental Studies, University of Tasmania, 1989, pp. 125-143.

Interdepartmental Committee on the Pollution of Waters. *Report of the Committee.* Wellington, Marine Department, 1952.

Interdepartmental Committee on Water. *N.Z. Law and Administration in Respect of Water.* Report to Cabinet. Wellington, Ministry of Works, 1965.

Jackson, K.E. "Government and Enterprise: The Early Days of Electricity Generation and Supply in New Zealand", *British Review of New Zealand Studies*, No.1, 1988, pp. 101-121.

Kellow, A.J. *Pollution Control in New Zealand: Making Policies and Prescribing Placebos.* Public

Sector Research Paper, New Zealand Institution of Public Administration, Vol. 4(2), 1983.

Kellow, A.J. "Electricity Planning in Tasmania and New Zealand: Political Processes and the Technological Imperative", *Australian Journal of Public Administration*, Vol. XLV(1), 1986, pp. 2-17.

Lees, A. "The Forest Service: Its Environmental Record." Nelson, Native Forest Action Council, undated.

Levine, S. (ed.) *New Zealand Politics: A Reader.* Melbourne, Cheshire Press, 1975.

McMahon, C.K. (ed.) *The Physical Environment Conference 1970. Reports, Papers and Proceedings.* Wellington, Environmental Council, 1972.

Mahuta, R.T. Ritchie, J.E. Parsons, S. and Wishart, P. "The Need for Change. A Maori Community View." Submission to the Environment Forum, March 1985.

Mascarenhas, R.C. *Public Enterprise in New Zealand.* Wellington, New Zealand Institute of Public Administration, 1982.

Mather, A.S. "Environmental Stress: Perception and Response in Two Examples from New Zealand", *International Journal of Environmental Studies*, Vol.20, 1982, pp. 7-15.

Meadows, D. H. Meadows, D. L. Randers, J. and Behrens, W.W. *The Limits to Growth.* New York, Universe Books, 1972.

Middlemass, K. *Politics in Industrial Society.* London, Andre Deutsch, 1979.

Miliband, R. *Marxism and Politics.* Oxford, Oxford University Press, 1969.

Mills, S.J. "Environmental Impact Reporting in New Zealand: A Study of Government Policy in a Period of Transition - Parts 1, II & III", *New Zealand Journal of Law*, 1979, pp. 472-484, 494-501 & 515-524.

Molloy, L.F. (ed.) *Land Alone Endures: Land Use and the Role of Research.* Wellington, Department of Scientific and Industrial Research, 1980.

Morgan, R.K. "The Evolution of Environmental Impact Assessment in New Zealand", *Journal of Environmental Management*, Vol.16, 1983, pp. 139-52.

Morgan, R.K. "Reshaping Environmental Impact Assessment in New Zealand", *Environment Impact Assessment Review*, Vol.8, 1988, pp. 293-306.

National Development Council, *Plenary Session: Report of Proceedings of the National Development Conference.* Wellington, Government Printer, 1969.

Nielsen, S.A. "Pollution in New Zealand", in Levine, S. (ed.) *New Zealand Politics: A Reader.* Melbourne, Cheshire Press, 1975, pp. 457-471.

Norman, R. G. "Central Government's Established Policies and Organisation for Management of the Environment." Background Paper for the Seminar on the Environment. Wellington, 1973.

O'Riordan, T. "New Zealand Resource Management in the Seventies: A Review of Three Recent Conferences", *N.Z. Geographer*, Vol.27(2), 1971, pp. 197-210.

O'Riordan. T. & Sewell, W.R.D. (eds.), *Project Appraisal and Policy Review.* Chichester, John Wiley, 1981.

Paehlke, P. and D. Torgerson, D. (eds.) *Managing Leviathan: Environmental Politics and the Administrative State.* Peterborough, Ont., Broadview Press, 1990.

Park, C.C. (ed.) *Environmental Policies: An International Review.* London, Croom Helm, 1986.

Pickvance, C.G. "Introduction", in Harloe, M. Pickvance, C.G. and Urry, J. (eds.) *Place, Policy and Politics: Do Localities Matter?* London, Unwin Hyman, 1990, pp. 1-41.

Polaschek, R.J. *Government Administration in New Zealand.* Auckland, OUP, 1958.

Roberts, A. *The Ecological Crisis of Consumerism.* Sydney, International Publications, 1973.

Roche, M.M. "Some Historical Influences on the Establishment of Protected Natural Areas in New Zealand, 1880-1980", in Dingwall P.R. (compiler) *People and Parks: Essays in Development and Use of Protected Areas.* Information Series No. 10, Department of Lands and Survey, Wellington, 1984a.

Roche, M.M. "Evolving Attitudes Towards New Zealand's Protected Areas System". A paper presented to the Seminar on Social and Historical Research in New Zealand's Parks and Protected Areas. Lincoln College, 27-30 August, 1984b.

Roche, M.M. *Forest Policy in New Zealand.* Palmerston North, Dunmore Press, 1987.

Sandercock, L. "Capitalism and the Environment: The Failure of Success", in Wheelwright,

E.L. and Buckley, K. (eds.) *Essays in the Political Economy of Australian Capitalism.* Vol.1. Sydney, Australia and New Zealand Book Company, 1975, pp. 153-177.

Sandercock, L. *Cities For Sale.* Melbourne, Melbourne University Press, 1977.

Thomas, W.L. (ed.), *Man's Role in Changing the Face of the Earth.* Chicago, University of Chicago Press, 1956.

Walker, K.J. "The State in Environmental Management: The Ecological Dimension", *Political Studies*, Vol. 37(1), 1989, pp. 25-38.

Weisberg, B. *Beyond Repair: The Ecology of Capitalism.* Boston, Beacon Press, 1971.

Wells, N.E. *A Guide to Environmental Law in New Zealand.* Wellington, Brooker and Friend, 1984.

White, L. *Machina ex deo: Essays in the Dynamics of Western Culture.* Cambridge, Mass., M.I.T. Press, 1968.

Williams, D.A.R. "Lawyers, Law Students and the Environment", in Levine, S. (ed.) *New Zealand Politics: A Reader.* Melbourne, Cheshire Press, 1975, pp. 249-251.

Williams, G.R. (ed) *The Natural History of New Zealand.* Wellington, A.H. & A.W. Reed, 1973.

Wynn, G. "Conservation and Society in Late Nineteenth-Century New Zealand", *New Zealand Journal of History*, Vol. 11(2), October 1977, pp. 124-136.

Wynn, G. "Pioneers, Politicians and the Conservation of Forests in Early New Zealand", *Journal of Historical Geography*, Vol.5(2), 1979, pp. 171-88.

Chapter 3

Boston J., Martin, J. and Walsh, P. (eds.) *Reshaping the State: New Zealand's Bureaucratic Revolution.* Wellington, Oxford University Press, 1991.

Clark, M. and Sinclair, E. (eds.) *Purpose Performance and Profit: Redefining the Public Sector.* Studies in Public Administration No 32. Wellington, Government Printer, 1986.

Cullen, M. "The Environment: The Prospects for the Future". Speech to the Auckland Minewatch/Auckland RFBPS, 3 August 1983.

Dean, R. "Public Sector Reform: A Review of the Issues", in Clark, M. and Sinclair, E. (eds.) *Purpose, Performance and Profit: Redefining the Public Sector.* Studies in Public Administration No.32. Wellington, Government Printer, 1987.

Department of Lands and Survey and New Zealand Forest Service. *Submissions on the Proposed Merger of the Department of Lands and Survey and the New Zealand Forest Service.* Wellington, April, 1983.

Emel, J. and Peet, R. "Resource Management and Natural Hazards", in Peet, R. and Thrift, N. (eds.) *New Models in Geography*, Vol. One. London, Unwin Hyman, 1989, pp. 49-76.

Environment Administration Task Group (on behalf of RFBPSNZ, Federated Mountain Clubs, NFAC, Environment Defence Society, Greenpeace & ECO). *Environmental Administration in N.Z. : An Alternative Discussion Paper.* Nelson, January 1985.

Environmental Council. *The Environmental Council's View on the OECD Review of Environmental Policies in New Zealand.* Wellington, 1981.

Memon, P.A. and Cullen, R. "Fishery Policies and their Impact on the New Zealand Maori", *Marine Resource Economics*, Vol. 7(3), 1992, pp. 153-157.

Memon, P.A. and Wilson, G.A. *Recent Indigenous Forest Policy Issues in New Zealand. An Annotated Bibliography.* Environmental Policy and Management Research Centre, Publication No. 2. Dunedin, University of Otago, 1992.

Ministry of Agriculture and Fisheries. *Sustainable Agriculture: A Policy Proposal.* Wellington, 1991.

NFAC. "Are Things Really Going to Change?", *Bush Telegraph*, No. 20, (May 1985a), pp. 1-2.

NFAC. "High Hopes of Success with Russell Marshall", *Bush Telegraph*, No. 21, (August 1985b), p.1.

NFAC. "Labour's Team Says: 'Trust Us'", *Bush Telegraph*, No. 29, (August 1987), p.1.

N.Z. Labour Party. "Environment Policy: Administration and Planning." Press statement by Cullen, M. Wellington, 28 April 1984a.

N.Z. Labour Party. "Natural Waters Policy." Press statement by Cullen, M. Wellington, 30 May

1984b.

N.Z. Labour Party. *Environment Policies.* Wellington, 1984c.

N.Z. National Party. *The Environment: Position Paper Prepared by the Government Research Unit.* Wellington, 21 June 1984.

N.Z. Planning Council. *Economic Strategy.* Wellington, 1979.

N.Z. Planning Council. Environmental/ Natural Resources Restructuring. Wellington, NZPC Working Paper, [1989].

OECD. *Environmental Policies in New Zealand.* Paris, 1980.

Paehlke, R. and Torgerson, D. (eds.) *Managing Leviathan: Environmental Politics and the Administrative State.* Peterborough, Ont., Broadview Press, 1990.

Peet, R. and Thrift, N. (eds.) *New Models in Geography*, Vol. One. London, Unwin Hyman, 1989.

RFBPSNZ, Federated Mountain Clubs of N.Z., NFAC, Environmental Defence Society, & Environment and Conservation Organisations of N.Z. *Environmental Management in N.Z: A Strategy.* Wellington, October 1982.

State Services Commission. *Environmental Administration in N.Z.: A Discussion Paper.* Wellington, 1984.

Synergy Applied Research Ltd. *Synopsis of Submissions and Forum Record.* Wellington, Environment Forum Secretariat, 1985.

The Treasury. *Economic Management.* Wellington, Government Printer, 1984a.

The Treasury. *Economic Management: Land Use Issues.* Wellington, Government Printer, 1984b.

Working Party on Environmental Administration. *Report of the Post-Environment Forum Working Party.* Wellington, State Services Commission, June 1985.

Chapter 4

Bassett, Hon. M. "Introductory Speech: Local Government Amendment Bill 1988." Hansard 1988 1R, 1988a, pp. 2883-2903.

Bassett, Hon. M. Statement on Reform of Local and Regional Government. Wellington, Office of the Minister for Local Government, 1988b.

Burke, Hon. T.K. "Labour Government Plan for Regions." *Otago Daily Times*, 15 January 1985.

Department of Internal Affairs. *Background Paper on Power of General Competence.* Wellington, 1990.

Elwood, B. "Address to Counties' Conference", *New Zealand Local Government*, July 1986, pp. 31-32.

Elwood, B. "Address to Regional, Territorial and Special Purpose Authority Representatives". Auckland, 28 September, 1988.

Government Economic Statement 1987. Wellington, 17 December 1987.

Local Government Commission. *Memorandum to Assist Authorities Affected by Local Government Re-organization.* Wellington, 22 July 1988a.

Local Government Commission. *Memorandum to Regional, Territorial and Special Purpose Authorities.* Wellington, 28 September 1988b.

Memon, P.A. "Decision Making for Multiple Utilization of Water Resources in New Zealand", *Environmental Management*, Vol. 13(5), 1989, pp. 553-562.

Memon, P.A. "Shaking Off a Colonial Legacy? – Town and Country Planning in New Zealand, 1870s to 1980s", *Planning Perspectives*, Vol. 6, 1991, pp. 19-32.

N.Z. Labour Party. *The 1984 Policy Statement.* Wellington, 1984a.

N.Z. Labour Party. *Local Government Backgrounder.* Wellington, 1984b.

Office of the Parliamentary Commissioner for the Environment. *Gisborne District Council Environmental Management: A Systems and Processes Review.* Wellington, 1990.

Officials Co-ordinating Committee on Local Government. *Reform of Local and Regional Government: Discussion Document.* Wellington, 1988a.

Officials Co-ordinating Committee on Local Government. *Reform of Local and Regional Government: Funding Issues. A Discussion Document.* Wellington, 1988b.

Officials Co-ordinating Committee on Local Government. *Bill for the Establishment of Maori*

Advisory Committees in Local Government and Explanatory Statement. Wellington, 1989.

"Schemes Create 'Modern Local Government System'". *Southland Times,* 13 June 1989.

Synergy Applied Research Ltd. *Synopsis of Submissions on Funding Issues.* Wellington, 1989.

The Bridgeport Group. *Synopsis of Submissions on Reform of Local and Regional Government: Report to the Officials Co-ordinating Committee on Local Government.* Wellington, Department of Internal Affairs, 1988.

The Bridgeport Group. *Reform of Local and Regional Government: Synopsis of Submissions on Bill for Establishment of Maori Advisory Committees in Local Government and Explanatory Statement. Report to the Officials Co-ordinating Committee on Local Government.* Wellington, Dept. of Internal Affairs, 1990.

The Treasury. *Economic Management: Land Use Issues.* Wellington, Government Printer, 1984.

Welch, R.V. "Local Government Commissions and Local Government Reform: The Failures and Now Success?", *Public Sector,* Vol. 12(1), 1989, pp. 3-6.

Working Party on Regional Government Funding. *Interim Report to the Officials Co-ordinating Committee on Local Government.* Wellington, 1990.

Working Party on the Future of Regional Councils. *The Future of Regional Councils. Report to the Minister of Local Government and the Minister for the Environment.* Wellington, 1991.

Chapter 5

Bromley, D. *Property Rights and the Environment. Natural Resource Policy in Transition: A series of lectures in August 1987.* Wellington, Ministry for the Environment, 1988.

Brown, Copeland and Co. Ltd. *District and Regional Planning in New Zealand: Objectives, Performance and Alternatives: A Report prepared for the Department of Trade and Industry and the Treasury.* Auckland, March 1987.

Economic Development Commission. *Town and Country Planning Reform.* Wellington, 1987.

Environment Administration Task Group (on behalf of RFBPSNZ, Federated Mountain Clubs, NFAC, Environmental Defence Society, Greenpeace and ECO). *Environmental Administration in N.Z.: An Alternative Discussion Paper.* Nelson, January 1985.

Fisher, D. "Clarity in a Little 'While'", *Terra Nova,* November 1991, pp. 50-51.

Hearn, A. *Report of the Review of the Town and Country Planning Act 1977.* Wellington, Department of Trade and Industry, 1987.

Interdepartmental Committee on The Review of Mining Legislation. *A Discussion Paper on Policy Issues for the Review of Mining Legislation.* March 1987.

International Union for the Conservation of Nature and Natural Resources. *World Conservation Strategy.* Gland, Switzerland, 1980.

Ministry for the Environment. *Directions for Change: A Discussion Paper.* Wellington, 1988a.

Ministry for the Environment. *People, the Environment and Decision Making: The Government's Proposals for Resource Management Law Reform.* Wellington, 1988b.

Ministry for the Environment. *Ecological Principles for Resource Management.* Wellington, 1988c.

Ministry for the Environment. *Equity in Resource Allocation: A Discussion Paper.* Wellington, 1988c.

Ministry for the Environment. *Economic Instruments for Environmental Management: An Overview.* Wellington, 1988c.

Ministry for the Environment. *Fundamental Issues in Resource Management.* RMLR Working Paper No.1. Wellington, 1988c.

Ministry for the Environment. *Analysis of Existing Statutes: Departmental Views.* RMLR Working Paper No.2. Wellington, 1988c.

Ministry for the Environment. *Review of Submissions on the Future Role of Local and Regional Government.* RMLR Working Paper No.3. Wellington, 1988c.

Ministry for the Environment. *The Role of Government in Pollution and Hazardous Waste Substances Management; The Management of Pollution and Hazardous Substances.* RMLR Working Paper No.4. Wellington, 1988c.

Ministry for the Environment. *The Rights To Use Land, Water, and Minerals.* RMLR Working Paper No.5. Wellington, 1988c.

Ministry for the Environment. *Users Group Working Papers.* RMLR Working Paper No.6. Wellington, 1988c.

Ministry for the Environment. *Analysis of Existing Statutes: Legal Analysis.* RMLR Working Paper No.7. Wellington, 1988c.

Ministry for the Environment. *The Treaty of Waitangi and its Significance to the Reform of Resource Management Laws.* RMLR Working Paper No.8. Wellington, 1988c.

Ministry for the Environment. *Waitangi Tribunal Findings Analysis.* RMLR Working Paper No.9. Wellington, 1988c.

Ministry for the Environment. *Resource Values.* RMLR Working Paper No.10. Wellington, 1988c.

Ministry for the Environment. *Analysis of Phase One Public Submissions.* RMLR Working Paper No.11. Wellington, 1988c.

Ministry for the Environment. *Public Participation.* RMLR Working Paper No.12. Wellington, 1988c.

Ministry for the Environment. *Objectives for Resource Management: Why, What and How.* RMLR Working Paper No.13. Wellington, 1988c.

Ministry for the Environment. *Compensation: An Examination of the Law.* RMLR Working Paper No.14. Wellington, 1988c.

Ministry for the Environment. *Part A: Natural Hazards and Resource Management Law; Part B: The Role of Information in Resource Management.* RMLR Working Paper No.15. Wellington, 1988c.

Ministry for the Environment. *The Various Roles of the Crown: as Resource Developer and as a Participant in Resource Management.* RMLR Working Paper No.16. Wellington, 1988c.

Ministry for the Environment. *Public Participation: Options for Legislation.* RMLR Working Paper No.17. Wellington, 1988c.

Ministry for the Environment. *Public Participation in Policy Formation and Development Consents.* RMLR Working Paper No.18. Wellington, 1988c.

Ministry for the Environment. *Decision Making Processes and Structures: Two Contributions to Resource Management Law Reform.* RMLR Working Paper No.19. Wellington, 1988c.

Ministry for the Environment. *Impact Assessment in Resource Management.* RMLR Working Paper No.20. Wellington, 1988c.

Ministry for the Environment. *Synopsis of Submissions Received in Response to Directions for Change.* RMLR Working Paper No.21. Wellington, 1988c.

Ministry for the Environment. *Resource Management Disputes: Part A: The Role of Courts and Tribunals; Part B: Mediation.* RMLR Working Paper No.22. Wellington, 1988c.

Ministry for the Environment. *Coastal Legislation: Options for Reform.* RMLR Working Paper No.23. Wellington, 1988c.

Ministry for the Environment. *Sustainability; Intrinsic Values and the Needs of Future Generations.* RMLR Working Paper No.24. Wellington, 1988c.

Ministry for the Environment. *Implementing the Sustainability Objective in Resource Management Law.* RMLR Working Paper No.25. Wellington, 1988c.

Ministry for the Environment. *Geothermal Energy: Maori and Related Issues* (by R P Boast). RMLR Working Paper No.26. Wellington, 1988c.

Ministry for the Environment. *A Treaty Based Model: The Principle of Active Protection* (by Mike Barns). RMLR Working Paper No.27. Wellington, 1988c.

Ministry for the Environment. *Part A: Town and Country Planning and the Treaty of Waitangi* (by Margaret Cotton); *Part B: The Planning System and the Recognition of Maori Tribal Plans* (by Kenneth Palmer); *Part C: Maori Participation in Resource Management* (by Mark Gray). RMLR Working Paper No.28. Wellington, 1988c.

Ministry for the Environment. *Part A: The Natural World and Natural Resources: Maori Value Systems & Perspectives* (by Rev. Maori Marsden); *Part B: Water Resources and the Kai Tahu Claim* (by David Palmer and Anake Goodall). RMLR Working Paper No.29. Wellington, 1988c.

Ministry for the Environment. *Enforcement and Compliance Issues in Resource Management* (by D. J. Berwick). RMLR Working Paper No.30. Wellington, 1988c.

Ministry for the Environment. *National Policy Matters in Resource Management* (by K. Cronin).

RMLR Working Paper No.31. Wellington, 1988c.

Ministry for the Environment. *Public Submissions in Response to People, Environment and Decision Making*. RMLR Working Paper No.32. Wellington, 1988c.

Nature Conservation Council. *Integrating Conservation and Development: A Proposal for a N.Z Conservation Strategy*. Wellington, 1981.

N.Z. Labour Party. *1984 Policy Statement*. Wellington, 1984.

N.Z. Labour Party. *Draft Proposals for Labour Party Environment Policy*. Wellington, 1987.

OECD. *Environmental Policies in New Zealand*. Paris, 1980.

Palmer, G. *Unbridled Power? An Interpretation of New Zealand's Constitution and Government*. 2nd edition. Auckland, Oxford University Press, 1987.

Palmer, G. *Environmental Politics: A Greenprint for New Zealand*. Dunedin, McIndoe, 1990.

Review Group on the Resource Management Bill. *Report on the Resource Management Bill*. Wellington, 11 February 1991.

Working Party on Environmental Administration. *Report of the Post-Environment Forum Working Party*. Wellington, State Services Commission, June 1985.

World Commission on Environment and Development. *Our Common Future*. Oxford, Oxford University Press, 1987.

Chapter 6

Department of Conservation. *Options for Conservation Quangos: Synopsis of Submissions on Discussion Paper*. Prepared by Synergy Applied Research. Wellington, December 1987.

Department of Conservation. *Review of Conservation Quangos: DoC Position Paper*. Wellington, February 1988.

Environment Forum Secretariat. *Environment Forum Papers, 7-9 March 1985*. Wellington, 1985.

Environmental Council. *A Citizens Voice for the Environment: Is there a Need for an Environmental Quango?* Discussion Paper. Wellington, August 1987.

National Parks and Reserves Authority. *General Policy for National Parks*. Wellington, Department of Lands and Survey, 1983.

Nature Conservation Council. *Integrating Conservation and Development: A Proposal for a N.Z. Conservation Strategy*. Wellington, 1981.

N.Z. Labour Party. "Environment Policy: Administration and Planning." Press Statement by Cullen, M. Wellington, 28 April 1984.

N.Z. National Party. *The Environment: Position Paper Prepared by the Government Research Unit*. Wellington, 21 June 1984.

OECD. *Environmental Policies in New Zealand*. Paris, 1980.

Palmer, G. *Unbridled Power? An Interpretation of New Zealand's Constitution and Government*. 2nd Edition. Auckland, Oxford University Press, 1987.

RFBPSNZ et.al. *Environmental Management in N.Z: A Strategy*. Wellington, October 1982.

State Services Commission. *Environmental Administration in N.Z: A Discussion Paper*. Wellington, 1984.

Task Force on Economic and Social Planning. *N.Z. at the Turning Point*. Wellington, 1976.

Working Party on Environmental Administration. *Report of the Post-Environment Forum Working Party*. Wellington, State Services Commission, June 1985.

Chapter 7

Dahlberg, K.A. "The Challenges of Making New Zealand Agriculture More Sustainable", *New Zealand Sociology*, Vol. 5(1), 1990, pp 27-43.

NZPC. Environmental/Natural Resources Restructuring. NZPC Working Paper. Wellington, 1989.

Sachs, W. "The Virtue of Enoughness", *New Perspective Quarterly*, Vol. 6(1), 1989, pp.16-19.

Glossary of Maori Terms

Iwi	Tribe
Hapū	Subtribe
Mana whenua	Customary authority exercised by an iwi or hapu in an identified area
Pākehā	A person of predominantly European descent
Rangatira Kaitiaki	Resource guardians
Rūnanga	Local representative groups. A Maori equivalent of local government formed to protect and defend the rangatiratanga, the tuurangawawae and the cultural and social values of their members
Tāngata whenua	In relation to a particular area, means the iwi or hapu that holds mana whenua over that area
Taonga	Treasured possessions, includes both tangible and intangible treasures (e.g. the Maori language)
Tapu	Spiritual protection or restriction
Te tino rangatiratanga	Full chieftainship and authority, including the right to permit or deny others inherent sovereignty
Tūrangawaewae	A person's right to stand on a particular piece of land or in a certain place and to speak and be heard on matters affecting them and their relationships to that land and its resources

Bibliography

A. Historical

Action for Environment. "When the Trees Start Falling", in Levine, S. (ed.) *New Zealand Politics: A Reader*. Melbourne, Cheshire Press, 1975, pp. 252-253.

Allsop, F. *The First Fifty Years of New Zealand's Forest Service*. New Zealand Forest Service Information Series, No. 59. Wellington, Government Printer, 1969.

Anderson, A.G. (ed.) *The Land Our Future: Essays on Land Use and Conservation in New Zealand*. Auckland, Longman Paul, 1980.

Armstrong, W.R. "Australasian Association: Implications for Industrialisation and Regional Development in New Zealand", *Tijdschrift voor Economische en Sociale Geographie*, Vol. 60, 1969, pp. 238-248.

Barton, C.J. *Statutory Functions and Responsibilities of New Zealand Public Service Departments: 1977*. Wellington, State Services Commission, 1977.

Barton, G.P. "Law and Environment". Hudson Lecture for 1975. Nature Conservation Council, Wellington.

Brown, G.S. "New Zealand: Conservation by the Forest Service", *Commonwealth Forestry Review*, Vol. 57(3), 1978, pp. 164-165.

Brown, J.B. (ed.) *Rural Land Administration in New Zealand*. Wellington, Institute of Public Administration, 1966.

Bryant, G.W. (ed.) *You and Your Environment: A Green Paper*. Wellington, New Guardian Publishing Company, 1973.

Buhrs, T. "The Co-ordination of Environmental Policy: An Unresolved Dilemma". Paper presented at the NZPSA Conference, University of Otago, Dunedin, May 1990.

Buhrs, T. Working Within Limits: the Role of the Commission for the Environment in Environmental Policy Development in New Zealand. Unpublished Ph. D. Thesis, University of Auckland, 1991.

Burrell, R. *Fifty Years of Mountain Federation, 1931-1981*. Wellington, Federated Mountain Clubs of New Zealand, 1983.

Cameron, C. *Town and Country Planning. The Right Use and Development of Land. Planning Legislation and Administration in England and New Zealand: A Comparison*. Wellington, Report prepared for the Ministry of Works, 1947.

Cameron, R.J. "Destruction of the Indigenous Forests for Maori Agriculture during the Nineteenth Century", *New Zealand Journal of Forestry*, Vol. 9(1), 1964, pp. 98-109.

Cleveland, L. *The Anatomy of Influence: Pressure Groups and Politics in New Zealand*. Wellington, Hicks Smith & Sons, 1972.

Cleveland, L. "The Major Agencies of Central Government in New Zealand", in Cleveland, L. and Robinson, A.D. (eds.) *Readings in New Zealand Government*. Wellington, A.H. & A.W. Reed, 1972, pp. 20-64.

Cleveland, L. *The Politics of Utopia: New Zealand and Its Government*. Wellington, Methuen, 1979. Chapter 4 entitled "Cabinet and the Machinery of Government", pp. 67-95.

Commission for the Environment, *Environmental Policy and Management in New Zealand*. Wellington, Government Printer, 1980.

Commission for the Environment. *Environmental Policy and Management in New Zealand*. A Working Document for the OECD Country Review. Wellington, 1980.

Commission of Inquiry into Housing. *Housing in New Zealand*. Report of the Commission of Inquiry. Wellington, Government Printer, 1971.

Cox, J. "Organisation for National Development: Its Role in Post War Development", *People and Planning*, No. 13, March 1980, pp. 19-21.

Cox, J. " Administrative Change: An Early Threat to Planning", *People and Planning*, No. 15, September 1980, pp.14-16.

Cumberland, K.B. "A Century's Change: From Natural to Cultural Vegetation in New Zealand", *Geographical Review*, Vol. 31, 1941, pp. 529-554.

Cumberland, K.B. *Soil Erosion in New Zealand*. Christchurch, Whitcombe & Tombs, 1947 (2nd ed.).

Cumberland, K.B. "Man in Nature", *New Zealand Geographer*, Vol. 17(2), 1961, pp. 137-154.

Cumberland, K.B. *Landmarks*. Sydney, Reader's Digest Services Pty Ltd., 1981.

Dale, W.R. *Land Use Policies*. Wellington, N.Z. Institute of Public Administration, 1976.

Davies, E. "Planning in the New Zealand National Parks", *New Zealand Geographer*, Vol. 43(2), 1987, pp. 73-78 & p. 94.

Debreceny, P. (ed). *The Restless Land: The Story of the Tongariro National Park*. Wellington, Department of Lands and Survey, 1981.

Dingwall, P.R. (compiler) *People and Parks: Essays in the Development and Use of Protected Areas*. Information Series No. 10, Wellington, Department of Lands and Survey, 1984.

Ecology Action (Otago) Inc. *Nuclear Power for New Zealand*. Submission to the Royal Commission on Nuclear Power Generation in New Zealand. Dunedin, 1977.

Environmental Council. *A Review of the Indigenous Forest Policy and its Implementation*. Wellington, 1979.

Familton, A. "The Experience of the New Zealand Forest Service", in Gregory, R.J. (ed.) *The Official Information Act: A Beginning*. Studies in Public Administration, No. 29, Wellington, 1984, pp. 62-70.

Fischer, P. "The New Zealand Planning Council: A Case Study." OECD Co-operative Action Programme, Papers for Meeting on Aids to Policy Makers, Part II. Paris, April 1981.

Franklin, S.H. *Trade, Growth and Anxiety: New Zealand Beyond the Welfare State*. Wellington, Methuen, 1978.

Gale, R. and Miller, M. "Professional and Public Natural Resource Management Arenas: Forests and Marine Fisheries", *Environment and Behavior*, Vol. 17(6), 1985, pp. 651-678.

Gibbs, H.S. "Management of Land and Water Resources", in Johnston, R.J. (ed.) *Society and Environment in New Zealand*. Christchurch, Whitcombe & Tombs, 1974, pp. 170-184.

Gilbert, J.T.E. "Environmental Assessment in New Zealand", *The Northwest Environmental Journal*, Vol. 2(2), 1986, pp. 85-106.

Gow, L.J.A. "Impact Assessment and Resource Management Law Reform." Paper presented to IAIA Seminar on Science, Assessment and Sustainability. Vancouver, Canada, March 1990.

Grant, P.S. "The Structure of the Forest Service and its Economic Performance." Nelson, Nature Forest Action Council, undated.

Greenall, A.F. and Hamilton, D. "Soil Conservation Surveys in New Zealand", *New Zealand Journal of Science and Technology*, Vol. 35(6), 1954, pp 505-517.

Gresham, P.H. "Establishing the Policy Framework for Economic Development and Environmental Management: A Perspective from Down Under." Paper presented at the IAIA Conference, Barbados, June 1987.

Harris, W.W. Three Parks: An Analysis of the Origins and Evolution of the New Zealand National Park Movement. Unpublished M.A. Thesis, University of Canterbury, Christchurch, 1974.

Hawke, G.R. *Government in the New Zealand Economy*. Planning Paper No. 13. Wellington, New Zealand Planning Council, 1982.

Hawke, G.R. *The Making of New Zealand: An Economic History*. Cambridge, Cambridge University Press, 1985.

Healy B, *A Hundred Million Trees: The Story of New Zealand Forest Products Ltd*. Auckland, Hodder and Stoughton, 1982.

Hearn, T.J. "Riparian Rights and Sludge Channels: A Water Use Conflict in New Zealand, 1869-

1921", *New Zealand Geographer* Vol. 38(2), 1982, pp. 47-55.

Hearn, T.J. "Mining and Land: A Conflict Over Use 1858-1953", *New Zealand Law Journal*, August 1983, pp. 235-238.

Holland, P.G. and Johnston, W.B. (eds.) *Southern Approaches: Geography in New Zealand*. Christchurch, N.Z. Geographical Society, 1987.

Horsley, P. "Recent Resource Use Conflicts in New Zealand: Maori Perceptions and the Evolving Environmental Ethic", in Hay, P. Eckersley, R. and Holloway, G. (eds.) *Environmental Politics in Australia and New Zealand*. Occasional Paper No. 23. Centre for Environmental Studies, University of Tasmania, 1989,pp.124-143.

Hughes, H.R. "Assessing Cultural Impacts: Industrial Effluents and the New Zealand Maori", *Environmental Impact Assessment Review*, Vol. 6(3), pp. 285-97.

Hunt, D. *Resources and Technology: Sustainability*. Wellington, Commission for the Future, 1979.

Institution of Professional Engineers & Royal Society of New Zealand. *Water Conference Proceedings*. Various Years.

Interdepartmental Committee on the Pollution of Waters. *Report of the Committee*. Wellington, Marine Department, 1952.

Interdepartmental Committee on Water, *New Zealand Law and Administration in Respect of Water*. Report to Cabinet. Wellington, Ministry of Works, 1965.

Jackson, K.E. "Government and Enterprise: The Early Days of Electricity Generation and Supply in New Zealand", *British Review of New Zealand Studies*, No.1, 1988, pp. 101-121.

Jackson, W.K. *New Zealand: Politics of Change*. Wellington, A.H. & A.W. Reed, 1973. Chapter 7 entitled "The Motivators? – Pressure Groups" pp. 82-100.

Johnston, R.J. (ed.) *Society and Environment in New Zealand*. Christchurch, Whitcombe and Tombs Ltd, 1974.

Jourdain, W.R. *Land Legislation and Settlement in New Zealand*. Wellington, Government Printer, 1925.

Kellow, A.J. Ideology and Environmental Politics: the New Zealand Values Party 1972-1975. Unpublished B.A. Hons. Thesis, Univ. of Otago, 1975.

Kellow, A.J. *Pollution Control in New Zealand: Making Policies and Prescribing Placebos*. Public Sector Research Paper. Wellington, New Zealand Institute of Public Administration, 1983.

Kellow, A.J. "Electricity Planning in Tasmania and New Zealand: Political Processes and the Technological Imperative", *Australian Journal of Public Administration*, Vol. XLV(1), 1986, pp. 2-17.

Kelly, G.C. "Landscape and Nature Conservation" in Molloy, L.F. et. al.(compilers) *Land Alone Endures: Land Use and the Role of Research*. Discussion Paper No. 3. Wellington, Department of Scientific and Industrial Research, 1980, pp. 63-88.

Kilmartin, L. and Thorns, D.C. *Cities Unlimited: The Sociology of Urban Development in Australia and New Zealand*. Sydney, George Allen and Unwin, 1978.

King, L.J. "Urbanisation in an Agriculturally Dependent Society: Some Implications in New Zealand", *Tijdschrift voor Economische en Sociale Geografie*, Vol. 56, 1965 pp. 12-21.

Lees, A. "The Forest Service: Its Environmental Record." Nelson, Native Forest Action Council, undated.

Le Heron R.B. and Roche, M.M. "Expanding Exotic Forestry and the Extension of a Competing Use for Rural Land in New Zealand", *Journal of Rural Studies*, Vol. 1(3), 1985, pp. 211-229.

Levine, S. "Structural Features of New Zealand Government", in Levine, S. (ed.) *New Zealand Politics: A Reader*. Melbourne, Cheshire Press, 1975, pp. 360-364.

Levine, S. (ed.) *New Zealand Politics: A Reader*. Melbourne, Cheshire Press, 1975.

Lewin J.P. "Towards Functional Administration", *N.Z. Journal of Public Administration*, Vol. 7(2), 1945, pp. 39-51.

Lister, R.G. "Looking Ahead – When the Party is Over...", Winter Lecture Series, Waikato University, 1985.

McCaskill, L.W. *A History of Scenic Reserves in New Zealand*. Wellington, Lands and Survey Department, 1972.

McCaskill, L.W. *Hold This Land*. Dunedin, A.H. & A.W. Reed, 1973.

McCaskill, M. (ed.) *Land and Livelihood: Geographical Essays in Honour of George Jobberns*. Christchurch, N.Z. Geographical Society, 1962.

McGlone, M.S. "Polynesian Deforestation of New Zealand: A Preliminary Synthesis", *Archaeology in Oceania*, Vol. 18, 1983, pp. 22-25.

McMahon, C.K. (ed.) *The Physical Environment Conference 1970. Reports, Papers and Proceedings*. Wellington, Environmental Council, 1972.

Mahuta, R.T. Ritchie, J.E. Parsons, S. and Wishart, P. "The Need for Change. A Maori Community View." Submission to the Environment Forum, March 1985.

Mark, A.F. "Manapouri-Te Anau: Case Study of its Hydro-Electric Development from Conflict to Resolution." Paper presented to the Ecopolitics III Conference, University of Waikato, Hamilton, 1989.

Mascarenhas, R.C. *Public Enterprise in New Zealand*. Wellington, New Zealand Institute of Public Administration, 1982.

Mather, A.S. "Environmental Stress: Perception and Response in Two Examples from New Zealand", *International Journal of Environmental Studies*, Vol. 20, 1982, pp. 7-15.

Memon, P.A. "Planning for Resource Utilization: A Political Administrative Perspective", *Public Sector*, Vol.8(1/2), 1985, pp. 29-33.

Memon, P.A. "Urban Renewal Policy in New Zealand: In Search of a Direction?", *Urban Law and Policy*, Vol. 8, 1986 pp. 53-75.

Memon, P.A. "Decision Making for Multiple Utilization of Water Resources in New Zealand", *Environmental Management*, Vol. 13(4), 1989, pp. 553-62.

Mills, S.J. "Environmental Impact Reporting in New Zealand: A Study of Government Policy in a Period of Transition - Parts 1, II & III". *New Zealand Journal of Law*, 1979, pp. 472-484, 494-501, & 515-524.

Molloy, L.F. (ed.) *Land Alone Endures: Land Use and the Role of Research*. Wellington, Department of Scientific and Industrial Research, 1980.

Moran, W. "Processes and Policies for Land-Use Diversification", *New Zealand Agricultural Science*, Vol. 15, 1981, pp. 113-122.

Moran, W. "Sectoral and Statutory Planning for Rural New Zealand", in Cloke, P. (ed.) *Rural Land Use Planning for Developed Nations*. London, Unwin Hyman, 1989, pp. 238-263.

Morgan, R.K. "The Evolution of Environmental Impact Assessment in New Zealand", *Journal of Environmental Management*, Vol. 16, 1983, pp. 139-52.

Morgan, R.K. "Reshaping Environmental Impact Assessment in New Zealand", *Environment Impact Assessment Review*, Vol. 8, 1988, pp. 293-306.

National Development Council. *Plenary Session: Report of Proceedings of the National Development Conference*. Wellington, Government Printer, 1969.

National Development Council. *Report of the Physical Environment Committee to the National Development Conference*, May 1969. Wellington, Government Printer, 1971.

National Development Council. *Newsletter*. Wellington, 1972.

National Water and Soil Conservation Authority & Land Settlement Board. *Review of Policies for Destocking and Land Surrender: South Island High Country*. Wellington, NWASCA and LSB, 1985.

Nature Conservation Council. *The New Zealand Environment 1968-1974: A Bibliography*. Wellington, 1975.

Nature Conservation Council. *The New Zealand Environment: A Bibliography*. Supplements No.1 to No.5. Wellington, 1976 to 1982.

Newsome, P.F.J. *The Vegetative Cover of New Zealand*. Wellington, NWASCA, 1987. Chapter One entitled "New Zealand's Vegetation History", pp 11-21.

New Zealand Forest Service. *Management Policy for New Zealand's Indigenous State Forests*. Wellington, Government Printer, 1977.

Nicholls, J.L. "The Past and Present Extent of New Zealand's Indigenous Forests", *Environmental Conservation*, Vol. 7, 1980, 309-310.

Nielsen, S.A. "Pollution in New Zealand" in Levine, S. (ed.) *New Zealand Politics: A Reader*.

Melbourne, Cheshire Press, 1975, pp. 457-471.

Noonan, R.J. *By Design: A Brief History of the Public Works Department, Ministry of Works 1870-1970*. Wellington, Government Printer, 1978.

Norman, R.G. "Central Government's Established Policies and Organisation for Management of the Environment." Background Paper for the Seminar on the Environment. Wellington, 1973.

Organisation for Economic Cooperation and Development (OECD). *Environmental Policies in New Zealand*. Paris, 1980.

O'Riordan, T. "The Geographer and the New Conservation", in *Proceedings of Sixth N.Z. Geography Conference*. Christchurch, 1970, pp. 86-92.

O'Riordan, T. "New Zealand Resource Management in the Seventies: A Review of Three Recent Conferences", *New Zealand Geographer*, Vol. 27(2), 1971, pp. 197-210.

O'Riordan, T. & Sewell, W.R.D. (eds.) *Project Appraisal and Policy Review*. Chichester, John Wiley, 1981.

Palmer, K.A. *Planning and Development Law in New Zealand*. Vols. I & II. Sydney, The Law Book Company, 1984.

Patrick, M. "Maori Values of Soil and Water", *Soil and Water*, 1987, pp.22-29.

Pearce, D.G. and Richez, G. "Antipodean Contrasts: National Parks in New Zealand and Europe", *New Zealand Geographer* Vol. 43(2), 1987, pp. 53-59.

Polaschek, R.J. *Government Administration in New Zealand*. Wellington, NZ Institute of Public Administration, 1958.

Poole, A.L. *Forestry in New Zealand: The Shaping of Policy*. Auckland, Hodder and Stoughton in association with English Universities Press, 1969.

Relph, D.H. "A Century of Human Influence on High Country Vegetation", *New Zealand Geographer*, Vol. 14(2), 1958, pp. 131-46.

Robson, J.L. (ed.) *New Zealand: The Development of its Laws and Constitution*. London, Stevens, 1954.

Roche, M.M. "Securing Representative Areas of New Zealand's Environment: Some Historical and Design Perspectives", *N.Z.Geographer*, Vol. 37(2), 1981, pp.73-77.

Roche, M.M. "Some Historical Influences on the Establishment of Protected Natural Areas in New Zealand, 1880-1980", in Dingwall P.R. (compiler) *People and Parks: Essays in Development and Use of Protected Areas*. Information Series No. 10, Department of Lands and Survey, Wellington, 1984.

Roche, M.M. "Evolving Attitudes Towards New Zealand's Protected Areas System." A paper presented to the Seminar on Social and Historical Research in New Zealand's Parks and Protected Areas. Lincoln College, 27-30 August, 1984.

Roche, M.M. *Forest Policy in New Zealand*. Palmerston North, Dunmore Press, 1987.

Roche, M.M. "A Time and Place for National Parks", *N.Z. Geographer*, Vol. 42(2), 1987, pp.102-107.

Roche, M.M. "Deteriorated Lands, Soil Erosion and Rivers Control: Towards a Political Geography of Soil Conservation in New Zealand During the 1920s & 1930s", *Proceedings of Fifteenth NZ Geography Conference*, Dunedin, August 1989, pp. 108-117.

Salmon, G. "The Native Forest Action Council: An Alternative View", in R.J. Gregory (ed.) *The Official Information Act: A Beginning. Studies in Public Administration*, No. 29, 1984, pp.70-87.

Salmon, J.T. *Heritage Destroyed: The Crisis in Scenery Preservation in New Zealand*. Wellington, Reed, 1960.

Seale, G. *Rush to Destruction: An Appraisal of the New Zealand Beech Forest Controversy*. Wellington, A.H. & A.W. Reed, 1975.

Shirley, I. *Planning For Community*. Palmerston North, Dunmore Press, 1979.

Simpson, P. "A History of Ecological Thinking in New Zealand". Paper read to the History of Science in New Zealand Conference, Wellington, February 1983.

Small, D. "Environmentalism in NZ: The Potential for a Neo-anarchist Approach", *NZ Environment*, No. 25, 1979, pp. 22-26.

Sutch, W.B. *Recent Economic Changes in New Zealand*. Wellington, Institute of Pacific Relations, 1936.

Sutch, W.B. *Poverty and Progress in New Zealand.* Wellington, Modern Books, 1941.

Sutch, W.B. *The Quest for Security in New Zealand.* Harmondsworth, Penguin Books, 1942.

Task Force on Economic and Social Planning, *New Zealand at the Turning Point.* Wellington, 1976.

Thompson, J. *The Origins of the 1952 National Parks Act.* Wellington, Department of Lands and Survey, undated.

Town, G.A. *Policies for Regional Development in New Zealand.* Wellington, N.Z. Institute of Public Administration, 1972.

Town and Country Planning Division. *Planning Research Index.* Wellington, Ministry of Works and Development, various years.

Turner, A.R. "The Changing Basis of Decision-Making: Is Reason Sufficient ?", *N.Z. Engineering,* 1985, pp. 13-23.

Victoria University of Wellington in conjunction with the Urban Development Association (Inc.). *Action on Environment: Seminar Proceedings and Papers.* Wellington, 1972.

Waghorne, M. The Environmental Movement in New Zealand. Unpublished M.A. Thesis, Univ. of Canterbury, 1978.

Watters, R.F. (ed.) *Land and Society in New Zealand.* Wellington, A.H. & A.W. Reed, 1965.

Wells, N.E. *A Guide to Environmental Law in New Zealand.* Wellington, Brooker and Friend, 1984.

Whirinaki Forest Promotion Trust. *To Save a Forest: Whirinaki.* Auckland, David Bateman, 1984.

Williams, D.A.R. "Lawyers, Law Students and the Environment", in Levine, S. (ed.) *New Zealand Politics: A Reader.* Melbourne, Cheshire Press, 1975, pp. 249-251.

Williams, D.A.R. *Environmental Law in New Zealand.* Wellington, Butterworth, 1980.

Williams, G.R. (ed.) *The Natural History of New Zealand.* Wellington, A.H. & A.W. Reed, 1973.

Wynn, G. "Conservation and Society in Late Nineteenth-Century New Zealand", *New Zealand Journal of History,* Vol. 11(2), October 1977, pp. 124-136.

Wynn, G. "Pioneers, Politicians and the Conservation of Forests in Early New Zealand", *Journal of Historical Geography,* Vol. 5(2), 1979, pp. 171-88.

B. Recent Reforms

Bassett, Hon. M. "Introductory Speech: Local Government Amendment Bill 1988." 1R, Hansard, 1988, pp. 2883-2903.

Bassett, Hon. M. "Statement on Reform of Local and Regional Government." Wellington, Office of the Minister for Local Government, 1988.

Blakeley, R. "Environmental Policies in N.Z.: A Post-Review Report prepared for the 1980 OECD Environment Committee". Wellington, Ministry for the Environment, 1988.

Blakeley, R. "Reform of Resource Management Statutes." Paper presented at the Law Society Seminar, University of Auckland, 22 March 1988.

Boston, J. and Holland, M. (eds.) *The Fourth Labour Government: Radical Politics in New Zealand.* Auckland, Oxford University Press, 1987.

Boston, J., Martin, J. and Walsh, P. (eds.) *Reshaping the State: New Zealand's Bureaucratic Revolution.* Auckland, Oxford University Press, 1991.

Bridgeport Group. *Review of the Restructuring of Environment Agencies. Report to the State Services Commission.* Wellington, 1988.

Britton, S., Le Heron, R. and Pawson, E. (eds.) *Changing Places in New Zealand: A Geography of Restructuring.* Christchurch, New Zealand Geographical Society, 1992.

Bromley, D. *Property Rights and the Environment. Natural Resource Policy in Transition: A series of lectures in August 1987.* Wellington, Ministry for the Environment, 1988.

Brown, Copeland and Co Ltd. *District and Regional Planning in New Zealand: Objectives, Performance and Alternatives: A Report prepared for the Department of Trade and Industry and the Treasury.* Auckland, March 1987.

Burke, Hon. T.K. "Labour Government Plan for Regions", *Otago Daily Times,* 15 January 1985.

Bush, G. "The Historic Reorganisation of Local Government", in Holland, M. and Boston, J. (eds.) *The Fourth Labour Government: Politics and Policy in New Zealand.* Auckland, Oxford

University Press, 1990, pp. 232-250.

Caldwell, J. *An Ecological Approach to Environmental Law.* Publication No.29. Auckland, Legal Research Foundation, 1988.

Clark, M. and Sinclair, E. (eds.) *Purpose, Performance and Profit: Redefining the Public Sector.* Studies in Public Administration No 32. Wellington, Government Printer, 1987.

Cocklin, C. "The Restructuring of Environmental Administration in New Zealand", *Journal of Environmental Management*, Vol.28, 1989, pp. 309-326.

"Conservation Underfunding Blow for Tourism". *Otago Daily Times*, Dunedin, 17/6/1991.

Cullen, M. "The Environment: The Prospects for the Future." Speech to the Auckland Minewatch/Auckland RFBPS, 3 August 1983.

Dahlberg, K.A. "The Challenge of Making New Zealand Agriculture More Sustainable", *New Zealand Sociology*, Vol.5(1), 1990, pp. 27-43.

Dean, R. "Public Sector Reform: A Review of the Issues" in Clark, M. and Sinclair, E. (eds.) *Purpose, Performance and Profit: Redifining the Public Sector.* Wellington, Government Printer, 1987.

Department of Conservation. *Options for Conservation Quangos: A Paper for Public Comment.* Wellington, 1987.

Department of Conservation. *Options for Conservation Quangos: Synopsis of Submissions on Discussion Paper.* Prepared by Synergy Applied Research. Wellington, December 1987.

Department of Conservation. *Report for the year ended 31 March, 1988.* Wellington, Government Printer, 1988.

Department of Conservation. *Review of Conservation Quangos: DoC Position Paper.* Wellington, February 1988.

Department of Conservation. *Report for the year ended 31 March, 1989.* Wellington, Government Printer, 1989.

Department of Conservation. *Corporate Plan 1990-91.* Wellington, July 1990.

Department of Conservation. *Draft N.Z. Coastal Policy Statement.* Wellington, DoC, 1990.

Department of Conservation. *Report for the year ended 30 June, 1990.* Wellington, Government Printer, 1990.

Department of Internal Affairs. *Background Paper on Power of General Competence.* Wellington, 1990.

Department of Lands and Survey and New Zealand Forest Service. *Submissions on the Proposed Merger of the Department of Lands and Survey and the New Zealand Forest Service.* Wellington, April, 1983.

Douglas, E. "The Maori", *Pacific Viewpoint*, Vol. 32(2), 1991, pp. 129-138.

Douglas, R. *There has to be a Better Way.* Wellington, Fourth Estate Books, 1982.

Econews. "Resource Management and Government Reforms." No. 10, Wellington, (July 1988).

Economic Development Commission. *Town and Country Planning Reform.* Wellington, 1987.

Elwood, B. "Address to Counties' Conference", *New Zealand Local Government*, July 1986, pp. 31-32.

Elwood, B. "Address to Regional, Territorial and Special Purpose Authority Representatives." Auckland, 28 September, 1988.

Environment Administration Task Group (on behalf of RFBPSNZ, Federated Mountain Clubs, NFAC, Environmental Defence Society, Greenpeace & ECO). *Environmental Administration in N.Z.: An Alternative Discussion Paper.* Nelson, January 1985.

Environment Forum Secretariat. *Environment Forum Papers, 7-9 March 1985.* Wellington, 1985.

Environment Forum Secretariat. *Environment Forum Synopsis of Submissions and Forum Record.* Wellington 1985.

Environmental Administration Task Group (on behalf of RFBPSNZ, Federated Mountain Clubs, N.Z., NFAC, Environment Defence Society, Greenpeace & ECO). *Environmental Administration in N.Z. – An Alternative Discussion Paper.* Nelson, January 1985.

Environmental Council. *The Environmental Council's View on the OECD Review of Environmental Policies in N.Z.* Wellington, 1981.

Environmental Council and Ministry for the Environment. *Environment Meets Economics: 1986*

Debate Series. Wellington, 1987.

Environmental Council. *A Citizens Voice for the Environment: Is there a Need for an Environmental Quango?* Discussion Paper. Wellington, August 1987.

"Environmentalists and the Treasury: Unholy Allies". *National Business Review*, Wellington, 6/2/1987.

Establishment Unit for the Parliamentary Commissioner and Ministry for the Environment. *Preliminary Draft Strategic Plan for the Office of Parliamentary Commissioner for the Environment.* Wellington, 1986.

Establishment Unit for the Parliamentary Commissioner and Ministry for the Environment. *Draft Strategic Plan.* Wellington, August 1986.

Establishment Unit for the Parliamentary Commissioner and Ministry for the Environment. *Policy Discussion Papers.* Wellington, August 1986.

"Financial Worries Make Young DoC Look Sick". *National Business Review*, Wellington, 29/9/1988.

Fisher, D. "The New Environmental Management Regime in New Zealand", *Environment and Planning Law Journal*, Vol 4(1), 1987, pp. 33-44.

Fisher, D. "Clarity in a Little 'While'", *Terra Nova*, November 1991, pp. 50-51.

Fookes, T.W. "New Zealand: New Environmental Administration", *Environmental Policy and Law*, Vol.17(3/4), 1987, 129-34.

Franklin, H. "New Zealand in the Eighties", *Pacific Viewpoint*, Vol. 32(2), 1991, pp. 119-120.

Garrad, I.M. *Commercialisation in the Management of New Zealand's Natural Resources.* Sydney, Soil Conservation Service of New South Wales. December 1989.

Glasby, G.P. "A Review of the Concept of Sustainable Management as Applied to New Zealand", *Journal of the Royal Society of New Zealand*, Vol. 21(2), 1991, pp. 61-81.

Government Economic Statement 1987. Wellington, 17 December 1987.

Gresham, P.H. "Some Reflections on the Origins, Evolution and Future of the Commission for the Environment." Wellington, Commission for the Environment, 14 September 1983.

Hearn, A. *Report of the Review of the Town and Country Planning Act 1977.* Wellington, Department of Trade and Industry, 1987.

"Hearn Report: Starting Point for New Mining Accord". *National Business Review*, Wellington, 21/9/1987.

Hide, R.P. "New Zealand's Resource Management Law Reform: the Wrong Direction", *Policy*, Spring 1989, pp.17-19.

Holland, M. and Boston, J. (eds.) *The Fourth Labour Government: Politics and Policy in New Zealand.* Auckland, Oxford University Press, 1990.

Interdepartmental Committee on The Review of Mining Legislation. *A Discussion Paper on Policy Issues for the Review of Mining Legislation.* March 1987.

International Union for the Conservation of Nature and Natural Resources. *World Conservation Strategy.* Gland, Switzerland, 1980.

Lawrence, J. and Lawrence R. "The Environment", *Pacific Viewpoint*, Vol. 32(2), 1991, pp. 201-209.

Local Government Commission. *Memorandum to Assist Authorities Affected by Local Government Re-organization.* Wellington, 22 July 1988.

Local Government Commission. *Memorandum to Regional, Territorial and Special Purpose Authorities.* Wellington, 28 September 1988.

McKinlay, P. "The Place of Planning in a Market Economy." Address to West Coast North Island Planning Group, Palmerston North, 6 May 1986.

McKinlay, P. (ed.) *Redistribution of Power? Devolution in New Zealand.* Wellington, Victoria University Press for the Institute of Policy Studies, 1990.

Memon, P.A. *Review of Regional Initiatives Under the Local Government Act 1974.* Wellington, Ministry For the Environment 1988.

Memon, P.A. "Decision Making for Multiple Utilization of Water Resources in New Zealand", *Environmental Management*, Vol.13(5), 1989, pp. 553-562.

Memon, P.A. "Shaking Off a Colonial Legacy?: Town and Country Planning in New Zealand, 1870s to 1980s", *Planning Perspectives*, Vol.6, 1991, pp. 19-32.

Memon, P.A. and Cullen, R. "New Zealand Fisheries Policies and Maori", in Whitwell, J. and Thompson, M.A. (eds.), *Society and Culture: Economic Perspectives*. Wellington, New Zealand Association of Economists, 1991, pp. 77-87.

Memon P.A. and Cullen, R. "Fishery Policies and their Impact on the New Zealand Maori", *Marine Resource Economics*, Vol.7(3), 1992, pp. 153-157.

Memon, P.A. and Wilson, G.A. *Recent Indigenous Forest Policy Issues in New Zealand. An Annotated Bibliography.* Environmental Policy and Management Research Centre, Publication No. 2. Dunedin, University of Otago, 1992.

Ministry for the Environment. *Land Allocations to the Department of Conservation and the State Owned Enterprises: Report on Public Submissions. Vol.2: Public Lands Coalition Submission.* Wellington, June 1987.

Ministry for the Environment. *Report for the period 1 December 1986 to 31 March 1987.* Wellington, Government Printer, 1987.

Ministry for the Environment. *Report for the year ended 31 March 1988.* Wellington, Government Printer, 1988.

Ministry for the Environment. *Directions for Change: A Discussion Paper.* Wellington, 1988.

Ministry for the Environment. *Ecological Principles for Resource Management.* Wellington, 1988.

Ministry for the Environment. *Economic Instruments for Environmental Management: An Overview.* Wellington, 1988.

Ministry for the Environment. *Equity in Resource Allocation: A Discussion Paper.* Wellington, 1988.

Ministry for the Environment. *People, the Environment and Decision Making: The Government's Proposals for Resource Management Law Reform.* Wellington, 1988.

Ministry for the Environment. *RMLR: A Collection of Discussion Papers.* Wellington, [1988].

Ministry for the Environment. *Fundamental Issues in Resource Management.* RMLR Working Paper No.1. Wellington, 1988.

Ministry for the Environment. *Analysis of Existing Statutes: Departmental Views.* RMLR Working Paper No.2. Wellington, 1988.

Ministry for the Environment. *Review of Submissions on the Future Role of Local and Regional Government.* RMLR Working Paper No.3. Wellington, 1988.

Ministry for the Environment. *The Role of Government in Pollution and Hazardous Waste Substances Management; The Management of Pollution and Hazardous Substances.* RMLR Working Paper No.4. Wellington, 1988.

Ministry for the Environment. *The Rights to Use Land, Water, and Minerals.* RMLR Working Paper No.5. Wellington, 1988.

Ministry for the Environment. *Users Group Working Papers.* RMLR Working Paper No.6. Wellington, 1988.

Ministry for the Environment. *Analysis of Existing Statutes: Legal Analysis.* RMLR Working Paper No.7. Wellington, 1988.

Ministry for the Environment. *The Treaty of Waitangi and its Significance to the Reform of Resource Management Laws.* RMLR Working Paper No.8. Wellington, 1988.

Ministry for the Environment. *Waitangi Tribunal Findings Analysis.* RMLR Working Paper No.9. Wellington, 1988.

Ministry for the Environment. *Resource Values.* RMLR Working Paper No.10. Wellington, 1988.

Ministry for the Environment. *Analysis of Phase One Public Submissions.* RMLR Working Paper No.11. Wellington, 1988.

Ministry for the Environment. *Public Participation.* RMLR Working Paper No.12. Wellington, 1988.

Ministry for the Environment. *Objectives for Resource Management: Why, What and How.* RMLR Working Paper No.13. Wellington, 1988.

Ministry for the Environment. *Compensation: An Examination of the Law.* RMLR Working Paper No.14. Wellington, 1988.

Ministry for the Environment. *Part A: Natural Hazards and Resource Management Law; Part B: The Role of Information in Resource Management.* RMLR Working Paper No.15. Wellington, 1988.

Ministry for the Environment. *The Various Roles of the Crown: as Resource Developer and as a Participant in Resource Management*. RMLR Working Paper No.16. Wellington, 1988.

Ministry for the Environment. *Public Participation: Options for Legislation*. RMLR Working Paper No.17. Wellington, 1988.

Ministry for the Environment. *Public Participation in Policy Formation and Development Consents*. RMLR Working Paper No.18. Wellington, 1988.

Ministry for the Environment. *Decision Making Processes and Structures: Two Contributions to Resource Management Law Reform*. RMLR Working Paper No.19. Wellington, 1988.

Ministry for the Environment. *Impact Assessment in Resource Management*. RMLR Working Paper No.20. Wellington, 1988.

Ministry for the Environment. *Synopsis of Submissions Received in Response to Directions for Change*. RMLR Working Paper No.21. Wellington, 1988.

Ministry for the Environment. *Resource Management Disputes: Part A: The Role of Courts and Tribunals; Part B: Mediation*. RMLR Working Paper No.22. Wellington, 1988.

Ministry for the Environment. *Coastal Legislation: Options for Reform*. RMLR Working Paper No.23. Wellington, 1988.

Ministry for the Environment. *Sustainability; Intrinsic Values and the Needs of Future Generations*. RMLR Working Paper No.24. Wellington, 1988.

Ministry for the Environment. *Implementing the Sustainability Objective in Resource Management Law*. RMLR Working Paper No.25. Wellington, 1988.

Ministry for the Environment. *Geothermal Energy: Maori and Related Issues* (by R P Boast). RMLR Working Paper No.26. Wellington, 1988.

Ministry for the Environment. *A Treaty Based Model: The Principle of Active Protection* (by Mike Barns). RMLR Working Paper No.27. Wellington, 1988.

Ministry for the Environment. *Part A: Town and Country Planning and the Treaty of Waitangi* (by Margaret Cotton); *Part B: The Planning System and the Recognition of Maori Tribal Plans* (by Kenneth Palmer); *Part C: Maori Participation in Resource Management* (by Mark Gray). RMLR Working Paper No.28. Wellington, 1988.

Ministry for the Environment. *Part A: The Natural World and Natural Resources: Maori Value Systems and Perspectives* (by Rev. Maori Marsden); *Part B: Water Resources and the Kai Tahu Claim* (by David Palmer and Anake Goodall). RMLR Working Paper No. 29. Wellington, 1988.

Ministry for the Environment. *Enforcement and Compliance Issues in Resource Management* (by D. J. Berwick). RMLR Working Paper No.30. Wellington, 1988.

Ministry for the Environment. *National Policy Matters in Resource Management* (by K. Cronin). RMLR Working Paper No.31. Wellington, 1988.

Ministry for the Environment. *Public Submissions in Response to People, Environment and Decision Making*. RMLR Working Paper No.32. Wellington, 1988.

Ministry for the Environment. *Corporate Plan 1989-1990*. Wellington, 1989.

Ministry for the Environment. *Report for the year ended 31 March, 1989*. Wellington, Government Printer, 1989.

Ministry for the Environment. *An Introduction for Local Government to Performance Standards in Resource Management. A Working Draft for Discussion Purposes*. Wellington, April 1991.

Ministry for the Environment. *Corporate Plan 1992/93*. Wellington, 1992.

Ministry of Agriculture and Fisheries. *Sustainable Agriculture: A Policy Proposal*. Wellington, 1991.

Ministry of Energy. *Position Papers on the Review of Minerals and Energy Legislation*. Wellington, October 1988.

Moriarty, M.J. "Alternative Approaches to Planning in a Free Market Economy." Wellington, 18 September 1986.

National Parks and Reserves Authority. *General Policy for National Parks*. Wellington, Department of Lands and Survey, 1983.

NFAC. "Are Things Really Going to Change?", *Bush Telegraph*, No. 20, (May 1985), pp. 1-2.

NFAC. "High Hopes of Success with Russell Marshall", *Bush Telegraph*, No. 21, (August 1985), p.1.

NFAC. "Labour's Team Says: 'Trust Us'", *Bush Telegraph*, No.29, (August 1987), p.1.

NFAC. "We Speak for the Trees: New Challenges for the NFAC 1987-1990." Nelson, [undated].

Nature Conservation Council. *Integrating Conservation and Development: A Proposal for a N.Z Conservation Strategy.* Wellington, 1981.

Nature Conservation Council. "Council to End, Conservation Department recommends", *Newsletter*, No.68, (Jan-April 1988).

Nature Conservation Council. *Nature Conservation Council 1962-1982.* Wellington [undated].

N.Z. Labour Party. *Policy for 1981: Environment Policy,* Wellington, 1981.

N.Z. Labour Party. *The 1984 Policy Statement.* Wellington, 1984.

N.Z. Labour Party. *Environment Policies.* Wellington, 1984.

N.Z. Labour Party. *Local Government Backgrounder.* Wellington, 1984.

N.Z. Labour Party. "Environment Policy: Administration and Planning." Press Statement by Cullen, M. Wellington, 28 April 1984.

N.Z. Labour Party. "Natural Waters Policy." Press statement by Cullen, M. Wellington, 30 May 1984.

N.Z. Labour Party. *Environment Policy: Progress Report.* Wellington, March 1985.

N.Z. Labour Party. *Draft Proposals for Labour Party Environment Policy.* Wellington, 1987.

N.Z. National Party. *The Environment: Position Paper Prepared by the Government Research Unit.* Wellington, 21 June 1984.

N.Z. Planning Council. *Economic Strategy.* Wellington, 1979.

N.Z. Planning Council. *Directions.* Wellington, 1981.

N.Z. Planning Council. Environmental/ Natural Resources Restructuring. NZPC Working Paper, 1989.

New Zealand Planning Institute. *The Challenge of Change. Proceedings of a National Conference on Planning and Resource Management.* Wellington, May 9-12, 1990.

New Zealand Regional Government Association. *Report of the First Annual Conference.* Whakatane, 30 April - 4 May, 1990.

OECD. *Environmental Policies in New Zealand.* Paris, 1980.

Office of the Parliamentary Commissioner for the Environment. *Gisborne District Council Environmental Management: A Systems and Processes Review.* Wellington, 1990.

Officials Co-ordinating Committee on Local Government. *Reform of Local and Regional Government: Funding Issues. A Discussion Document.* Wellington, 1988.

Officials Co-ordinating Committee on Local Government. *Reform of Local and Regional Government: Discussion Document.* Wellington, 1988.

Officials Co-ordinating Committee on Local Government. *Bill for the Establishment of Maori Advisory Committees in Local Government and Explanatory Statement.* Wellington, 1989.

Palmer, G. *Unbridled Power?: An Interpretation of New Zealand's Constitution and Government.* 2nd edition. Auckland, Oxford University Press, 1987.

Palmer, G. *Environmental Politics: A Greenprint for New Zealand.* Dunedin, McIndoe, 1990.

Palmer, G. "Sustainability: New Zealand's Resource Management Legislation." Unpublished Manuscript, June 1991.

Parliamentary Commissioner for the Environment. *Report for the three months ended 31 March 1987.* Wellington, Government Printer, 1987.

Parliamentary Commissioner for the Environment. *Report for the year ended 31 March 1988.* Wellington, Government Printer, 1988.

Parliamentary Commissioner for the Environment. *Report for the year ended 31 March 1989.* Wellington, Government Printer, 1989.

Parliamentary Commissioner for the Environment. *Corporate Plan 1990-91.* Wellington, 1991.

Public Lands Coalition. *Public Land News.* Dunedin, November 1988.

"Resource Management and Government Reforms." *Econews,* No.10, Wellington, July 1988.

Review Group on the Resource Management Bill. *Report on the Resource Management Bill.* Wellington, 11 February 1991.

Royal Forest and Bird Protection Society (RFBPSNZ). "1984 Election Policies." Supplement to *Bush Telegraph* No.16, June 1984.

RFBPSNZ, Federated Mountain Clubs of N.Z., NFAC, Environmental Defence Society, and Environment and Conservation Organisations of N.Z. *Environmental Management in N.Z: A Strategy.* October 1982.

"Schemes Create 'Modern Local Government System'". *Southland Times*, Invercargill, 13/6/ 1989.

Smith, D.L. "Address to the Seminar on Local and Regional Implications of Recent and Proposed Changes in Environmental Administration." Dunedin, University of Otago, October 1987.

State Services Commission. *Environmental Administration in N.Z.: A Discussion Paper.* Wellington, 1984.

Suggate, R. "Management Planning Provisions in the Conservation Law Reform Bill." Paper for Management Planning Seminar. Wellington, DoC, 7-9 March 1991.

Synergy Applied Research Ltd. *Synopsis of Submissions and Forum Record.* Wellington, Environment Forum Secretariat, 1985.

Synergy Applied Research Ltd. *Synopsis of Submissions on Funding Issues.* Wellington, 1989.

Synergy Applied Research Ltd. *Synopsis: The Resource Management Bill 1989.* Wellington, December 1989.

Tapsell Hon. Peter, "High Country Pastoral Leases and the Need for Natural Historic and Environmental Protection." Speech to the North Canterbury High Country Section of Federated Farmers, 29 March 1989.

Task Force on Economic and Social Planning. *New Zealand at the Turning Point.* Wellington, 1976.

The Bridgeport Group. *Review of the Restructuring of Environment Agencies: Report to the State Services Commission.* Wellington, 1988.

The Bridgeport Group. *Synopsis of Submissions on Reform of Local and Regional Government: Report to the Officials Co-ordinating Committee on Local Government.* Wellington, Department of Internal Affairs, 1988

The Bridgeport Group. *Reform of Local and Regional Government: Synopsis of Submissions on Bill for Establishment of Maori Advisory Committees in Local Government and Explanatory Statement. Report to the Officials Co-ordinating Committee on Local Government.* Wellington, Dept. of Internal Affairs, April, 1990.

The Treasury. *Economic Management.* Wellington, Government Printer, 1984.

The Treasury. *Economic Management: Land Use Issues.* Wellington, Government Printer, 1984.

Town and Country Planning Directorate. *Mission Statement, Functions and Activities.* Wellington, MOW&D, 1987.

Town and Country Planning Directorate. *Submission on Review of the Town and Country Planning Act 1977.* Wellington, MoW&D, 1987.

Town and Country Planning Division. *Report of the Committee on the Review of the District Scheme.* Wellington, MoW&D, 1981.

Upton, Hon. S. "Resource Management Bill." Press Statement, Wellington, February 27 1991.

Upton, Hon. S. "Resource Management Bill 1991." 3R, Hansard, 1991, pp. 3018-3020.

Water and Soil Directorate. *1987/1988 Management Plan.* Wellington, MoW&D, 1987.

Welch, R.V. "Local Government Commissions and Local Government Reform: The Failures and Now Success?", *Public Sector*, Vol.12(1), 1989, pp. 3-6.

Wheeler, P.B. "Changing the Ground Rules of the Planning System." Palmerston North, City Planning Dept, [undated].

Wilson, M. *Labour in Government, 1984-1987.* Wellington, Allen and Unwin/Port Nicholson Press, 1989.

Wood, G.A. (ed.) *Ministers and Members in the New Zealand Parliament. Part 1: NZ Ministries 1912-1987.* Dunedin, Tarkwode Press, 1987.

Wood, G.A. (ed.) *Supplement to Ministers and Members in the New Zealand Parliament. NZ Ministries 1987-1991.* Dunedin, Tarkwode Press, 1992.

Woollaston, Hon. P.T.E. "DoC Structure and Function." Address to the Hill and High Country Seminar, Lincoln College, July 1987.

Working Party on Environmental Administration. *Report of the Post-Environment Forum Work-*

ing Party. Wellington, State Services Commission, June 1985.

Working Party on Regional Government Funding. *Interim Report to the Officials Co-ordinating Committee on Local Government*. Wellington, August 1990.

Working Party on the Future of Regional Councils. *The Future of Regional Councils. Report to the Minister of Local Government and the Minister for the Environment*. Wellington, 1991.

Archive of Material in the Ministry for the Environment on the Reorganisation of Environmental Administration During the Period 1984 to 1987:

Folio No.　　Folio Title

1. N.Z. Labour Party Pre-election Environment Policy Parts I to IV.
2. Cabinet Policy Committee, P(84) 30, 5 November 1984. Creation of Ministry for the Environment.
3. CPC Minutes P(84) M12 Part 2, 13 November 1984. Creation of Ministry for the Environment.
4. *Environmental Administration in NZ: A Discussion Paper*. November 1984.
5. Acting CfE/Under-Sectretary for the Environment, 13 December 1984. Briefing on developments among officials following CPC decisions on 13/11/84.
6. Principal Planning Judge Turner/Under-Secretary for the Environment, 31 January 1985.
7. Cabinet Minute CM 85/3/7, 4 February 1985. Environmental Forum.
8. SSC/Environment Related Departments, 5 February 1985. Environmental Adminstration: Progress Report.
9. *Environment Forum 1985: Background Papers*.
10. Terms of reference etc. for Post-Forum Working Party.
11. News release. Minister for the Environment, 15 March 1985. Follow-up to Environment Forum.
12. *Environment Forum 1985: Synopsis of Submissions and Forum Record*. April 1985.
13. CfE/Minister for the Environment. Briefing note for meeting with Minister of Works and Development re: Ministry for the Environment, 22 May 1985.
14. File note, 21 May 1985. Environmental Administration: Further Consultations.
15. CfE/SSC, 28 May 1985. *Report of the Working Party on Environmental Administration*.
16. Social Impact Working Group/Ministry for the Environment, 28 May 1985.
17. CfE/President Federated Farmers, 5 June 1985. Development/Conservation/Preservation.
18. Minister of Maori Affairs, Lands and Forests/ Chairman CPC, 10 June 1985. Environmental Administration: Implementation of Policy.
19. Treasury Report 2864. *Report of the Working Party on Environmental Administration*. Minister for the Environment's Proposals, 10 June 1985.
20. Minister for the Environment/CPC. Environmental Administration: Implementation of Policy.
20a. SSC/Permanent Heads (early June). Departmental response to the Report of Working Party on Environmental Administration.
21. SSC/Acting Minister of State Services, 10 June 1985. Report on extent of consultations by Working Party on Environmental Administration, and comments on significant issues raised by departmental responses.
22. CPC Minutes, P(85) M21 Part 4, 11 June 1985. Environmental Administration.
23. Treasury report 2864, *Report of the Working Party on Environmental Administration*, 10 June 1985.
24. Minister for the Environment/Cabinet. Memorandum on Environmental Administration, 14 June 1985. SSC/Minister for the Environment, 13 June 1985. Report òf departmental meeting (12 June 1985) to consider the report of the Minister for the Environment and Treasury (No 2864) to CPC (11 June 1985).
25. CfE/Minister for the Environment, 14 June 1985. Briefing on issues to go before Cabinet.
26. DG, Department of Social Welfare/Minister of Social Welfare, 14 June 1985. Working Party Report on Environmental Administration.

27. Note on Working Party on Environmental Administration. David Butcher, MP.
28. Hon. Russell Marshall/Hon. David Caygill, 17 June 1985. Briefing on issues to go before Cabinet.
29. CfE/Acting Minister for the Environment, 17 June 1985. Briefing on issues to go before Cabinet.
30. Cabinet Minute CM 85/21/12, 17 June 1985. Environmental Administration.
31. Prime Minister. Press Release, 18 June 1985. Government Decisions on Environmental Administration.
32. SSC/CfE, 19 June 1985. Procedures for officials' reports and external consultations.
33. *Environment 1986*. Report of the Post-Environmental Forum Working Party, June 1985.
34. File Note, 3 July 1985. Officials Working Party – Ministry for the Environment issues.
35. Parliamentary Under-Secretary for the Environment and Local Government. Opening Address to the Environmental Defence Society Annual Meeting. 22 July 1985.
36. CfE/SSC, 2 August 1985. Degree of consultation between WPEA and the Forest Service during the final stages of drawing up *Environment 1986*.
37. Minister of Lands and Forests/Minister for the Environment, 5 August 1985. Finding an effective mechanism of meeting policy commitments on a nature conservancy division which can be put in place with a minimum of disruption of existing structures.
    An integrated approach to the management of lands of the Crown. Some alternative proposals to those contained in the *Environment 1986* report. Department of Lands and Survey and NZ Forest Service. August 1985.
38. CfE/Minister for the Environment, 8 August 1985. Briefing on the options for nature conservation.
39. Minister for the Environment. Address to ECO Conference 10 August 1985.
40. Minister for the Environment. Press release, 16 August 1985. Options for a nature conservancy.
41. Minister of Works and Development/Chairman, Officials Coordinating Committee, 30 August 1985. Views on role and functions of MfE as proposed by WPEA.
42. Officials Report on the recommendations of the WPEA regarding the Ministry for the Environment, 2 September 1985.
43. Minister for the Environment/Minister of State Services, 3 September 1985. Submission to CPC on matters raised in the WPEA report and which the Officials Co-ordinating Committee had been directed to report on.
44. CPC Agenda, P(85) A 34, for a meeting on 10 September 1985.
45. CPC paper, P(85)116, 6 September 1985. Environmental Administration: Heritage NZ.
46. CPC paper, P(85)117, 6 September 1985. Environmental Administration: Ministry for the Environment. Includes Statement of Government Aims as Appendix 1 of SSC report to Minister of State Services.
47. *Environmental Administration in NZ*. A summary of submissions and consultative meetings on environmental administration. Synergy Applied Research Ltd. 9 September 1985.
48. CPC Minute, P(85) M34 Part 1, 10 September 1985. Environmental Administration.
49. CfE/Minister for the Environment, 12 September 1985. MfE-Budget 1986/87.
50. Cabinet Minute. CM 85/34/13, 16 September 1985. Environmental Administration: (Establishment of DoC, LDMC, commercial forestry agency, DOSLI; MfE not to have direct responsibility for administration of Town and Country Planning and Water and Soil statutes.)
51. Minister for the Environment and State Services. Press statement, 16 September 1985. Environmental Administration.
52. SSC/Ministers for the Environment, State Services, Lands and Forests. September 1985. Aide-memoire Environmental Administration.
53. CfE/SSC. 19 September 1985. Environmental Administration: Implementation. (Includes a paper bringing together the decisions made by Government to date on the MfE.)
54. Officials Steering Committee. Environmental Administration: A Discussion Paper – Outstanding Matters.
55. Draft paper to Minister of State Services seeking clarification of some aspects of Cabi-

net's decision on 1 September 1985.

56. Ministerial Ad Hoc Committee, 30 September 1985. Agenda and Papers.
57. Ministerial Ad Hoc Committee, 30 September 1985. Minutes.
58. Ministerial Ad Hoc Committee, 7 October 1985. Agenda and papers (includes EPP, Crown leases).
59. Ministerial Ad Hoc Committee, 7 October 1985. Minutes.
60. SSC/Union Delegates, 9 October 1985. Environmental Administration.
61. Ministerial Ad Hoc Committee, 14 October 1985. Agenda and papers (includes EPP).
62. Ministerial Ad Hoc Committee, 14 October 1985. Minutes.
63. CPC Minute, P(85) M 39 Part 1, 15 October 1985. Resource Recovery Grant Scheme.
64. Under-Secretary for the Environment/Ministerial Ad Hoc Committee. 21 October 1985. Environmental Planning Procedures.
65. Minsterial Ad Hoc Committee, 21 October 1985. Agenda and papers (includes EPP).
66. Ministerial Ad Hoc Committee, 21 October 1985. Minutes.
67. KP/PG, 21 October 1985. Relationship between the Town and County Planning Act and the EP&EP.
68. Environmental Assessment Procedures.
69. Note by K. A. Edmonds on meeting with Woollaston 23 October 1985 re: EAP.
70. File note on discussions between CfE and Federated Farmers re proposed changes to environmental administration, 23 October 1985.
71. CfE/Under-Secretary for the Environment, 24 October 1985. Relationship of the functions and responsibilities of the DoC to those of the MfE and to the Office of Parliamentary Commissioner.
72. Minister for the Environment/Ministerial Ad Hoc Committee. Environmental Planning Procedures and their legislation requirements.
73. Ministerial Ad Hoc Committee, 31 October 1985. Minutes (includes EPP).
74. Prime Minister/Mr Guy Salmon, Group of Six. 31 October 1985. Group of Six/Prime Minister, 5 September 1985.
75. Note of in-house CfE meeting on draft functions for MfE, 1 November 1985.
76. Ministerial Ad Hoc Committee, 4 November 1985. Agenda and papers (includes DoC – legislation and functions; DoC - transfer of land; MfE - legislation and functions.
77. Ministerial Ad Hoc Committee, 4 November 1985. Minutes.
78. S. Arnold, Environmental Secretariat/Officials Steering Committee. MfE – breadth of values to be considered by MfE.
79. References to Somerville draft of Environment Bill and Environmental Assessment Regulations.
80. Ministerial Ad Hoc Committee, 11 November 1985. Agenda and papers (quangos).
81. Ministerial Ad Hoc Committee, 11 November 1985. Minutes.
82. CfE/SSC, 12 November 1985. Structure for the MfE.
83. Treasury/CfE. Thoughts on what approach may be taken to the review of EAP.
84. CPC, Agenda for 12 November 1985.
85. CPC, P(85) 141, 11 November 1985. Environmental Administration - Progress and Strategy Report.
86. CPC, P(85) 142, 11 November 1985. DoC - legislation, mission and functions.
87. CPC, P(85) 143, 11 November 1985. Transfer of Lands to the Department of Conservation.
88. CPC, P(85)144, 11 November 1985. Proposed Department of Survey and Land Information.
89. CPC, P(85) 145, 11 November 1985. Drafting Instructions: MfE and Parliamentary Commissioner for the Environment(PCFE).
90. CPC, P(85) 147, 11 November 1985. Environmental Planning Procedures and their Legislative Requirements.
91. CPC, Minute, P(85) M43 Part 1, 13 November 1985. Environmental Administration – Progress and Strategy Report.

92. CPC, Minute, P(85) M43 Part 2, 13 November 1985. DoC – legislation, mission and functions.
93. CPC, Minute, P(85) M43 Part 3, 13 November 1985. Transfer of Lands to DoC.
94. CPC, Minute, P(85) M43 Part 4, 13 November 1985. Proposed Purpose: Department of Survey and Land Information.
95. CPC, Minute, P(85) M43 Part 5, 13 November 1985. Drafting Instructions: MfE and Parliamentary Commissioner for the Environment.
96. CPC, Minute, P(85) M43 Part 7, 13 November 1985. Environmental Planning Procedures and their Legislative Requirements.
97. Ministerial Ad Hoc Committee, 18 November 1985. Agenda and papers (includes EAP).
98. Ministerial Ad Hoc Committee, 20 November 1985. Minutes.
99. HRH/KP 20 November 1985.
100. Assist. CfE/Minister for the Environment, 20 November 1985. Briefing on Environmental Assessment Procedures.
101. HRH. Note on MfE structure, 22 November 1985.
102. Minister for the Environment. Opening Address to Seminar on Environmental Administration, University of Waikato, 22 November 1985.
103. SSC/CfE. Principles and procedures for consultation with various service organisations affected by environmental reorganisation.
104. Assist. CfE/Minister for the Environment. 25 November 1985. Briefing on EAP and their Legislative Requirements.
105. Assist. CfE/Minister for the Environment. 26 November 1985. Briefing on EAP and their Legislative Requirements.
106. CPC, P(85) 153, 25 November 1985. Environmental Assessment Procedures and their Legislative Requirements -Draft Environment Bill.
107. CPC, Minute, P(85) M45 Part 8, 26 November 1985. Environmental Assessment Procedures and their Legislative Requirements.
108. PHG/CfE. 26 November 1985. EAP: Proposed Regulations.
109. Minister of State Services. Press statement, 28 November 1985. Recent Decisions on Environmental Administration.
110. Asst. CfE/Under-Secretary for the Environment, 29 November 1985. Decisions taken by Government on MfE and Parliamentary Commissioner for the Environment to date.
111. CfE/SSC Environment Secretariat, 3 December 1985. Reorganisation of Environmental Administration: Freshwater.
112. Ministerial Ad Hoc Committee, 9 December 1985. Agenda and papers (includes Crown Estate Commission).
113. Ministerial Ad Hoc Committee, 9 December 1985. Minutes.
114. Notes by AH on a structure for the new MfE. 28 November 1985.
115. File Note, 16 November 1985. Record of first meeting of the new working group on EAP.
116. RA/DP. Draft discussion paper re: establishment of Maori Secretariat.
117. Cabinet Minute, CM 86/1/5, 21 January 1986. Establishment of Crown Estate Commission.
118. Under-Secretary for Environment/Professor A. F. Mark. 10 March 1986. Role, mission, functions and powers of MfE.
119. CPC, P(86)82, 16 May 1986. Environment Bill.
120. CPC, Minute, P(86) M20 Part 6, 20 May 1986. Environment Bill.
121. Treasury Report 6865. Environment Bill, 26 May 1986.
122. CPC, P(86)87, 26 May 1986. Foreshores and Coastal Waters
123. CPC minute, P(86)M21 Part 1, 27 May 1986. Foreshores and Coastal Waters.
124. CPC, P(86)91, 30 May 1986. Environment Bill: Establishment of Parliamentary Commissioner and Ministry for the Environment.
125. CPC minute, P(86)M22 Part 3, 3 June 1986. Environment Bill, P(86)82; Environment Bill: Establishment of Parliamentary Commissioner and Ministry for the Environment, P(86)91.
126. CPC, P(86)96, 6 June 1986. Environment Bill: Treaty of Waitangi.

127. CPC, P(86)97 (originally numbered P(86)95), 6 June 1986. Environment Bill.
128. CPC, P(86)98, 9 June 1986. Conservation Bill.

C. General

Bartlett R.V. "Comprehensive Environmental Decision Making: Can it Work ?", in Vig, N. and Kraft, M. (eds.) *Environmental Policy in the 1990s: Towards a New Agenda*. Washington, D.C., Congressional Quarterly Press, 1990, pp. 235-254.

Birkeland-Corro, J. "Redefining the Environmental Problem: Some Impediments to Institutional Reform", *Environmental and Planning Law Journal*, Vol. 5, 1988, pp. 109-133.

Caldwell, L.K. *Environment: A Challenge for Modern Society*. New York, Natural History Press, 1970.

Caldwell, L.K. *Between the Two Worlds: Science, the Environmental Movement and Policy Choice*. Cambridge, Cambridge University Press, 1990.

Churchill, R. Gibson, J. and Warren L.M. *Law, Policy and the Environment*. Oxford, Basil Blackwell, 1991.

Commoner, B. *The Closing Circle*. London, J. Cape, 1972.

Cullingworth, J.B. *Town and Country Planning in Britain*. London, George Allen & Unwin, 1964.

Dryzek, J.S. "Designs for Environmental Discourse: The Greening of the Administrative State?", in Paehlke, R. and Torgerson, D. (eds.) *Managing Leviathan: Environmental Politics and the Administrative State*. Peterborough, Ontario, Broadview Press, 1990, pp. 97-111.

Emel, J. and Peet, R. "Resource Management and Natural Hazards", in Peet, R. and Thrift, N. (eds.) *New Models in Geography*. Volume One. London, Unwin Hyman, 1989, pp. 49-76.

Fernie, J. and Pitkethly, A.S. *Resources: Environment and Policy*. London, Harper and Row, 1985.

Gold, H. and Webster, A. *New Zealand Values Today*. Palmerston North, Massey University, 1990.

Hill, M. and Bramley, G. *Analysing Social Policy*. Oxford, Basil Blackwell, 1986.

Kivell, P.T. "Geography, Planning and Policymaking", in Kivell, P.T and Coppock, J.T. (eds.) *Geography, Planning and Policymaking*. Exeter, Geo Books, 1986.

Meadows, D.H., Meadows D.L., Randers J. and Behrens W.W. *The Limits to Growth*. New York, Universe Books, 1972.

Meadows, D. H., Meadows D.L. and Randers J. *Beyond the Limits: Confronting Global Collapse, Envisioning a Sustainable Future*. Toronto, McClelland & Stewart, 1992.

Mercer, D. "Institutional and Counter-Institutional Forces in Australian Environmental Decision-Making." Working Paper No. 21. Clayton, Victoria, Department of Geography, Monash University, 1986.

Middlemass, K. *Politics in Industrial Society*. London, Andre Deutsch, 1979.

Miliband, R. *Marxism and Politics*. Oxford, Oxford University Press, 1969.

O'Riordan, T. "Institutions Affecting Environmental Policy", in Flowerdew, R.T.N. (ed.) *Institutions and Geographical Patterns*. London, Croom Helm, 1982, pp. 103-140.

O'Riordan, T. "The Challenge for Environmentalism", in Peet, R. and Thrift, N. (eds.) *New Models in Geography, op. cit*. pp. 77-102.

Paehlke, R. and Torgerson, D. (eds.) *Managing Leviathan: Environmental Politics and the Administrative State*. Peterborough, Ont., Broadview Press, 1990.

Park, C.C. (ed.) *Environmental Policies: An International Review*. London, Croom Helm, 1986.

Park, C.C. "Environmental Policies in Perspective" in Park, C.C. (ed.) *Environmental Policies: An International Review. op. cit*. pp. 1-44.

Peet, R. "Introduction", in Peet, R. and Thrift, N. (eds.) *New Models in Geography, op. cit*. pp. 43-47.

Peet, R. and Thrift, N. (eds.) *New Models in Geography*. Volume One. London, Unwin Hyman, 1989.

Pickvance, C.G. "Introduction", in Harloe, M. Pickvance, C.G. and Urry, J. (eds.) *Place, Policy and Politics. Do Localities Matter?* London, Unwin Hyman, 1990, pp. 1-41.

Portney, P.R. (ed.) *Public Policies for Environmental Protection*. Washington, Resources for the Future, 1990.

Redclift, M. *Development and the Environmental Crisis*. London, Methuen, 1984.

Rees, J. *Natural Resources: Allocation, Economics and Policy*. London, Methuen, 1985.

Rees, J. *Natural Resources: Allocation, Economics and Policy*. Second edition. London, Routledge, 1990.

Roberts, A. *The Ecological Crisis of Consumerism*. Sydney, International Publications, 1973.

Sachs, W. "The Virtue of Enoughness", *New Perspective Quarterly*, Vol.6(1), 1989, pp. 16-19.

Sandercock, L. "Capitalism and the Environment: The Failure of Success", in Wheelwright, E.L and Buckley, K (eds.) *Essays in the Political Economy of Australian Capitalism*. Vol. 1. Sydney, Australia and New Zealand Book Company, 1975, pp. 153-177.

Sandercock, L. *Cities For Sale*. Melbourne, Melbourne University Press, 1977.

Thomas, W.L. (ed.) *Man's Role in Changing the Face of the Earth*. Chicago, University of Chicago Press, 1956.

Walker, K.J. "The State in Environmental Management: The Ecological Dimension", *Political Studies*, Vol. 37(1), 1989, pp. 25-38.

Weisberg, B. *Beyond Repair: The Ecology of Capitalism*. Boston, Beacon Press, 1971.

White, L. *Machina ex deo: Essays in the Dynamics of Western Culture*. Cambridge, Mass., M.I.T. Press, 1968.

Wildavsky, A. *Speaking Truth to Power: The Art and Craft of Policy Analysis*. Boston, Little Brown, 1979.

World Commission on Environment and Development. *Our Common Future*. Oxford, Oxford University Press, 1987.

Index

State Services Commission 51, 54, 59, 61, 63, 74, 76
sustainable development 17, 92, 97, 121, 122–123, 124–125
sustainable management 13, 96–99, 104

technocentrism 19–20
"Think Big" development strategy 32, 33, 36, 57, 91
town and country planning 14, 27, 35–37, 44, 56, 61, 87, 96, 106
  – Town and Country Planning Act 1953 30, 36
  – Town and Country Planning Act 1977 37, 98
  – Townplanning Act 1926 30, 35
Treasury 21, 51, 53–54, 59–64, 65, 76, 88, 91–93, 98, 105

Treaty of Waitangi 13, 21, 33, 58, 92, 99–100, 101, 104, 106, 124, 128, 131–132
Treaty of Waitangi Act 1975 34, 69
  – Waitangi Tribunal 34, 69, 132

unitary authorities 74, 81, 82, 84
United and Regional Councils 37, 90

Waitangi Tribunal 34, 69, 132
water and soil planning 14, 27, 37–39, 44
  – Soil Conservation and Rivers Control Act 1941 30, 35, 37–38
  – Water and Soil Conservation Act 1967 30, 38
World Conservation Strategy 55, 97

Values party 43